Walking on Water

Walking on Water

Living into a New Way of Thinking

ROBERT P. VANDE KAPPELLE

WIPF & STOCK · Eugene, Oregon

WALKING ON WATER
Living into a New Way of Thinking

Copyright © 2020 Robert P. Vande Kappelle. All rights reserved. Except for brief quotations in critical publications or reviews, no part of this book may be reproduced in any manner without prior written permission from the publisher. Write: Permissions, Wipf and Stock Publishers, 199 W. 8th Ave., Suite 3, Eugene, OR 97401.

Unless otherwise noted, Bible quotations are from the New Revised Standard Version of the Bible, copyright © 1989 by the Division of Christian Education of the National Council of the Churches of Christ in the United States of America. Used by permission.

Wipf & Stock
An Imprint of Wipf and Stock Publishers
199 W. 8th Ave., Suite 3
Eugene, OR 97401

www.wipfandstock.com

PAPERBACK ISBN: 978-1-7252-5974-4
HARDCOVER ISBN: 978-1-7252-5975-1
EBOOK ISBN: 978-1-7252-5976-8

Manufactured in the U.S.A.   01/15/20

To Richard Rohr, OFM
ecumenical teacher, courageous visionary,
wise guide, friend to all.

We don't think ourselves into a new way of living,
we live ourselves into a new way of thinking.

—Richard Rohr, OFM

Love all God's creation, the whole and every grain of sand in it. Love every leaf, every ray of God's light. Love the animals, love the plants, love everything. If you love everything, you will perceive the divine mystery in things. Once you perceive it, you will begin to understand it better every day. And you will come at last to love the whole world with an all-embracing love.

—Fyodor Dostoyevsky

Contents

Preface | ix
Acknowledgements | xv

Mindfulness
    Chapter 1: Personal Awareness | 3
    Chapter 2: Social Awareness | 15

Mystery
    Chapter 3: Perennial Wisdom and Ultimate Reality, Part I | 33
    Chapter 4: Perennial Wisdom and Ultimate Reality, Part II | 47
    Chapter 5: Perennial Wisdom and the True Self, Part I | 57
    Chapter 6: Perennial Wisdom and the True Self, Part II | 66

Metaphor
    Chapter 7: The Power of Metaphor | 83
    Chapter 8: Death and Resurrection as Metaphor | 96

Myth
    Chapter 9: The Power of Myth | 111
    Chapter 10: The Quest for the Grail, Part I | 123
    Chapter 11: The Quest for the Grail, Part II | 137
    Chapter 12: The Power of Love | 156

Appendix A: Twelve Ways to Practice Resurrection Now | 167
Appendix B: Modern Approaches to Reality | 169
Bibliography | 171
Index | 175

Preface

ARISTOTLE SAID DEMOCRACY WOULD only work in a culture committed to virtue; Jesus said we must know the truth, for only truth can set us free (John 8:32); the book of Proverbs maintains that where there is no vision, there is no common restraint (29:18). In the past, society was guided by common principles, inspired truth. Today there is no communal myth to guide us, no common vision to inspire us, no transcendent images to shape us.[1] It is a sad and dismal world if I alone am its center. If we have to start at zero, our lives are too short to discover wisdom on our own, too brief to learn how to love, too arrogant to identify our place and role, and too myopic to define our proper significance and value.

Given our divisive attitudes and perspectives, a single cultural myth or national story may no longer be possible. Many today are unable to offer one another basic respect, engage in civic dialogue, or honor the human struggle. Modern humans have become adept at dissecting, critiquing, disagreeing, shaming. Despite its ubiquity, however, faultfinding is not an art form. It does not represent the kind of deep passion or positive faith that can stand up to war, vengeance, or injustice. To survive, we must learn to walk on water.

The story of Jesus walking on water is familiar. After feeding the multitudes, Jesus dismissed the crowd and went into the hills to pray. When evening came, his disciples went down to the Sea of Galilee, got into a boat, and started across the sea. As they rowed, a strong wind arose, and the sea became rough. When they had gone about three or four miles, they saw Jesus approaching them, walking on the water. It was dark and they were afraid, believing they were seeing a ghost. Immediately Jesus spoke to them, saying "It is I; do not be afraid." Then Jesus got into the boat with them, and the wind ceased.

---

1. For a chart contrasting the modern and postmodern consciousness, see appendix B: "Modern Approaches to Reality."

This story is found in three Gospels—Matthew (14:21-33), Mark (6:45-52), and John (6:16-21). Only Matthew's Gospel, however, adds the story of Peter's attempt to walk on water. "If it is you," Peter says to Jesus, "command me to come to you on the water." And Jesus bid him, "Come." So Peter got out of the boat, started walking on the water, and came toward Jesus. But when he noticed the strong wind, he became frightened and started to sink. Jesus reached out his hand and caught him, saying to him, "You of little faith, why did you doubt?" And together they got in the boat.

As we ponder this story and its meaning, there is one correction I would like to make to the text, changing "You of *little* faith" to "You of *literal* faith." That simple change, I believe, can transport us to the level of application. A veiled form of rationalism, literalism is the lowest level of meaning. Reactive and trapped in critique, literalism places severe limits on God's possibilities and on our own freedom for creative action (see 2 Cor. 3:6). To alleviate this entrapment, I recommend reading more poetry, literature, and mythology. Only then can we be entrusted with the scriptures.

God seemingly works best underground, when we are not in control. If we try to understand how God is changing us, or try to be overly rational about the process of transformation, we will only fight grace, try personally to control our journey, and, of course, take argumentative and divisive sides. However, if our imagination is rich, intelligent, and not overly defended, we will continue growing spiritually.

"How did Jesus do it?" people always ask after reading the story, meaning, "How did Jesus walk on water?" Reading this story literally, solely as an account of a miracle, leads them to miss its metaphorical message, that walking on water is not something only Jesus could do, but also something all people of faith can and should do. Perhaps this is what Jesus had in mind when he declared in John's Gospel, "Very truly, I tell you, the one who believes (trusts)[2] in me will also do the works that I do and, in fact, will do greater works than these" (John 14:12).

Human beings need to find that rare ability to live happily in a broken world and still work for its reform. It is a way of living that I believe only

---

2. Prior to the seventeenth century, "to believe" meant, "to give one's heart to someone or something"; the concept indicated loyalty, commitment, and trust. In the centuries following the Enlightenment, the terms "belief" and "believe" came to be associated with ideas in one's mind rather than with the disposition of one's heart. By the nineteenth century, when knowledge consisted chiefly of empirical facts, belief became the opposite of knowledge. From that point, a person's belief in God was reduced to his or her belief system, that is, to unprovable statements of faith that person judged to be true. The greatest downside to this conflation is that when faith is reduced to belief in creeds and doctrines, many thoughtful people decide they no longer have faith, thereby experiencing a great loss.

spirituality can achieve. Mere ideology is not sufficient for the task. Conservative ideologues, in my opinion, often have no practical goal beyond preserving the status quo, and liberal ideologues no useful objective beyond maintaining personal and social freedom. While this is a generalization, what ideologues often lack is a spiritual center, a reference point beyond the individual "I" or corporate "We." Lacking a God who gives source, pattern, and external goal, they create gods in their own image, becoming their own god. Contrast that to the prophets of old, all claiming an authority beyond their own, a Center outside of themselves.

What does it mean to be human? we ask. What makes a person unique? Does biology have priority? Are personality and spirituality equally significant factors? What about race, gender, and social class? To what extent are we shaped by our upbringing or education, by our friends and loved ones? What roles do our jobs and accomplishments play in our self image and identity?

When our Western forebears thought of personhood, they searched the realm of art and drama for guidance, settling on the term "person" as definitive. The word "person" comes from the Latin word for "mask" or for the actor's role in a drama. The Judeo-Christian tradition built on this idea, viewing human personhood as an organic participation in the one personhood that is God. In other words, the human self has no meaning or substance apart from the Selfhood of God. God's personhood, however, is not a mask, but the face behind all masks. We humans are the masks of God, and we play out God's image in myriad ways.

The problem we face in a secular society is that we do not know we are the masks of God. Hence, we are compelled to create our own significance, our own masks and personhood. This makes us—like atoms—inherently unstable. When we do not see our lives as a participation in Another, we are forced to manufacture our own private significance. Needing a word for this phenomenon, modern psychology chose the Latin word for "I," or "ego." This is the atomized self, the small self, the false self, which does not really "exist" at all. In such a state of insecurity, it overly defends and overly defines itself. This imperial ego becomes the basis for all illusion and evil. It is Adam and Eve trying to survive outside of the Garden, something they cannot do.[3]

Many people, I find, have a God who is too small, a God they fear, hate, or ignore. Naturally, we cannot admit that to ourselves. However, if we are afraid of God, or experience God as cold and absent, as someone who toys with us or sabotages our plans, we have only one alternative: Lose the false images that no longer serve us, the images of God that are insufficient and the images of ourselves that are likewise inadequate. God is transcendent,

---

3. Rohr, *What Mystics Know*, 24–25.

even of the name "God." God is beyond names and forms. The medieval Christian mystic, Meister Eckhart, said it best when he declared that the ultimate and highest leave-taking is leaving God for God, leaving our notion of God for an experience that transcends all notions.

Faith is first a verb before it becomes a noun, a way of trusting and living before it becomes a way of believing. Unfortunately, most of us reverse that equation. We start with belief, and then we try to act accordingly. That approach only lasts so long before it collapses from failure, inertia, or exertion. To discover the truth, we must become the truth. First, we must act, and then we will understand. That is the mysterious wisdom of faith. Called the "primacy of action," it is the wisdom we learn only when we are on the way. This is a lesson nobody can teach us; we must go down this road ourselves. This is the place of the soul, the place of wisdom, toward which we must move. In the end, truth is an encounter much more than a concept that can be argued. We are realigned with truth when the real person meets the real God, which is exactly the stuff of spirituality, theology, and conversion.

There are two necessary paths enabling us to move toward wisdom: a radical journey inward and a radical journey outward. For too long we have confined people to a sort of secure middle position, a safe midpoint between these two great teachers. Failure and falling short are the best teachers; success has practically nothing to teach on the spiritual path. Through education or by temperament, most of us fall into one of two camps, mysticism (the focus is inward) or activism (the focus is outward). Unfortunately, these two types seldom come together, and thus they both miss half the truth.

The great temptation of Western Christians has been to imprison the gospel in their heads. Up there, one can be right or wrong, a position correct or false, but in any case, everything must remain firmly under one's control. On the other hand, action never allows the illusion of control, at least not for long. For this reason alone, it seems obvious that we must begin primarily with action.

This book describes a path, based on unfailing vision and enduring truth. Exploring ideas common to the Perennial Tradition and the Judeo-Christian heritage, *Walking on Water* can help you become wise at the deepest level, living harmoniously with yourself, others, the earth, and the Creator.

The following ideas summarize this book:

1. The goodness of God fills all the gaps of the universe, without discrimination or preference. The space between everything is not space at all but God's Spirit.
2. Death is not just physical dying, but hitting bottom, going the distance beyond when the ego is in control, fully beyond what I am now.

Grace is found at the depths and in the death of everything. After these smaller deaths, the only "deadly sin" is to swim on the surface of things, where we never see, find, or desire God and love. This includes even the surface of religion, which might be the worst danger of all.

3. When we go into the full depths and death, even the depths of our own sin, we come out the other side—and the word for that is resurrection. None of us crosses over by our own effort or merits, purity or perfection. We are all carried across by unearned grace. The tomb is always finally empty. There are no exceptions to death, and there are no exceptions to grace or resurrection.

QUESTIONS FOR DISCUSSION AND REFLECTION

1. Do you agree with the author's statement that modern societies lack common myths, common vision? Explain your answer. If you agree, can such a loss be regained? If so, where can such myths (vision) be found?

2. Should we take the account of Jesus walking on water literally, figuratively, or somehow both literally and figuratively? Explain your answer.

3. In your estimation, can people of faith (Jesus people) replicate or improve on Jesus' deeds? If so, how? If not, how do you interpret Jesus' statement about "doing greater works" in John 14:12?

4. In your estimation, what does the author mean by "living happily in a broken world and still working for its reform?" Can you provide an example from your own experience?

5. In your estimation, what does it mean to view humans as "masks of God" and God as "the face behind all masks?"

6. In your estimation, what did Meister Eckhart mean when he suggested that Christians "leave God for God?" Can you provide an example from your own experience?

7. Perhaps the most intriguing question of this study is embedded in the book's subtitle. This is a question we must ask now, at the beginning of our study, and again at the end: "How does 'acting' lead to understanding, 'living' to a new way of thinking?"

8. Do you agree with the idea that failure and falling are better spiritual teachers than success and getting ahead? If so, how has this been true in your life?

Acknowledgements

I RECENTLY COMPLETED A summer-long residence at Chautauqua Institution, America's premier community combining the arts, religious life, education, and recreation. During the 2019 nine-week summer assembly season, I faithfully attended the weekly interfaith conversations on the topic of suffering, evil, and a loving God led by speakers representing different faith traditions, including evangelical and progressive Christianity, Islam, humanism, orthodox and reconstructionist Judaism, Quakerism, Zen Buddhism, and Sikhism. Other highlights from the season included lectures on topics such as Moments that Changed the World, Communities Working toward Solution, The Many Faces of Grace, The Power of Soft Power, and Exploring Racism.

Those themes were expounded in lectures delivered by luminaries such as Dan Egan, James Fallows, John Dominic Crossan, Richard Rohr, James Geary, Krista Tippett, Rabbi Rami Shapiro, Serene Jones, Katherine Ozment, Robin Wright, Bill Moyers, Bill McKibben, angel Kyodo williams, Debby Irving, Jennifer Eberhardt, Episcopal Bishop Eugene Taylor Sutton, and Wynton Marsalis, together with sermon series delivered by Rabbi Sharon Brouse, Father Richard Rohr, and Revs. Otis Moss, Susan Sparks, and Miguel De La Torre, among others. Worship culminated with a sermon by Chautauqua's Senior Pastor, Bishop Gene Robinson, titled "O Say Can You See!?" a retrospective of the season's topics and a call to enact the vision we had received that summer in our lives and communities.

The 2019 summer season marked thirty-five years of attendance by my wife Susan and me at Chautauqua, one week per summer initially and then for the entire assembly season. When I leave Chautauqua, it is with sadness at the conclusion of an inspiring and enjoyable season, but also with anticipation as to how I might incorporate what I have learned into my life and teaching vocation. Topics for books and ideas for old and new courses regularly emerge at Chautauqua, and 2019 was no exception. However, something new and unexpected occurred this season for which I am grateful.

Five years ago, when I retired as college professor teaching in the field of philosophy and religious studies, I went to Chautauqua in search of a cause to which I could commit. My search finally ended in 2019, not only with a potential topic for my next book, but with a twofold challenge, to commit to the issues of climate change and racism by addressing the ignorance, denial, and hidden prejudices that shape my own thoughts, actions, and priorities.

To walk on water, we need reliable guides. My primary aquatic instructor is Jesus, the pioneer and perfecter of the art of walking on water. You will find in this book many references to his life and teachings. In addition, I rely on the wisdom and experience of mentors such as Joseph Campbell, Richard Rohr, Carl Jung, Rami Shapiro, Jim Wallis, Karen Armstrong, Bill McKibben, James Geary, Bill Moyers, Serene Jones, Marcus Borg, Huston Smith, Eugene Taylor Sutton, and Martin Luther King Jr.

Of these mentors, my greatest indebtedness is to Franciscan priest Richard Rohr, founding director of the Center for Action and Contemplation in Albuquerque, New Mexico. In addition to his daily online newsletter, I rely on his insight found in writings such as *Falling Upward*, *Immortal Diamond*, *The Universal Christ*, *The Naked Now*, *Quest for the Grail*, and *What the Mystics Know*.

Acknowledging my admiration and esteem, I dedicate this book to Father Richard Rohr, mindful of his courage, faithfulness, and ecumenical vision. His pioneering work in second-half-of-life values has transformed my own living and thinking.

Mindfulness

Chapter 1

Personal Awareness

In the 1980s, when my children were growing up, transformer action figures were the rage. The top line of transforming figures has come a long way since its inception in 1984, including not only toys that transform, but also action figures, mini-figures, vehicles, model kits, role-playing items, and even computer accessories generated by a galaxy of highly entertaining pictures, comic books, animation, and video games. Whether your experience dates to the early beginnings or you have been lured by more recent enticements like *The Last Knight* or *Bumblebee* films, TV series such as *Titans Return* or *Power of the Princes*, or the array of video games available for play, practically every adult and child in America today has been exposed to this phenomena. Why are Transformer toys and action figures so popular, pervasive, and enduring? Why are we humans so fascinated with the concept of transformation?

In addition to the fun and excitement of transforming animate objects into inanimate objects and vice versa, or combining the two, such as adding superhuman qualities to humanoid beings or artificial intelligence to machines and technology, children and adults alike find an outlet for adventure in unlimited possibilities and imaginative universes. Transformers feed the modern need for fantasy and escapism. They also encourage us to "play God," to postulate and even create alternative realities while plumbing the depths of our own potential as human beings. In so doing, such creativity explores the limits of biology, physics, cosmology, psychology, philosophy, and spirituality.

Our ultimate fascination, of course, is with the world within, exploring the limits and possibilities of our humanity, individually and corporately. The ultimate adventure, the grandest game, the greatest challenge, is the spiritual transformation of the self. As we learn in chapters 5, 6, and 8, the role of authentic spirituality is letting go of the False Self, one's incomplete self trying to pass for one's True Self. Our True Self, our inherent soul, is that part of us that sees reality accurately, truthfully. It is divine breath passing through us, dwelling with us. Our False Self is the egoic self that is limited and constantly changing. It masquerades as true and permanent but in reality is passing, tentative, and fearful of change. It is that part of us that will eventually die. The role of true spirituality, of mature religion, is to help speed up this process of dying to the False Self.

Not surprisingly, we cannot accomplish—or even understand—what we have not been told to look for or to expect. This staggering change of perspective—that our ego is not our True Self—is what Jesus came to convey to humanity. It led Thomas Merton, the Trappist monk who first suggested use of the term False Self, to his radical rediscovery of the meaning of Jesus' teaching that his followers must lose their False Self in order to discover their True Self (see Mark 8:35).

This realization—what some people call "mindfulness" and mystics call "being present"—is the heart of religious transformation (meaning, "to change forms"). For Christians, the model and exemplar of such transformation is Jesus, who came to tell us—and show us—that our human form is also divine, that what is human also shares in the divine nature, a divinely implanted reality that can be experienced here and now, in our present mortal state. Initially, that possibility might sound far-fetched, but I assure you, that concept is both true and truly Christian.

The Greek word *theosis*, often used by Eastern Christians and perhaps best translated as "divinization" or "deification," speaks of this reality. Bishop Irenaeus taught the concept in the second century when he wrote that "God had become what we are, that He might bring us to be even what He is Himself."[1] Likewise, Bishop Athanasius of Alexandria at the end of the fourth century declared: "Jesus Christ was made human so that he might make us gods."[2] The clearest biblical antecedents for this teaching are 2 Peter 1:3–4, "His divine power has given us everything needed for life and godliness . . . so that through them you may escape the corruption that is in the world . . . and may *become participants in the divine nature*," and 2 Corinthians 5:16–17, "From now on, therefore, we regard no one from a

---

1. *Against Heresies* 4, 38.
2. *De Incarnatione* 54, 3.

human point of view.... So if anyone is in Christ, there is a new creation: everything old has passed away; see, everything has become new!" Elsewhere Paul uses words like "adopted" (Gal. 4:5) and "joint heirs with Christ" (Rom. 8:17) to make the same point.

Unfortunately, many people today, including religious and non-religious conservatives and other traditionalists, have become and remain quite rigid in their thinking, living, and believing because they have been taught that happiness, success, and stability require adherence to the religious status quo, and with it unquestioned obedience to the guardians of tradition. Such people are often moral and productive—even model citizens—but they simply never learned much about wisdom, paradox, or mystery, and their centrality to the faith traditions they espouse. When so many religious practitioners, including most professional clergy, attend worship and observe rituals faithfully without experiencing spiritual transformation at any deep level, religion becomes a duty that actually prevents transformation from taking place. This has been going on for centuries, and in all faith traditions.

In Jesus' day, most of his contemporaries, particularly social, religious, and political leaders, simply could not see what he saw (Matt. 13:13–17). This was not due to Jesus' unique identity or access to truth, for he keeps saying, in effect, "You should all know better. You do not know your own wonderful Jewish tradition." The same could be said of conventional Muslims, Buddhists, Hindus, or Christians today, "You do not know your own wonderful religious heritage."

Like any true reformer or prophet, Jesus evaluates his tradition from within, by its own criteria and its own documents. This is what I hope to do here for Christianity or any religion. Too often, religion offers doctrinal conclusions, additional competing truth claims in the increasingly growing marketplace of religious claims, but seldom does it give people a vision or process whereby they can legitimate those truth claims for themselves by inner experience and actual practice. As German Jesuit theologian Karl Rahner often remarked, "Devout Christians of the future will either be 'mystics' or else cease being anything at all."[3]

LEARNING HOW TO SEE

As all mystics know and teach, spirituality is about seeing rightly, for "how one sees is what one sees." As Jesus says in Matthew 6:22, "The eye is the lamp of the body. So, if your eye is healthy, your whole body will be full of

---

3. Cited in Rohr, *Naked Now*, 38.

light." Moses could never have seen burning bushes as divine, could never have persevered with so much unknowing, unless he had moved to a higher level of seeing. William Blake, the seminal mystic poet who worked to bring about change both in the social order and in common ways of thinking, taught that "All we need to do is cleanse the doors of perception, and we shall see things as they are—infinite."

While Western religions have been preoccupied with telling people *what* to know and believe, mystics approach things differently, teaching people *how* to see. That, according to Luke's Gospel, is what took place when the resurrected Jesus joined two ordinary travelers on their way home in Emmaus. He invites them to "open up" by telling their story of heartbreak. In the process, he explains to them his own life narrative. Through this act of intimacy and disclosure, they learn to see; their eyes are opened "and they recognized him" (Luke 24:31). Later that day, Jesus also appears to his sequestered disciples, transforming their vision from despondency to resurrection reality (Luke 24:36–49).

In the Gospels, Jesus praises God for hiding divine wisdom "from the wise and the intelligent" and for having revealed it "to infants" (Matt. 11:25). What is it that the learned and the clever often miss, and why is it that only infants and children see it? The learned and self-sufficient ones often see themselves as "having arrived," and by such arrogance, they remain outsiders to divine mystery. Their resistance and cleverness block its possibilities and hinder its reciprocity. Because of their vulnerability and dependence, children are avid learners, open to growth and newness. That is why children have a head start. When vulnerable exchange happens, there is always an augmentation of being on both sides. We are improved people afterward, bigger and better selves.

During the medieval period, two influential Christian philosophers at the monastery of St Victor in Paris—Hugh of St. Victor and Richard of St. Victor—wrote that humanity was given three different sets of eyes. The first was the eye of sensation, the second the eye of reason, and the third the eye of understanding. The third eye—the mystical gaze—builds on the first two, yet goes further. It represents the full goal of all seeing and knowing.

The first two ways of seeing, when separated from the third, result in dualistic thinking, an "us versus them" way of seeing, the foundation of much violence and discontent in the world. The third way of seeing—typifying the seer, the poet, the saint, and the authentic mystic—grasps the whole picture. Today's world has many eccentrics, fanatics, rebels, and self-promotors. What the world needs is more mystics who see with all three sets of eyes. Such people are both humble and compassionate, for knowing that they do not know, they experience the unknowable.

Some call such knowing conversion, some call it enlightenment, some transformation, and some holiness. This way of knowing is Paul's "third heaven," where he "heard things that are not to be told, that no mortal is permitted to repeat" (2 Cor. 12:2–4). Far too often, organized religion has a stake in keeping members in the first or second heaven, for this keeps them coming back, and keeps clergy in business. This is not always intentional, but rather an extension of the principle that you can lead others only as far as you yourself have gone. Lacking the contemplative gaze, such leaders remain functionaries and technicians, their parishioners without the resources to guide them into Mystery. Theological training without spiritual experience is protectionist, not progressive.

What I call the contemplative gaze is not a technique for acquiring benefit, for getting ahead, or even a requirement for entry into heaven; nor is it a pious exercise that somehow pleases God. It is much more like practicing heaven now.

Paradoxically, if we misuse spiritual awareness, or keep it to ourselves, it "hides," and we cannot go deeper. This is why many remain at the level of mere "religion," and it is surely what Jesus means when he says, "For to those who have, more will be given, and they will have an abundance; but for those who have nothing, even what they have will be taken away" (Matt. 13:12). How does the "secret" of God's kingdom, of God's reality and nature, become "unhidden"? It is disclosed when people stop hiding—from God, themselves, and others. The emergence of our True Self discloses the secret of God's kingdom, the mystery of reality.

All who witness this mystery, who experience its reality, "become children of God" (John 1:12), and, as Paul puts it, if children, then also "heirs of God and joint heirs with Christ" (Rom. 8:15–17; see also Gal. 4:7). While the Judeo-Christian tradition tells us we are already children of God, made in "God's image and likeness" (Gen. 1:26–27), most of us have no clue what this means, and far fewer live out of its resources.

Twenty-five hundred years ago the Indian sage Siddhartha Gautama—the historical Buddha—experienced enlightenment. After years of training in the austerities of his native Hinduism, he was no closer to Truth than before he began. Then something changed. He took responsibility for his own awakening. He ceased to walk the path his teachers followed and simply sat down. He sat beneath a large fig tree in Bodh Gaya, India, and observed what he could of the world within and without. Then the veil lifted, and he realized what he was unable to see previously. Transformed, he knew what he was—he was awake.

LIFELONG LEARNING

Personal transformation—openness to change; the desire to be all that we are; to defeat negative habits, attitudes, and beliefs; to overcome fear, anxiety, and distress—underlies the concept of lifelong learning, so widespread in academia today.

What does it mean to be a learner, particularly a lifelong learner? What does it mean to truly grow and evolve over a lifetime? Defined pedagogically, learning often involves the acquisition of requisite information about such disciplines as math, science, language, literature, and communication. Socially, learning cultivates emotional intelligence, the ability to live happily and harmoniously with others and oneself. Philosophically, learning introduces a mode of thinking about "fact," "theory," and "truth," that discerns their commonalities as well as their distinctions.

Defined scientifically, learning requires openness. Scientific facts, for example, are never final; hence, they are labelled "theories." The same should hold true for other disciplines, including philosophy and religion, yet in these areas, particularly religion, bias and arrogance often masquerade as revelation. When science and philosophy speak with finality, they are falling short of their own standards. When it is true to its own principles, science does not seek to impose its findings on nature, but instead humbly interrogates nature and takes seriously what it finds. Such science constantly prods, challenges, and seeks contradictions or persistent errors, proposing alternative explanations, encouraging heresy. Science gives its highest rewards to those who convincingly disprove established beliefs.

Whenever possible, religion should follow suit. In religion there should be something comparable to scientific humility. Such a perspective, attitude, and approach to life, learning, and truth is what we call spirituality.

Humans love labels; in the field of political science, as in economics and religion, we create spectrums of perspective, of thinking and living, and then we place people in categories along that spectrum, using terms such as conservative, moderate, progressive, and liberal to type people and their views. Of course, others may be extremists, but most of us seem to place ourselves conveniently and consistently in the moderate mean, never at the fanatical poles. There is a place for specificity, but when we use such terms stereotypically, we lose the greater perspective of the fluidity and dynamism of life. The Romantic poet William Wordsworth put it best in his poem *The Tables Turned*: "We murder when we dissect." When we define categories rigidly, placing others into static perspectival straightjackets, we embark on a path that leads ultimately to conflict and futility.

Take, for example, the supposed conflict between science and religion, "supposed conflict" because opposition between the two requires a "winner take all" mindset. Using the notion of "a hierarchy of explanation," namely, that most phenomena can be explained from numerous levels that make sense at their own level, we can affirm an approach that in religion, as in science and all of life, various explanations can coexist without contradicting or competing with one another.

Ultimately, it doesn't matter what you call yourself, what your worldview is, or where you place yourself on the ideological spectrum. There is only one reality that works. This reality, which we call spirituality, embraces all perspectives and exemplifies them all. It represents adulthood, citizenship, maturity, health, and wellbeing; it is organic, dynamic, growing, and ever changing. This is what Jesus meant by the kingdom, by eternal life, and why John's Gospel depicts Jesus as the only way to God (John 14:6).

Lifelong learning is attitudinal, for it espouses that one can and should be open to new ideas, decisions, skills, or behaviors. For lifetime learning to occur, the following six attitudes are essential:

1. Awareness. While not all learning happens consciously, lifelong learners are attuned to opportunities to learn. As learners, their devotion to learning often puts them into situations where they absorb a great deal unconsciously.

2. Commitment. Lifelong learners believe that time spent learning is time well spent. They have a mindset that tells them learning is always possible regardless of age, current abilities, criticism, or other factors that may deter or hold individuals back.

3. Engagement. Lifelong learners do not just sit by passively and let the world flow by. They take action; they take risks, and are not afraid of failure.

4. Reflection. Lifelong learners pause. They do not fear silence. They can do without computers, television, or media. They take time to review and rethink what they have learned. They connect new knowledge to things they already know. They do this often.

5. Curiosity. Lifelong learners are inquisitive; they probe, and ask questions. Living in a digital age, where information is literally at their fingertips, they know how to feed their curiosity. Ultimately, lifelong learners recognize the need to remain spiritually open, to satisfy the longing in their souls and find spiritual happiness.

6. Humility. Lifelong learners are optimists, believing great change is possible. Ready to learn from others, they have the ability to listen, to learn in silence, to teach by example. Eager to share, they know they must not impose their insights or awareness on others. They know they and others are capable of great things. But they also know there are things humans can never know, mysteries they can never solve, situations beyond their control.

THE FURTHER JOURNEY (SECOND HALF OF LIFE)

While many models—biological, social, psychological, cognitive, moral, ecological, religious, existential, mystical—exist to help conceptualize life's journey, one I find compelling is known as the "second half of life." It links beautifully what I am saying about learning and lifelong learning. Adult learning involves "second-half-of-life" thinking and living, a concept I have inserted into my books since the publication of *Dark Splendor* in 2015, my response to Richard Rohr's groundbreaking book *Falling Upward* in 2011. The reason I refer frequently to "second-half-of-life spirituality" is that the concept is transformative. In short, first-half-of-life living, thinking, and learning is characterized by the term "religion," a man-made system largely designed to keep human beings dependent and spiritually immature, using catechisms and creeds to raise and answer predesigned questions. This approach is no longer working, resulting in passivity, suspicion, and conformity for those who stay, and disdain and disinterest for those who leave. Fortunately, another option exists. Second-half-of-life living, thinking, and learning is characterized by the term "spirituality," a dynamic, organic, and unsystematic approach designed to promote wisdom, compassion, maturity, and independence, a transformational journey nourished by myth, metaphor, and mystery.

This "further journey" is not chronological, nor does one magically stumble upon it at midlife or in times of crisis, though these often serve as catalysts. While the second journey represents the culmination of one's faith journey, it is largely unknown today, even by people we consider deeply religious, since most individuals and institutions remain stymied in the preoccupations of the first half of life, establishing identity, creating boundary markers, and seeking security. The first-half-of-life task, while essential, is not the full journey. Furthermore, one cannot walk the second journey with first-journey tools. One needs a new toolkit.

While disagreements over matters such as the role of religion, the Christian life, the interpretation of scripture, the meaning of God, and doctrines such as belief in heaven and hell are attributable to upbringing, chronological age, social standing, and academic training, many disagreements are affected by our spiritual journeys, particularly by our place on that journey. This explains why some people are more open to growth, change, and transformation than others are. While intellect and background are factors, spiritual growth, curiosity, and development are often indicative of second-half-of-life spirituality.

The second-half-of-life journey has been likened to a second simplicity or a second naiveté. Whatever we call it, this condition is the very goal of mature adulthood and mature religion. First naiveté is the earnest and dangerous innocence we sometimes admire in young zealots, but it is also the reason we should not elect them or follow them as leaders. It is probably necessary to be impetuous when we are young, taking risks and eliminating most doubt. In the long run such approaches to life are not wise. Mature wisdom is content to live with mystery, doubt, and "unknowing," and in such living ironically resolves that very mystery to some degree. It takes a great deal of learning to finally "learn ignorance," as so many religious sages discovered. As T. S. Eliot puts it in the *Four Quartets*: "We had the experience but missed the meaning." Eliot's verse suggests that people in the second half of life need not expect to have the same experience as others; rather, simple meaning now suffices.

This new coherence, a unified field that embraces paradox, is precisely what characterizes second-half-of-life people. It feels like a return to simplicity after having learned from all the complexity. Finally, one understands that "everything belongs," even the sad, absurd, and futile parts. In the second half of life we can devote ourselves to integrating even the painful parts of our life into the now unified field, including people who are different or marginalized. If we can forgive ourselves for being imperfect and falling, we can now do it for others.

This talk of the first and second half of life is not new. It has been embodied for centuries in the scriptures, tales, and experiences of men and women who found themselves on the further journey. In this second half of life, people have less interest in judging or punishing others, or in harboring superiority complexes. Life is more spacious now, the boundaries of one's life having been enlarged by the addition of new experiences and relationships. Life is more participatory than assertive, and there is less need for self-assertion and self-definition. In the second half of life, people live in the presence of God. In that reality, the brightness comes from within, a reflection of the divine that is more than adequate.

The second half of life is transformative, producing individuals who are

- less fearful
- less hostile and combative
- less self-absorbed
- less assertive
- less self-concerned
- less dogmatic
- less possessive

The second half of life is not about precepts or commandments, for there is only one guideline: to love the Lord your God with your entire mind, heart, soul, and strength, and your neighbor as yourself.

A MODERN PARABLE: ADAPTED FROM MARK 10:17–31 AND 8:34–38

One day, as Jesus and his disciples approached Jericho on their way to Jerusalem, Jesus paused at the Jordan River, removed his sandals and tunic, and entered the water, welcoming newcomers by baptism. A young man stepped from the crowd, and standing at the bank of the river, addressed Jesus.

"Good Teacher," he said, "what must I do to inherit eternal life?" And Jesus replied, "Why do you connect eternal life with doing? Eternal life is more a matter of being than doing."

The young man answered, "I was brought up to believe that God would not accept me unless I was a good person. Hence, I have kept all the moral commandments. All my life I have sought wealth and success," he continued, "and have attained them. I believe I am a good person. Others admire me, and I have tried to be a model citizen, paying my taxes, giving my tithe to the synagogue, and giving alms to the poor. But something is lacking, and I sense I am too selfish, too possessive, and too self-assured. I am fearful of losing what I have achieved, and fearful of strangers, of change, of letting go. I am struggling with racism, sexism, and homophobia, and I fear I am succumbing to entitlement, exceptionalism, and white supremacy. Despite my social success, I feel morally inadequate and spiritually immature. Can you help me?"

And Jesus, looking at him, loved him, and said, "Enter the water and come to me." The young man did as Jesus commanded, and as he drew near to Jesus, the latter said, "Will you trust me?"

Nodding assent, the young man presented himself for baptism. Placing his hands on the young man's shoulders, Jesus gently nudged him into the water. Taking a deep breath and trusting Jesus, the young man felt his upper body engulfed by water. Under the water, he felt relaxed and confident. However, after a while, running short of air, he struggled upward, only to encounter pressure downward. Jesus seemed to be fighting him, holding him under. He relaxed further, knowing he could survive a few seconds longer. Finally, frantic and desperate for air, he struggled with all his might, and only then did Jesus relinquish his forcible hold.

Unfazed, Jesus embraced him while saying, "If you seek eternal life—if you desire spiritual transformation—you must want it as desperately as you cling to your own mortal life, and even more. If you wish to be my disciple, you must deny yourself and follow me. For those who want to save their life will lose it, and those who lose their life for my sake, and for the sake of the gospel, will save it. Young man, you are too self-assured: give up your pride, your accomplishments, your prejudice, your sense of supremacy, and your fear of change; then come, follow me." And the young man did as Jesus said.

Then Jesus looked around and said to his disciples, "How hard it is for those who are successful and self-assured to enter the kingdom. It is easier for a cable to go through the eye of a needle than for someone who is self-obsessed to enter the kingdom of God." His disciples were greatly astounded and said to one another, "Then who can be saved?" Jesus looked at them and said, "For mortals, personal transformation is impossible, but not for God; for God all things are possible."

This parable, a modern adaptation of Jesus' encounter with the rich young man, addresses many of the problems in our world today. Our planet is unhealthy, our civilization fragile, our nation overly hostile, our communities vulnerable, and our neighborhoods unsafe. American corporations are too greedy and immoral, and American citizens too fearful, impulsive, and self-obsessed. To change our planet, we must change global civilization; to change our world, we must change our nation; to change America, we must change our communities; and to change our neighborhoods, we must change ourselves, beginning with you and me.

Global health begins with social transformation, and social transformation with personal transformation. How personal transformation occurs is the subject of this book. It begins with self-reflection, sincerity, honesty, integrity, and right intent. Before we humans can change, we must discover our need for change—what the mystics in our religious traditions call "awareness" or "awakeness"—and desire transformation as desperately as the air we breathe.

QUESTIONS FOR DISCUSSION AND REFLECTION

1. In your own words, explain your understanding of "the transformation of the self."
2. Do you agree with the idea that "the role of true spirituality is to help speed up the process of dying to the False Self?" Explain your answer. While we will return to the idea of the False Self in later sessions, at this point, provide a working definition of the False Self.
3. In your estimation, what do Christians mean by "*theosis*" or by humans participating in the divine nature? At this point in your thinking, does the idea of "deification" sound far-fetched to you? Why or why not?
4. In your own words, explain your understanding of the phrase, "how one sees is what one sees."
5. In your estimation, do children have a "head start" on spirituality? Explain your answer.
6. In terms of "seeing" reality, explain the difference between mystics and fanatics.
7. In your estimation, what does it mean to be a lifelong learner? Would you place yourself in this category? Why or why not?
8. Of the six learning attitudes, which qualities do you find most important? Which least important?
9. In your estimation, what is the most important quality of second-half-of-life living? Explain your answer.
10. In your estimation, what is the primary insight gained from this chapter? Does this chapter raise any issues you might need to address in the future?

Chapter 2

Social Awareness

Last night I had the strangest dream. I saw myself standing next to another person, a tall, handsome, white male in his mid-thirties. His back was erect, his hair brown and short cropped, his demeanor confident yet not cocky or proud. He embodied the model of attractive, authentic humanity. Suddenly, without warning or explanation, I found myself looking through his eyes. We had exchanged identities! I had been transformed into this ideal, virile young adult, and he, alas, had put on my stooped, aging body. The dream ended as suddenly as it began, and I awoke with the realization that something significant had transpired.

Like most dreams, this one emerged from an active process, an ongoing awareness of discernment around three occurrences: (1) a regimen of physical therapy to rehabilitate an unstable back; (2) a realization of the plight of planet earth due to global warming, and the consequent looming demise of the human race; and (3) a recognition of my racist biases.

Mindfulness begins with personal and social awareness, and in my opinion, no issues have greater priority today than global warming and racism, the topics we examine in this chapter. While issues such as LGBTQ rights, gender equity, classism, violence, militarism, and xenophobia weigh upon our minds at this time and demand action, they are interrelated with racial and environmental concerns, and have a common solution. How we love anything is how we must love everything. When we learn to love the planet and all its gifts—human and nonhuman—as extensions of ourselves, our social and ecological problems will dissipate.

GLOBAL WARMING: THE FIGHT OF OUR TIME

Due to human activity and negligence, we humans are responsible for such destructive environmental acts as deforestation, overfishing, and species loss. According to Bill McKibben, there are currently half as many wild animals on the planet as there were in 1970. Furthermore, many plant species, including the planet's oldest and largest trees, are dying rapidly, as climate change attracts new pests and diseases. The baobab tree can live as long as 2,500 years, but five of the six oldest species on the planet have died in the last decade. Yet nothing seems to slow human destructiveness—just the opposite. "By most accounts," McKibben notes, humans have "used more energy and resources during the last thirty-five years than in all of human history that came before."[1] Around the world, human pollution is the biggest public health crisis, killing 9 million people a year, far more than AIDS, malaria, TB, and warfare combined. The list of severe environmental problems grows longer each day, including dead zones in the oceans and lakes where fertilizer pours off farms along with irreplaceable topsoil; vast quantities of plastic waste gathering in the sea; suburbs spilling across agricultural lands and agriculture overrunning tropical forests; and water tables quickly sinking as aquifers drain.

When the modern environmental movement came of age in 1972 with the publication of *The Limits of Growth*, the authors warned that the most probable result of unleashed human growth would be "a sudden and uncontrollable decline in both population and industrial capacity." Though modern societies have taken the environmental challenge semi-seriously, passing laws to clear air and water, they remain committed to further growth. Now, McKibben warns, it may be too late for change. The American way of life is unsustainable, and the human game on earth may be starting to play itself out. In 1989, when McKibben wrote *The End of Nature*, he painted a bleak picture. The situation since has not improved; instead it has become bleaker, possibly dire.

In 2015, at the Paris climate talks, the world's governments set a goal of holding temperature increases to 1.5 degrees Celsius and, at the very least, below 2 degrees. However, by 2018 researchers reported the temperature would surpass the 1.5-degree mark by 2030.[2] For the first time in history, humanity has cut off all lines of retreat. When that happens, human history will be much closer to its end, and the future will hold prospects we cannot comprehend.

---

1. McKibben, *Falter*, 12.
2. The environmental statistical information in this segment is taken from McKibben, ibid.

When we speak of climate change, we need to recall its cause and its magnitude, for it is by far humanity's greatest calamity. Over the past two centuries, humans have consumed immense quantities of fossil fuels, burning them in car motors, basement furnaces, power plants, and steel mills. When we burn fossil fuels, the carbon atoms combine with oxygen atoms in the air to produce carbon dioxide. The molecular structure of carbon dioxide traps heat that would otherwise radiate back out to space. This means that human usage of fossil fuels has changed the energy balance of our planet, trapping excess amounts of solar heat that would otherwise have returned to space.

If we consumed small amounts of fossil fuels, it wouldn't matter. But we have burned enough to raise the concentration of carbon dioxide in the atmosphere from 275 parts per million to 400 parts per million in the course of 200 years. We are currently on our way to 700 parts per million or worse.[3] To clarify what this means, the extra heat we trap near the planet because of the carbon dioxide we have created is equivalent to the heat from 400,000 Hiroshima-sized bombs every day, or four each second. At present, we are pushing about forty billion tons of carbon dioxide into the atmosphere annually, an amount unprecedented in the earth's 4.5-billion-year history. Even during the end of the Permian Age, when most life went extinct, the carbon dioxide content of the atmosphere grew at perhaps one-tenth the current pace.

The results of our current pollution have been extraordinary. The past thirty years have seen the twenty hottest years ever recorded. "Faster than expected," is the watchword of climate scientists, that is, regarding the damage to ice caps and oceans. In January 2019, scientists concluded that the earth's oceans were warming 40 percent faster than previously believed. Droughts are intensifying globally, and in unexpected places such as Cape Town, South Africa; São Paulo, Brazil; and the Po River Valley, Italy's agricultural heartland.

As land dries out, it often burns, which explains the rash of forest fires in Northern California in 1987, when a thousand blazes broke out simultaneously. And every year seems to be worse. Since 2000, more than a dozen U.S. states have reported the largest wildfires in their recorded histories. Furthermore, each degree Fahrenheit we warm the planet increases the number of lightning strikes by 7 percent, and once the fires get going in our hot, dry new world, they are all but impossible to fight, as we saw in the devastating Camp Fire burning of Paradise, California in 2018.

3. According to experts, 350 parts per million is considered the limit for healthy atmosphere. The limit has now been crossed, and we surpassed 400 several years ago, climbing steadily beyond that figure annually.

According to experts, global warming is affecting the earth negatively in polar opposite ways, namely by making dry areas drier and wet areas wetter. As ocean temperatures rise, there is an increase of water in the atmosphere, increasing the level and intensity of storms. It wasn't the winds that made 2017's Hurricane Harvey the most damaging storm in American history; it was the amount of rain that hit Houston, Texas—127 billion tons worth, enough to fill 26,000 New Orleans Superdomes—its weight alone causing the city to sink by several centimeters. In places, the rainfall topped 54 inches, by far the largest rainstorm in American history. When Hurricane Florence hit the Carolinas in 2018, it set a new record for East Coast rainfall—the storm dumped the equivalent of all the water in the Chesapeake Bay.

The effects of global warming are now irreversible, at least for the near future. A 2018 study concluded that even if human beings stopped emitting *all* greenhouse gases today, more than a third of the planet's glacial ice would melt anyway in the coming decades. Beside the damage, the cost associated with global warming is staggering. Climate change is currently costing the U.S. economy about $240 billion a year, and the world, $1.2 trillion annually.

Climate related disasters are also resulting in increased poverty and hunger globally. In 2017, a United Nations agency announced that after a decade of decline, the number of chronically malnourished human beings had started growing again, by 38 million, to 815 million. The planet is becoming crowded, and climate change is pushing people closer together, resulting in civil conflict and unrest and producing more migrants and refugees. In addition, if carbon dioxide levels continue rising, human cognitive ability will fall. If carbon levels increase to a thousand parts per million (a possibility by the year 2100), human cognitive ability will fall by as much as 21 percent.

As ice sheets melt, they take weight off land, increasing the risk of earthquakes—seismic activity is already increasing in Greenland and Alaska due to this effect. As faults are activated, landslides and tsunamis will increase in number and intensity. Climate change will also affect food supply. Since World War II, human ingenuity has kept crop yields growing ahead of fast-rising populations. That climb, however, now seems to be thwarted by rising heat and drought.

Assuming increased temperatures and rainfall, in June 2018, researchers found that a two-degree Celsius rise in temperature could cut U.S. corn yield by 18 percent. A four-degree increase would cut the crop almost in half. The effects of such a loss are incalculable, since the United States is the world's largest producer of corn, which is the planet's most widely grown crop. Global warming is also making food less nutritious, resulting in a loss of minerals such as calcium, iron, and zinc. Global warming studies also reveal an increase in crop pests, which thrive in the heat. Even if we hit the UN target of limiting temperature rise to two degrees Celsius, pests should cut wheat yields by 46 percent, corn by 31 percent, and rice by 19 percent.

Even if crops could be grown, research reveals that the transportation system that distributes it runs through fourteen major chokepoints, areas vulnerable to massive disruption from climate change. For example, Brazil accounts for 17.9 percent of the world's grain exports, but heavy rainfall in 2017 stranded 3,000 trucks.

Just as people have gotten used to eating certain amounts of food every day, they have gotten used to living in particular places, such as by oceans or in river valleys. From the earliest cities to the largest metropolises, proximity to saltwater meant wealth and power. Now, however, such proximity means increased vulnerability and potential fatality. As polar ice thaws, sea levels are rising. In 2018, researchers concluded that Antarctica had lost three trillion tons of ice in the last three decades, with the rate of melt tripling since 2012. As a result, scientists are now predicting not a half-meter or even a meter in sea level rise, but "several meters in the next 50 to 150 years," according to James Hansen, the world's premier climatologist. As Jeff Goodell notes, such a rise would "create generations of climate refugees that will make today's Syrian war refugee crisis look like a high school drama production." The UN estimates that climate change will produce from 200 million to 1 billion refugees this century alone. Where will they go? As Bill McKibben reminded his listeners at Chautauqua, "if we don't solve this problem soon, we will not solve it. We must respond with all that we have. It is the fight of our time."

A good place to start might be with the view astronauts have given us of the earth. Viewing the earth from their cosmic perspective, we see no divisions of nations or states. The symbol of the earth as a "blue marble" reminds us of the view of the earth held by primal peoples on the American continent. Such a view is found in a letter written to President Franklin Pierce by Chief Seattle. Around 1852, when the United States government inquired about buying tribal lands, Chief Seattle wrote a marvelous letter in reply. His letter, which I quote selectively, expresses the solution to our current crisis, and I recommend that you go online and read it in its entirety.

> The President in Washington sends word that he wishes to buy our land. But how can you buy or sell the sky? The land? The idea is strange to us. If we do not own the freshness of the air and the sparkle of the water, how can you buy them? Every part

of this earth is sacred to my people . . . The shining water that moves in the streams and rivers is not just water, but the blood of our ancestors. If we sell you our land, you must remember that it is sacred. Each ghostly reflection in the clear waters of the lakes tells of events and memories in the life of my people. The water's murmur is my father's father. The rivers are our brothers. They quench our thirst. They carry our canoes and feed our children. So you must give to the rivers the kindness you would give any brother. . . .

This we know: the earth does not belong to man, man belongs to the earth. All things are connected like the blood that unites us all. Man did not weave the web of life, he is merely a strand in it. Whatever he does to the web, he does to himself. One thing we know: our god is also your god. The earth is precious to him and to harm the earth is to heap contempt on its creator. . . . We love this earth, as a newborn loves its mother's heartbeat. So, if we sell you our land, love it as we have loved it. Care for it as we have cared for it. Hold in your mind the memory of the land as it is when you receive it. Preserve the land for all children and love it, as God loves us all.

As we are part of the land, you too are part of the land. This earth is precious to us. It is also precious to you. One thing we know: there is only one God. No man, be he Red Man or White Man, can be apart. We are brothers after all.[4]

WHITE SUPREMACY: AMERICA'S ORIGINAL SIN

While I agree with McKibben's assessment that climate change makes all other problems pale by comparison, one other issue affects Americans profoundly at this time, which we can ignore only at our common peril. That issue, labelled "America's original sin" by evangelical activist Jim Wallis, is racism. Chautauquans addressed the intersection of race and culture powerfully, pervasively, and persuasively during the final week of the 2019 season. The topic was taken seriously and driven home not only by the morning program lecturers and by Miguel De La Torre, the chaplain of the week, but also by the afternoon religion speakers and the evening entertainers, headlined by the renowned trumpeter Wynton Marsalis and the Jazz at Lincoln Center Orchestra.

America, we learned, rests upon myths deeply embedded in religious, political, economic, and social institutions, which regularly leave

---

4. Cited in Campbell, *Power of Myth*, 34–35.

out marginalized people who—metaphorically and physically—built this nation. According to Zen Buddhist teacher angel Kyodo williams—black, queer, and female—one myth is that America was founded upon meritocracy, namely, "the hard work of a limited number of people, most often relegated to a small group of heterosexual, white, Protestant, Anglo-Saxon males." With a history of oppression and prejudice in this country that continues to the present, williams said that the myth of meritocracy blindly supports ideas of opportunistic nationalism and freedom in the United States, rendering white Americans confused and dazed by ignorance, wondering why African-Americans and many other people of color appear unable to take advantage of the opportunities promised by American democracy.

As African Americans have been saying for over 150 years, the playing field was never equal. Despite the promises of what religion scholar Richard Hughes calls "the American creed," found in the American Constitution and captured in the immortal words of the Declaration of Independence: "We hold these Truths to be self-evident, that all Men are created equal, that they are endowed by their Creator with certain unalienable Rights, that among these are Life, Liberty, and the Pursuit of Happiness," America failed to implement those promises.[5]

Martin Luther King Jr. offered a striking example of this paradox in his "I Have a Dream" speech, the keynote address at the March on Washington of 1963. King registered his disappointment in America when he recalled that one hundred years after emancipation, African Americans still were not free, "still sadly crippled by the manacles of segregation and the chains of discrimination . . . living on a lovely island of poverty in the midst of a vast ocean of material prosperity . . . still languishing in the corners of American society and finding themselves in exile in their own land." At the same time, King expressed his hope for realistic change when he said,

> In a sense, we've come to our nation's capital to cash a check. . . . It is obvious today that America has defaulted on this promissory note in so far as her citizens of color are concerned. Instead of honoring this sacred obligation, America has given the Negro people a bad check; a check which has come back marked "insufficient fund." We refuse to believe that there are insufficient funds in the great vaults of opportunity of this nation. And so we've come to cash this check, a check that will give us upon demand the riches of freedom and the security of justice.[6]

---

5. Hughes, *Myths America Lives By*, 2.
6. King Jr., *A Testament of Hope*, 217.

You ask most African Americans today whether America has been true to its promise, and the answer will be a resounding No. Racism, in the form of prejudice, segregation, and injustice, abounds in American society to this day. "We have this enormous gap, not just in our sense of a race divide, but actually in our imagination, of what each other are and of what we are capable," Rev. williams proclaimed to a mostly white audience in Chautauqua's Hall of Philosophy. In America, "people who are slow to cross the finish line are deemed incapable, ill-equipped, and untalented. Conversely, those who win the [capitalist] race are dubbed talented and endowed with great capacity . . . No one acknowledges this fact, that actually, the race had begun and the firing gun had already gone off, allowing a certain set of people to run and run, and run further. They got to tie the others up first, bind them, leave them behind the starting line, and begin running—this has gone on for 200 years, give or take," williams noted.

The vestiges of this narrowed view of the "fruits of meritocracy," whereby the success of some is the detriment of others, is imprinted in American culture, something not easily changed. The remnants of racial prejudice appear in American institutions such as the justice system and in our Constitution, which intentionally excludes women, people of color, and immigrants. According to williams, this judicial foundation created a sense of "social madness," where minorities continued to participate and pin their hopes on a system intent on belittling over half of the population—in the eighteenth century, certainly, but even to this day. Such a system positions "whiteness" at the pinnacle of society and creates, particularly in white males, an inability to recognize the brokenness in society that directly affects people of color, but indirectly all of us. Williams likened the myth of white supremacy, of white male exceptionalism, to a large-scale social illness that has prevented Anglo Americans and other whites in the United States from recognizing, affirming, and relating to people of color as equals, withholding from them the capacity for full humanity that is their birthright.

Comparing this phenomenon to taking a pill that removes all feeling of empathy, compassion, and racial equality, williams noted that that pill had been taken for generations. The pill has been so prolific, she said, that American society cannot remember when it was first "seduced" into the idea of white supremacy. White Americans no longer recognize their own history, the ways laws were enacted to induce citizens to participate in a system of enslaving black human beings and treating them as inhuman chattel, that it, as property or currency, thereby reducing collective humanity to a myth based on the notion of racial superiority, a system that exists exclusively for profit or gain.

Dismantling this myth is harder than tackling racism, williams said. It requires engaging a culture rooted in celebrating whiteness. Beyond lectures, scholarly works, and historical evidence, the answer lies in an internal conversation—confronting one biases and prejudices—as well as in disavowing the pill that has seduced America into the myth of white supremacy. "If we are happy with the pill that has induced us into this myth," williams said, "then we should simply carry on. But if we are even slightly curious as to what it would be like not to have the myth of race obscuring our vision, our sense of possibility, our sense of promise, then we owe it to ourselves to ask the tough questions, to be in honest conversation, and thereby to redeem ourselves and the generations left behind."[7]

From the outset, two questions arise: "Where does the conversation begin?" and "How should we proceed?" Of course, there are many excellent books on racism and white supremacy in America, including *Waking Up White* by Debby Irving, *Biased*, by Jennifer Eberhardt, and *Myths America Lives By*, by Richard Hughes. There is no better place to begin, however, than with Jim Wallis's book, *America's Original Sin*. In the Foreword to Wallis's book, Bryan Stevenson, a black lawyer and acclaimed founder of the Equal Justice Initiative in Montgomery, Alabama, speaks of an incident when, having recently moved to a neighborhood in Atlanta, he was sitting in his car outside his home when a policeman pointed a gun at him and threatened to "blow your head off." To that officer, Stevenson looked dangerous and guilty. Why? Simply because he was a young black man in a country where such people are presumed dangerous and guilty.

Versions of this event occur regularly across the United States, experienced regularly by hundreds of thousands of black and brown people. Stevenson writes:

> As a consequence of our nation's historical failure to address the legacy of racial inequality, the presumption of guilt and the racial narrative that created it *have significantly shaped every institution in American society* [emphasis mine], especially our criminal justice system. . . . We are currently in an era of mass incarceration and excessive punishment in which the

---

7. In her dramatic novel, *Small Great Things*, Jodi Picault writes about racism and white supremacy. In the "Author's Note," she points out that "racism is more than just discrimination based on skin color. It is also about who has institutional power. Just as racism creates disadvantages for people of color that make success harder to achieve, [racism] also gives advantage to white people that make success easier to achieve." When it comes to racial justice, she concludes, the role of white allies is not to be a savior or a fixer but rather to make other white people "see that many of the benefits they have enjoyed in life are direct results of the fact that someone else did *not* have the same benefits," 460–61.

> politics of fear and anger reinforce the narrative of racial difference. [America] imprison[s] people of color at record levels by making up new crimes, which are disproportionately enforced against those who are black or brown. We are the nation with the highest rate of incarceration in the world, a phenomenon that is inexorably linked to our history of racial inequality. The Justice Department projects that one in three black males born in the twenty-first century is expected to go to jail or prison at some point during his lifetime. Only in a country where we have learned to tolerate evidence of racial injustice would this be seen as something other than a national crisis.... No historic presidential election, no athlete or entertainer's success, no silent tolerance of one another is enough to create the truth and reconciliation needed to eliminate racial inequality or presumption of guilt. We're going to have to collectively acknowledge our failures at dealing with racial bias. People of faith are going to have to raise their voices and take action.[8]

As Stevenson notes, millions of Africans were brought to America in chains during the colonial period and the first century of nationhood. While involuntary servitude was banned by the Thirteenth Amendment to the Constitution, America did nothing thereafter to confront the ideology of white supremacy. Slavery didn't end in 1865; it simply evolved. "Until the 1950s, thousands of black people were routinely lynched while many in the white community watched and even cheered. Throughout much of the twentieth century, African Americans were marginalized by racial segregation and silenced by humiliating Jim Crow laws that denied basic economic, social, and political rights."[9]

Overt attacks and atrocities by white supremacists continue, epitomized by the 2015 murder by twenty-one-year-old Dylann Roof of nine African Americans gathered for prayer in Charleston, South Carolina; by the 2017 Unite the Right rally in Charlottesville, Virginia; and the shooting rampage of Latinos at a Walmart in El Paso, Texas, one of the deadliest racist attacks in recent history, events either anticipating or precipitated by the 2016 presidential campaign, the most vitriolic in modern American history. While many white voters—of all economic levels, ages, and genders—voted for Donald Trump, animated by his "Make America Great Again" slogan, the vast majority of people of color—of every economic background, gender, and religion—knew what that slogan meant, voting against Trump. As Wallis notes, "in the aftermath of the election, many people of color are

---

8. Stevenson, in Wallis, *America's Original Sin*, xiv–xvi.
9. Ibid., xiv.

losing hope for an America that values diversity—and them—and losing trust in white Christians who loudly claim not to be racist but who clearly decided that Trump's racial bigotry was not enough to dissuade them from voting for him. These voters ultimately set aside his statements, which even other Republicans called 'textbook racism,' in favor of their other concerns . . . . , with no seeming understanding of or empathy toward families of color. . . . Not surprisingly, the voters who ultimately chose Donald Trump were the most racially isolated white people in America."[10]

In the face of the implicit and often unconscious structures of racism, Wallis writes, it is time for white Christians to be more Christian than white; time to focus on "the least of these," as Jesus commands in Matthew 25, supporting the poor and vulnerable and defending those weakened and marginalized by unjust laws and racist policies. To do so, Wallis recommends a course of action involving six principles:

1. Tell the truth (American Christians need to replace fear with facts when it comes to public discourse about race, national security, immigrants, refugees, and Muslims).
2. Love your neighbor (American Christians must protect minorities and marginalized groups from hate speech and attack and surround them with supportive community).
3. Welcome the stranger (American Christians should obstruct mass deportation of immigrants who are law-abiding and hard-working members of our communities, inviting them and their families into their congregations, particularly when they become vulnerable).
4. Expose and oppose racial profiling in policing (American Christians should monitor police activity in their communities).
5. Defend Muslims and Jews (American Christians should embrace Muslims and Jews as fellow Americans, standing with mosques and synagogues in individual and congregational solidarity, and resisting anti-Semitism in the face of rising white nationalism).
6. Listen to people of color (American Christians must renounce bigotry and befriend "the other" in their midst as their own. American communities should guarantee safety for all, citizens and strangers alike, its places of worship spaces for hearing and sharing one another's stories, pains, fears, and hopes).[11]

---

10. Ibid., xix.
11. Ibid., xx–xxii.

Simply increasing compassion and racial diversity, however, is not enough; we must change the narrative of racial division in America, and that begins with self-examination. I did this at Chautauqua in 2019, beginning with the challenging question, "Am I a racist?" Taking inventory, I identified the following racist tendencies and attitudes. First, I admitted to having benefitted socially—primarily financially and vocationally but also personally and existentially—from systemic racism in America. Being white in America had never put me at a disadvantage, but rather had been advantageous. Second, I admitted to having bought into the myth of meritocracy described by Rev. williams.

Having been born and raised in Costa Rica and later, as a teenager, having spent summers with my parents while they lived in Colombia, I felt I knew what it was like being a foreigner in another culture, a white North American living in a predominantly Latino culture. Black and Hispanic neighbors, many of them friends and playmates, surrounded me, and I saw myself as colorblind. I may have felt culturally superior, but not racially so— or so I thought. As an outsider, I had never experienced prejudice. In fact, quite the opposite. I found being North American in Latin America prestigious, beneficial. Thus, when I settled in the United States as a teenager, and later, as a young adult, I couldn't acknowledge race as disadvantageous, having never experienced racial discrimination directly. As an adult, and throughout my working years, I believed people of color in North America had an equal opportunity with whites, and, since the success of civil rights in the 1960s, an actual advantage over whites, particularly in academia, where affirmative action favored disadvantaged minorities. All people had to do to succeed, I believed, was to work hard and be thrifty. Such thinking, I later realized, was faulty and naïve. Affirmative action and related equalizing laws often backfired, producing frustration, resentment, and even despair. Racial bias was too entrenched, and affirmative policies were powerless to level the playing field for people of color. Meanwhile, discrimination continued and even intensified, despite token accommodation to racial justice such as removal of "White Only" signs and increased black representation in entertainment, law enforcement, and industry.

Third, I admitted to having opposed the concept of reparations for slavery. Having gained wide attention recently, the concept has been brought to national attention as three 2020 presidential candidates—Kamala Harris, Elizabeth Warren, and Julián Castro—have endorsed it. Additionally, David Brooks made the case for reparations on the March 7, 2019 editorial page of *The New York Times*, as did Ta-Nehisi Coates in his acclaimed 2014 essay, "The Case for Reparation" in *The Atlantic*, and the publication in 2000 of Randall Robinson's bestselling book *The Debt: What America Owes Blacks*.

Such interest, however, is not new. A bill calling for the federal government to consider how to provide reparations to African Americans has been introduced into every session of the U.S. Congress for the last thirty years. The bill only once got a hearing (in 2007), but may again in 2019, since House Speaker Nancy Pelosi voiced support for the proposal. The bill's aim is "to address the fundamental injustice, cruelty, brutality, and inhumanity of slavery in the United States and the thirteen American colonies between 1619 and 1865," or, as Rev. Eugene Sutton, Episcopal Bishop of Maryland told an audience at the Hall of Philosophy during the final week of the Chautauqua season, "I learned something in Sunday School . . . that if you steal something, you have to pay it back." Reparations was not the topic of Bishop Sutton's lecture, but it is what resonated most with me, a blockage in my racist psyche.

While celebrating the struggles and accomplishments of those who fostered commitment to racial equality in the United States, Sutton also recognized the millions of descendants of slaves who are entrapped, this day, in a pernicious cycle of hopelessness, poverty, and rage "due to segregation, redlining, inferior schools, false arrests and incarcerations, and other forms of racism and injustice." Americans, he said, "have been raised in a racist society. We all swim in an ocean of racism. Only we are like fish in the water, who don't know they are wet." For people interested in tangible, anti-racist actions, Sutton reminded his audience that "social critique of our nation's history and current practice is both healthy and patriotic. . . The only chance that a liberal democracy such as ours has to succeed is if there is an informed populace deeply in love with their country, who love it enough to challenge, critique, and protest when that nation does not live up to its ideals." The nation's founders knew that dissent in a democracy is not a synonym for disloyalty. For them, blind subservience was unpatriotic.

Reparation, Sutton noted, is not "throwing money at the problem of racism . . . It is not a transfer of money from individual white people to individual black people," he clarified. "The word literally means 'to repair what is broken.' Descendants of slaves are loyal," he added, "and they do not desire to leave the United States. We built this country, and we're going to stick around."

Reparations are needed to repair the mess African Americans have inherited. Suggesting a price tag for the damage, Sutton proposed $500 billion, half of one year's worth of federal deficit, and contrasted it with the $6 trillion the U.S. government has spent on wars since 2001. In his estimation, that money could be allotted to schools, job training, housing, environmental sustainability, and nursing homes. "You cannot repay four hundred years of abject degradation," he stated, "but unless we do something, we are in a moral ditch."

Concluding with Micah 6:8, a verse that asks, "What does the Lord require of you?" Sutton urged the audience "to do justice, to love kindness, and to walk humbly with your God. Nobody has all the answers," he said. "But I have a feeling that if we can just be kind enough, and committed enough to justice, the answers will come."

Sutton's talk, spoken frankly and truthfully, exposed my racist bias, and my agreement with his assessment eliminated my hidebound prejudice. I had become a believer, a convert to racial justice. I would forever know the difference between equality (treating everyone the same) and equity (acknowledging the unfairness of privilege and working to create a climate where everyone has a chance to succeed). While the former *sounds* fair, only the latter *is* fair. Hence, I was heartened to learn that my alma mater, Princeton Theological Seminary, had recently adopted a five-year plan to repent for the Seminary's past relationship to slavery, committing to tangible action by enacting over twenty initiatives to reshape the institution's future. The plan would establish increased investment in the Center for Black Church Studies; enact changes in the Seminary curriculum, including a required cross-cultural class for all first-year students; designate five doctoral fellowships and thirty additional scholarships for entering students descended from slaves or from underrepresented groups; rename the library after an African-American graduate; and hire new faculty to teach and research the legacy of slavery and African American experience in America and in ecclesial life. Institutions such as Princeton Seminary can make a huge difference in our society by helping to turn the rhetoric of "liberty and justice for all" into reality.

In my self-examination, there was one additional racist attitude I needed to address. I opposed interracial marriage, viewing it as a betrayal of one's culture and race. Thus, when my daughter dated an African-American in high school, I discouraged it, believing it would bring her undue pain. While I recognized and legitimated my bias, I failed to acknowledge my racism.

Confronting my own racist tendencies at Chautauqua left me with this final issue to resolve. By chance, I came across *The Color of Life*, Cara Meredith's account of falling in love, marrying, and raising two biracial boys with the son of James Meredith, a Civil Rights Movement figure famous as the first African American admitted to the segregated University of Mississippi during the presidency of John F. Kennedy. Cara's account, written by a white evangelical, convinced me that interracial marriages can work when love, maturity, and sincerity are undergirded by familial and societal support. When racism is not present, interracial marriage, particularly between whites and blacks, can succeed. While I still believe such marriages should be the exception rather than the rule, when they occur authentically and maturely, I will be their biggest fan.

Am I still racist? I trust not, but my yearning to be freed from racism or sexism can be achieved when in my dreams I am transformed not into a younger, better version of white maleness, but rather into a black male or Hispanic female of any age and appearance. If our dreams expose our deepest desires and truest identity, when identity change occurs there, my transformation will be complete.

QUESTIONS FOR DISCUSSION AND REFLECTION

1. Do you agree with the author's point that genuine love of our planet is a good place to start in solving many social and economic problems humans face today, or do you find such thinking false or misplaced?
2. Has humanity reached a point of no return in terms of climate change and other ecological concerns? Explain your answer. When you think of our planet's health, what hope do you have for the future? If you were placed in charge of the planet, what one thing would you change to ensure a better ecological future?
3. Ecologically speaking, are your attitudes and lifestyle part of the problem or part of the solution?
4. In your estimation, what is the underlying principle in Chief Seattle's letter to the American president?
5. According to Rev. williams, America was founded upon the "myth of meritocracy." Explain and assess her use of this phrase.
6. In your estimation, what is the chief malady or sin underlying America's racist past?
7. According to Rev. williams, disassembling "white supremacy" will be harder than tackling racism. Do you agree? Explain your answer.
8. Assess the merits of Stevenson's idea, "Slavery didn't end in 1865; it simply evolved."
9. Assess Jim Wallis's statement that "it is time for Christians to be more Christian than white."

10. Do you agree with the concept of reparation for African-American descendants of slaves? Explain your answer. If so, where should we begin?
11. After reading this chapter, has your perspective on racism or privilege changed? Do you agree with the distinction between equality and equity? Explain your answer.
12. In your estimation, what is the primary insight gained from this chapter? Does this chapter raise any issues you might need to address in the future?

Mystery

Chapter 3

Perennial Wisdom and Ultimate Reality, Part I

GIVEN THE QUANDARY WE face, socially and environmentally, exacerbated by our complicity with racism and our propensity for exploiting natural resources, America needs help. Ironically, if solutions exist, they must come not from exclusively American expertise—from uniquely modern, scientific, or Christian values—but from the Perennial Tradition, from peoples, beliefs, and customs North Americans have traditionally overlooked, discarded, or displaced in their strident surge onward.

When I speak of the Perennial Tradition, sometimes called Perennial Philosophy or simply "the wisdom tradition," I am referring to the view that the world's major religions share common teachings, and that these truths transcend culture, time, and place. Jews, Christians, or members of any specific religion, should not feel they were the first to know God's eternal patterns and presence. After all, those patterns are perfectly plain, because God has made it plain. "Ever since the creation of the world [God's] eternal power and divine nature, invisible though they are, have been understood and seen through the things [God] has made" (Rom. 1:19–20). How else could it be? How could any God worthy of the name squeeze Being itself into any specific timeframe, culture, or vocabulary? That is what we mean by the Perennial Tradition.

People who value perennial wisdom share core existential questions with other human beings, only they do not confine their search for answers to any one religion. What I call "core existential questions," what philosophers call "ultimate questions," can be reduced to four: (1) "Is there an ultimate reality?" (2) "Can I relate to that reality?" (3) "How does that relationship affect the way I live?" and (4) "For what can I hope?" Because these questions never go away, they form the heart of almost every spiritual quest.

It is the main business of religion to answer life's existential questions. And this is why, even when we try to distance ourselves from it, we remain intrigued by religion. Religion responds to the preoccupations that arise when life comes up against barriers beyond which ordinary—including scientific—ways of coping cannot take us. For our purposes, therefore, religions may be understood very simply as pathways or "route-findings" through the ultimate limits on our lives. These limits include not only death and meaninglessness but also anything that threatens our wellbeing, anything that stands between us and lasting peace or happiness.

To accomplish this task, every generation of believers benefits by reexamining its theology, thereby providing society with vision. A useful place to start is the Perennial Tradition, by which I mean not the distinct perspectives of other religious traditions—for the goal of spiritual transformation is a deeper understanding of one's own faith tradition, not conversion to some alternative religious tradition—but rather the congruence of values and beliefs (absolutes) across cultures, those unchanging beliefs that unite human traditions that seek wisdom in ancient texts and modes of life. According to perennial wisdom, every religious tradition, when one explores its mystical side, articulates common answers to humanity's existential questions, answers that emerge repeatedly throughout human history and across human culture.

The term "perennial philosophy," often attributed to the German philosopher Gottfried Leibnitz (1646–1716) but frequently associated with the English writer and philosopher Aldous Huxley, whose 1946 text *The Perennial Philosophy* popularized a universalist interpretation of religion, originated with a group of Renaissance thinkers who took inspiration from neo-Platonism and the idea of the One, from which all existence emanates. Giovanni Pico della Mirandola (1463–1494) proposed harmony between the thought of Plato and Aristotle, suggesting that truth could be found in many rather than in only two traditions.

Agostino Steuco (1497–1548), likely the first to coin the phrase "perennial philosophy," used it with reference to four timeless truths taught by the great sages and mystics of every civilization throughout human history:

1. There is only one ultimate Reality—called by many names, including God, Tao, Allah, Brahman, Emptiness, or Great Spirit—that is the source and substance of all existence.

2. Each human being is a manifestation of this Reality, though most identify with a smaller, culturally conditioned individual ego.

3. This identification with the individualized self gives rise to needless suffering and anxiety, leading to cross-cultural competition and violence.

4. Identifying with one's True Self, that is, realizing that one's true nature is a manifestation of the singular Reality, gives rise to peace and love, enabling human beings to engage others with compassion and justice.[1]

This is an excellent summary of perennial wisdom. As we apply this perspective to the four "core existential questions" listed above, I will add my own views where appropriate, applying the teachings of two of America's foremost teachers of the Perennial Philosophy—Rabbi Rami Shapiro, a Jewish practitioner of perennial wisdom, and Father Richard Rohr, a Christian (Franciscan) practitioner of the Perennial Tradition. Both lectured to Chautauqua audiences during the 2019 assembly season.

ULTIMATE REALITY: THE SOURCE AND SUBSTANCE OF ALL EXISTENCE

Perennial wisdom, found in most human cultures, religions, and civilizations, begins not with time, space, matter, or even with ontology (speculation about divine essence or Being), but with a common singularity we call Unity, or better yet, Mystery. As Lao Tzu, the sixth-century BCE author of the *Tao Te Ching*, says in his opening poem, "The Tao that can be named is not the eternal Tao. The name that can be named is not the eternal name ... Darkness within darkness. The gate to all mystery."

The Perennial Tradition says that there is a capacity for divine reality inside all humans, but we initially cannot see what we are looking for because what we are looking for is doing the looking. God, the name most of us give to Ultimate Reality, is never an object to be found or possessed as we find other objects, but the One who shares our deepest subjectivity by virtue of being only Subject, never object. Furthermore, we do not see things as *they* are, but rather we see things as *we* are, through our own level of development and consciousness. This affects not only how we view Reality, but also how we read scripture. We see the text through our available eyes. Punitive people love punitive texts; loving people hear in the same text calls to discernment, clarity, choice, and decision. In the world of spirituality, nondualists are the only experts.

More than with any other personality trait in our lives, all-or-nothing thinking causes huge mistakes and bad judgments. It results in withholding

---

1. Shapiro, *Perennial Wisdom*, xiv.

love, misinterpreting situations, and hurting both others and ourselves. This pattern of dualistic or polarity thinking is deeply entrenched in most of us, despite its severe limitations. Dualistic thinking is not wrong or bad in itself—in fact, it is necessary in most situations. However, it is completely inadequate for the major questions and dilemmas of life.

Dualistic people use knowledge, even religious knowledge, for the purposes of ego enhancement, shaming, and the control of others and themselves, for it works very well in that way. Nondual people use knowledge for the transformation of persons and structures, but especially to experience transformation, seeing reality with a new eye and heart.

This realization helps to explain the great paradox we all must face—and embrace—that God is both perfectly hidden and perfectly revealed in all things. God has written the pattern in things as they are, and yet we never see the full pattern without divine assistance. Thus, faith (trust in the divine) is always necessary to see what is "natural."

Despite their commonality, the many names for the Ultimate Reality, viewed culturally, theologically, and religiously, do not mean the same thing. For example, in the context of Islam, Allah has no son, chooses Muhammad as his final prophet, and the Qur'an as final revelation. In the context of Christianity, God has a son, knows nothing about Muhammad, and does not reveal the Qur'an. Similarly, the Jewish God knows nothing of Jesus and has nothing to do with the New Testament, which Christians regard as the Word of God. Likewise, Krishna, God for many Hindus, has nothing to do with the Hebrew Bible, the Greek New Testament, or the Arabic Qur'an. If you wish to understand Krishna, you must read the Bhagavad Gita, the revelation of Lord Krishna to Arjuna, about which the Jewish, Christian, and Muslim Gods know nothing.

Hence, in the context of comparative religion, it is wrong to claim that all Gods are the same, or that all Gods are variations of a specific context. If you want to study Allah, study Islam. If you want to learn about Krishna, Vishnu, Shiva, and the rest of the Gods of India, study the many schools of Hinduism. In the study of world religions, each deity must be allowed to speak in its own way, or at least to reflect the values of its priests, prophets, sages, and gurus.

The Perennial Tradition, however, does not seek such distinctions. Rather, it sifts through the scriptures and teachings of many cultures looking for those teachings that transcend the limits of specific cultures and point to the Reality that cannot be named, defined, or figured out. Augustine, the great fifth-century theologian, articulated that very idea when he declared, "*Si comprehenderis, non est Deus*" (If you understand, then what you understand is not God). God, it seems, cannot really be known, but only related to.

Such teaching, central to scripture, is regularly overlooked by people committed to religious uniqueness or denominational distinctives. Due to scripture's narrative nature, essential teachings about God are not dealt with abstractly, dogmatically, or systematically, but rather in pastoral or social settings, such as by caring for the poor and needy (Jer. 22:16) and by loving fellow human beings in general (1 John 4:20; see also James 1:27).

Alternatively, as mystics assert, we know God by loving God, by trusting God, by placing our hope in God. Such relating is always non-possessive, a non-objectified way of knowing. It is always I-thou and never I-it, to use Martin Buber's insightful perspective.

Is the Perennial Tradition, the perspective that all the world's religions share a single truth or origin, consonant with Christianity? For many, this perspective is false, misleading, and heretical. For others, however, it is not only compatible with Christianity, but it represents an essential and oft overlooked aspect of Christianity, perhaps its deepest insight and teaching.

A person's view of God is vital because it serves as a lens through which people view reality, influencing their perspective of life, the cosmos, others, and of themselves. As one's view of self provides a microcosm of reality, so one's view of God serves as a macrocosm of that reality. If one's view of God is positive—such as lover or friend—then the universe seems benevolent, others are valued, and the self is considered good. However, if one's view of God is negative—such as angry antagonist or vindictive judge—then the universe seems harsh, others are devalued, and the self is considered evil or sinful.

Theology is "talk about God." The majority of people who use the term "God," particularly in the Western world, have in mind a theistic concept of God, meaning an all-powerful and supreme ruler of the universe. Supernatural theism, by implication, includes the view that all finite things are dependent in some way on this ultimate reality, a reality generally described in personal terms. After all, imaging God as a personal being is very common in the Bible. It is also the natural language of worship and prayer, and there is nothing wrong with it in such contexts. A transcendent reality that does not possess at the very least those qualities that constitute the dignity of human beings, qualities such as intelligence, feeling, freedom, power, initiative, and creativity, could not adequately inspire trust or reverence in human beings. In this sense, God would have to be "personal" to be God. It is doubtful whether believers could worship something that does not have at least the stature of personality.

While the idea of a "personal God" is beneficial in that it makes God relational and accessible to humanity, the extremes of this position, such as presented in the Hebrew scriptures, raise insuperable problems for people in the modern era. This God fights wars and defeats enemies, chooses people and works through them, sends storms, heals the sick, spares the dying, rewards goodness, and punishes evil. Many people have trouble intellectually with these anthropomorphic renderings of God and with the seeming irrationality of belief in a personal God. While only the most traditional believers and the most literal readers of scripture believe such things anymore, this deity remains the primary object and substance of the Christian church's faith. It is this understanding of God that is becoming meaningless to increasing numbers in the modern world.

While it is attractive to speak of intimacy with God and accessibility to God, religious philosophers have long warned against ascribing human qualities and attributing human feelings to God. Still, the joy of familiarity with God and the need to recognize and be recognized by God override the philosopher's critique. There is, however, a critical flaw in this perspective: Once we conceive of God as a person like ourselves, God becomes open to criticism.

To protect God, apologists and theologians urge us to discard this way of thinking. God is not like us, says twentieth-century theologian Karl Barth; God is "Totally Other." This understanding views God as different not only in degree but also in kind. Humans can only speak of God indirectly, says thirteenth-century theologian Thomas Aquinas, for they cannot "know" God directly. Humans can only speak of God or "know" God indirectly, by saying what God is not (the *via negativa*), or by saying what God is like, thereby resorting to analogies or metaphors (the *via analogia*).

In using models of transcendence, whereby God is said to be all-knowing, all-powerful, and all-good, we instinctively know that we are not referring to the same kind of qualities we understand when speaking of attributes in humans. Does this mean, then, that God cannot be said to be moral in the manner that we are said to be moral? If so, that raises deep resentments. We hear it in the outburst of the philosopher John Stuart Mill: "I will call no being good who is not what I mean when I apply the epithet to my fellow creatures, and if such a being can sentence me to hell, to hell I will go."[2]

In his publication, *The Sins of Scripture*, Bishop Spong examines biblical moral principles attributed to the will of God and concludes that those who wish to base their morality literally on the Bible have either not read it or not understood it. Bishop Spong spoke forcefully and shockingly when he wrote:

> There is no supernatural God who lives above the sky or beyond the universe. There is no supernatural God who can be

---

2. Cited by Schulweis, *Those Who Can't Believe*, 132.

understood as animating spirit, Earth Mother, masculine tribal deity or external monotheistic being. There is no parental deity watching over us from whom we can expect help. There is no deity whom we can flatter into acting favorably or manipulate by being good. There are no record books and no heavenly judge keeping them to serve as the basis on which human beings will be rewarded or punished. There is also no way that life can be made to be fair or that a divine figure can be blamed for its unfairness. Heaven and hell are human constructs designed to make fair in some ultimate way the unfairness of life. The idea that in an afterlife the unfairness of this world will be rectified is a pious dream, a toe dip into unreality. Life is lived at the whim of luck and chance, and no one can earn the good fortune of luck and chance.[3]

With Spong, I too recoil at these words, for the traditional understanding of God has been my guide from the beginning. Unlike some who have concluded that God is no more, Spong does not mean to say that God once existed but has since died. Nor does he mean to say that there is no God. What he calls "God" is real, only not as popularly conceived.[4]

But what are the alternatives? Is atheism (a-theism) the only alternative to theism? Technically, of course, there are numerous options, including polytheism (the belief that there are numerous deities), pantheism (the belief that God is in everything for everything is divine), henotheism (the notion of worshipping a territorial god, conceived as one god among many), animism (the belief that nature is filled with spirits or souls, which must be worshipped or appeased), and panentheism.

UNDERSTANDING GOD PANENTHEISTICALLY

Many people today are finding the case for panentheism increasingly attractive in an age of science and reason. One can find historical traces of panentheism in both Western and Eastern orthodox theology, though the word itself was popularized by English philosopher Alfred North Whitehead (1861–1947). Panentheism is not the same as pantheism, the concept

---

3. Spong, *Eternal Life*, 121–22.

4. The conventional understanding of God, based in part on medieval debates and the language of certain classical theologians, attributes to deity such qualities as impassibility (that God cannot experience pain and suffering), transcendence (that God is eternal and unchanging and largely unrelated to this world), and omnipotence (unlimited in power and capable of doing all things). Overall, such views are unbiblical and, with regard to the concept of "omnipotence," philosophically indefensible.

that "all things are God." Rather, pan*en*theism is the concept that "all things are *in* God." Panentheism views God not as a supernatural being separate from the universe, beyond nature and history, but as the encompassing Spirit around us and within us. According to this conception, God is more than the universe, yet the universe is in God. Viewed spatially, God is not "out there" but "right here." Whereas supernatural theism emphasizes God's transcendence—God's otherness, God as more than the universe—panentheism affirms both the transcendence and immanence of God. It does not deny or subordinate one in order to affirm the other. For panentheism, God is both more than the universe and yet everywhere present in the universe.

In this regard, panentheism is located between traditional theism and pantheism. As David Ray Griffin describes it, panentheism "combines features of both pantheism, which regards God as 'essentially immanent and in no way transcendent,' and traditional theism, which regards God 'as essentially transcendent and only accidentally immanent.'"[5] Griffin's work helps to explain why panentheism isn't just pantheism with a new name: "Panentheism is crucially different from pantheism because God transcends the universe in the sense that God has God's own creative power, distinct from that of the universe of finite actualities. Hence, each finite actual entity has its own creativity with which to exercise some degree of self-determination, so that it transcends the divine influence upon it."[6]

Theologians in various traditions have offered different ways of defining and modeling this God-world relationship. According to the influential German evangelical theologian Jürgen Moltmann, in the panentheistic view God, having created the world, also dwells in it, and conversely the world which he has created exists in him. He writes of God "making space," a *nothing* (*nihil*) to which God gives being (*creatio ex nihilo*). "God does not create merely by calling something into existence . . . In a more profound sense he 'creates' by letting-be, by making room, by withdrawing himself."[7] Moltmann's language expresses the idea of the world, including humanity, as "enveloped by God without losing its true distinctiveness."[8] Consonant with Moltmann's theology, Anglican theologian Arthur Peacocke writes that "God is best conceived of as the circumambient [i.e., surrounding] reality enclosing all existing entities, structures and processes, and as operating in and through all, while being 'more' than all. Hence, all that is not God

---

5. Griffin, *Reenchantment*, 141.
6. Ibid., 142.
7. Moltmann, *God in Creation*, 88–89.
8. Clayton and Peacocke, *In Whom We Live*, 145.

has its existence within God's operation and Being."[9] Other panentheistic models have been suggested, but all reveal a common theme: the world is given existence, energy, life, nourishment, and continuous creation by the God in whom "we live and move and have our being" (Acts 17:28).

Fortunately there are alternatives to the concept of theism, for "theism" and "God" need not be the same. Supernatural theism is but one human definition of God. Panentheists affirm that "God" does not refer to a supernatural being "in heaven," apart from nature, but rather to the sacred at the center of existence, the holy mystery that is around us and within us. Panentheism affirms the centrality of mystery in the universe and the possibility of relating intellectually and experientially to that mystery. It is possible, then, to be an agnostic or even an atheist regarding the God of supernatural theism and yet be a believer in God in the way offered by panentheism.

In 1986 John F. Haught, one of our most insightful Christian scholars, wrote a short work titled *What is God? How to Think About the Divine*. Writing for skeptical individuals who question whether talk about God is obsolete, Haught proposed that we alter the way we think about God; instead of using personal terms to describe God—asking "who" God is—he suggests that we focus instead on "what" God is, focusing on the transpersonal or superpersonal aspect to God found in many religious traditions, aspects of deity that cannot be adequately represented in personalistic imagery. This approach is helpful ontologically as well as intellectually.

Ontologically, an examination of the transpersonal dimension of God's nature, that side of God's being that cannot be adequately represented in personalistic terms, may help us to make some sense of the "scandal" of the divine hiddenness. Intellectually, thinkers ask questions like "What is nature?" "What is history?" "What is the universe?" Those are the questions of inquiry, so in that intellectual environment it seems appropriate to ask also "What is God?" Haught's project isn't to demonstrate the existence of God, but rather to help us think about God, thereby arguing that a case can be made for taking seriously the possibility that God is.

The suspicion of God's existence that one finds in the writings of Nietzsche, Marx, and Freud is shared by many intellectuals today. Noting a serious question today among scientific thinkers, philosophers, and many other intelligent people as to whether the word "God" actually refers to any genuinely real dimension of our experience, Haught claims that talk about "God" may be little more that whistling in the dark or a cover-up for human weakness. Given the trite and personalistic ways the idea of God has been

9. Ibid., 146.

employed by many "religious" people, such suspicion is often justified. But the word "God" can mean much more than this.

Haught contends that the idea of God was not a theoretical construct invented by theologians but came to human consciousness spontaneously as the product of religious experience, as a response to the sense of the "sacred," a phenomenon Rudolf Otto termed the *mysterium tremendum et fascinans*. Originally described in the language of symbol and myth, this experience "was acted out in ritual and other kinds of human activity long before it became a topic of philosophical or theological discussion."[10] Modern reflection on God should utilize similar symbolic categories, ones that can be identifiable in the experience of all human beings and not simply "religious" people.

Building on the contributions of depth psychology, process theology, and the insights of important twentieth-century religious thinkers such as Whitehead, Paul Tillich, Paul Ricoeur, Bernard Lonergan, and Karl Rahner, Haught identifies five experiential human notions as the locus for conceptualizing deity: depth, future, freedom, beauty, and truth. While there is something undeniably "real" about each of these aspects of conscious existence, there is something elusive about them as well. Like our idea of God, such experiences are either bio-psychological phenomena that refer to nothing beyond themselves, or they point beyond themselves to a Source that grounds them—which Source is a God candidate.

Utilizing these five categories enables Haught to emphasize what he calls the "neuter" rather than the masculine and feminine images ordinarily evoked by religious symbolism, the "whatness" rather than the "whoness" of God. Considered the leading figure in the development of twentieth-century hermeneutics, German philosopher Hans-Georg Gadamer relates how his teacher, Martin Heidegger, once observed: "Who is God? That is perhaps beyond the possibilities of our asking. But what is God? That we should ask."[11] And Gadamer thinks that we should pay more attention to neuter expressions such as "the divine" or "the sacred," terms that occurs frequently in poetry: "I think the neuter is one of the most mysterious things in human language . . . To use the neuter—for example, "the beautiful"—expresses something of ungraspable presence. It is no longer "this" or "that," male or female, here or there; it is filling empty space . . . The neuter represents in a way the plenitude of presence, the omnipresence of something. Hence the divine is indeed an expression for such omnipresence."[12] Thus, while

---

10. Haught, *What is God?*, 2–3.
11. Cited in Haught, ibid., 8.
12. Cited in Haught, ibid.

inadequate in itself, the neuter in our thinking of God is a helpful corrective to a one-sided personalistic understanding.

In selecting ordinary aspects of human experience, Haught demonstrates that humans react to concepts such as depth, future, freedom, beauty, and truth "in the same way that Rudolph Otto's *homo religiosus* reacts to the sacred. We experience these realities first of all as *mysteria*, that is, as incomprehensible, overwhelming, and majestic... Secondly, they are *tremenda*, in that they are terrifying in their demands upon us, and so understandably we shrink from them, fearing that we shall be lost if we surrender completely to them. Finally they are *fascinosa*, inasmuch as there is something ultimately fascinating, attractive, and satisfying about them. They have the same features Otto saw in the religious experience of the sacred,"[13] particularly when one examines these as dimensions that appear more as the horizon of our experience than as qualities or objects of our experience. As the geographical horizon is elusive since it recedes as we explore further, so God might be understood in part as the ultimate horizon of all our experience, always receding, encompassing, illuminating, but never falling within our comprehending grasp.

One of the most persistent aspects of the "problem of God" is that there is no unambiguous evidence in our ordinary experience of any providential, transcendent, divine presence. Many atheists and agnostics point to this and wonder how truly intelligent persons can be believers. But the point here is that the reality of God is no less capable of immediate validation than are the dimensions of depth, future, freedom, beauty, and truth. For God not to be accessible to our senses or our wishes should be no more outrageous than that these dimensions are incapable of being brought under our comprehending control. God is not one object among others in our experience. Rather, God may be understood as the ultimate horizon that makes all experience possible in the first place. The sacred does not force itself into the range of objects or events that make up the content of ordinary experience. Instead, God may be viewed as the inexhaustible depth and ground out of which all our experiences arise.

The most important way of responding to the question "What is God?" is to say that essentially God is mystery. Haught's five metaphors, while helpful, do not exhaust and should not be substituted for that of mystery. Unfortunately, in a world where the methods and techniques of science have become dominant, the sense of mystery often leaves us feeling insecure. In the face of this eclipse of mystery, the very possibility of speaking

---

13. Ibid., 5–6.

meaningfully about God has likewise diminished. For that reason, it is essential today that leaders emerge to provide a sort of pedagogy of mystery.

The term "mystery" is often misunderstood simply as a gap in our knowledge, a temporary hiatus that might be closed as scientific consciousness advances. Thus, the realm of "mystery" will allegedly be gradually diminished, and "knowledge" will take its place. As B. F. Skinner, the noted psychologist, has put it, the objective of science is to eliminate mystery. However, when "mystery" is understood in this way, namely as a gap to be replaced by scientific knowledge, it is little wonder that the word no longer functions to evoke a religious sense of the *tremendum et fascinans*. For in this case "mystery" is merely a vacuum that begs to be filled with our intellectual achievements rather than an ineffable depth summoning our awe and allegiance.

Haught encourages us to address the gaps in our present understanding and knowledge as "problems" rather than as "mysteries." "Problem" points to an area of ignorance that may be solved eventually by the application of human ingenuity. "Mystery," on the other hand, denotes a region of reality that, instead of growing smaller as we grow wiser and more powerful, can actually be experienced as growing larger and more incomprehensible as we solve more of our scientific and other problems. Mystery is the horizon that keeps expanding and receding into the distance the more our knowledge advances. In contrast to problems, mystery is incapable of any "solution." Whereas problems can be solved and eliminated, mystery becomes more prominent the deeper our questions go and the surer our answers become.[14]

For Haught, there are only two major "truths" that a genuine religious sense requires. All dogmas of religion are derivatives of these two truths: the first is that our lives are embraced by mystery, and the second is that this mystery is gracious. Keeping these two propositions before us "provides us with criteria to evaluate and criticize the actual religious lives of others and ourselves. For there is no doubt that religious traditions which have their origin in a decisive encounter with mystery and its graciousness can themselves deviate from their founding insights and end up participating in the eclipse of mystery. Religions can become entangled in the pursuit of domination or the legitimation of oppression and thus themselves become obstacles to the sense of liberating mystery. Hence they should constantly be evaluated in accordance with the criteria of mystery and its graciousness."[15]

---

14. Ibid., 118–20.
15. Ibid., 127–28.

THE VULNERABLE GOD

Alfred North Whitehead characterized God's relationship to the world as that of a "Persuasive Lover;" and Haught, Peacocke, and others have offered variations on Whitehead's theme. The love relationship is an apt metaphor, for love is the fundamental and most intimate of relationships. Two qualities make this analogy particularly attractive: (1) that the essence of love is persuasive rather than coercive, and (2) that the experience of the beloved is to flourish and grow and emerge into fullness of life as a result of being loved. If this is so in human experience, then in a much more profound way God's unconditional love for the creation must be such as to invite the creation into ever more complex levels of being. To accomplish this, the God of infinite love freely accepts the integrity of nature, its processes and its laws, thereby inviting the world through the complex interplay of all of its elements to emerge into more novel forms and greater beauty through the evolutionary process.

QUESTIONS FOR DISCUSSION AND REFLECTION

1. In your own words, define "Perennial Philosophy" or "wisdom tradition." Are these concepts identical or merely similar? Explain your answer.

2. In your own words, name the four existential or ultimate questions addressed by Perennial Philosophy. Why are these questions central to the spiritual quest? Are there other questions or issues you would add to the list? Explain your answer.

3. Explain the difference between viewing Ultimate Reality as Subject or as object.

4. Assess the validity of the author's statement, "In the world of spirituality, nondualists are the only experts."

5. Do you agree with the idea that "God is both perfectly hidden and perfectly revealed in all things?" Explain your answer.

6. Explain the meaning of Augustine's dictum, "If you understand God, then it is not God."

7. In the Perennial Tradition, is the perspective that all the world's religions share a single truth or origin consonant with Christianity? Explain your answer.

8. Assess the author's statement that a person's view of God influences his or her view of reality (of life, the cosmos, others, and themselves).

9. What are the advantages and disadvantages of the idea of a "personal God"?

10. Explain the meaning of the term "panentheism." Do you find merit in Haught's preference for the "whatness" of God over the "whoness" of God? What are the advantages and disadvantages of the idea of an "impersonal God"?

11. In your estimation, what is the primary insight gained from this chapter? Does this chapter raise any issues you might need to address in the future?

Chapter 4

Perennial Wisdom and Ultimate Reality, Part II

WHILE TRADITIONAL THEISTS HAVE been one-sided in speaking of the remoteness of God from the ordinary realm of experience, mystics have emphasized the "nearness" of the sacred. In fact, because there is no contradiction between the absence and the nearness of God, God's absence may even be understood as essential for the sake of the nearness. By not intruding into or forcing itself upon the world and personal subjects, the divine mystery can be understood as caringly involved with the world. Concerned that the world not lose its integrity by being absorbed into the divine or diluted into an overbearing divine "presence," God may be seen to "withdraw" from the world and from persons in order to let them be. This withdrawal, this self-absenting of God, however, is not abdication but rather essential in order to give the world its autonomy and human subjects their freedom. In this sense the absence and inscrutability of mystery may be understood as the other side of its intimacy with us.[1]

GOD AS SPIRIT

In his accessible book titled *The God We Never Knew*, biblical scholar Marcus Borg examined the variety of images of God in the biblical and Christian traditions and discerned therein two primary "models":

---

1. Haught, *What is God?*, 130–31.

1. The *"monarchical model,"* which clusters images of God as king, lord, and father. This approach leads to what Borg calls a "performance model" of the Christian life.

2. The *"Spirit model,"* which clusters images of God that point to intimate relationship and belonging. This model leads to a "relational model" of the Christian life.

Both models, Borg discovered, are found throughout all periods of Christian history, though the first is more common. From roughly the fourth century—when Christianity became the dominant religion of Western culture—through the present, the monarchical model has dominated. But alongside it, as an alternative voice, the Spirit model has also persisted. These models reflect two different voices within the Christian tradition.

The monarchical model portrays God as male, as all-powerful, as lawgiver, and as judge. Images of God in this model suggest that God is distant. Within this model, humans have offended divine majesty and deserve judgment. But because God loves his subjects, God creates a way for his people to escape the punishment they deserve: through appropriate sacrifice and true repentance. In the royal theology of ancient Israel, atonement was institutionalized in temple rituals. In the Christian version of the monarchical model, the king's (Lord's) love is seen especially in Jesus. Because God loves us, he sends his son into the world to die on a cross as the sacrifice that makes our forgiveness possible.[2]

The Spirit model, as used in the Bible, is broader than the specific Christian doctrine of "the Holy Spirit," which sees the Spirit as one aspect of God. In the Bible, Spirit is used comprehensively to refer to God's presence in creation, in the history of Israel, and in the life of Jesus and the early church. While the monarchical model also affirms that God is Spirit, of course, and that affirmation can be a source of confusion that limits our understanding of God, there is a difference. When Spirit is assimilated to the monarchical model, God is not Spirit but a spirit—that is, a spiritual being out there, not here. But when Spirit is set free from the monarchical understanding, Spirit retains the suggestive meanings associated with breath and wind: God is the encompassing Spirit both within and outside us.[3]

In addition to wind and breath, the Bible provides other non-anthropomorphic images, such as rock (meaning a place of refuge and safety). Additional non-masculine images include mother, wisdom, lover, and shepherd. These metaphors for the Spirit affect our root image of God in

---

2. Borg, *God We Never Knew*, 63–64.
3. Ibid., 72.

quite obvious ways: (1) they emphasize *the nearness of God* rather than the distance implied by the monarchical model, thereby suggesting the language of relationship; (2) they utilize *both male and female metaphors* (as well as some that are neuter), rather than the exclusively male images of the monarchical model; and (3) they include *both anthropomorphic and nonathropomorphic images*. Taken together, both models suggest that the relationship to God is personal, even as God is more than a person. The sacred is not simply an inanimate mystery but a presence. Using an ancient biblical analogy, these metaphors lead to a covenantal understanding of the divine-human relationship, which emphasizes belonging and connectedness. This model is intrinsically dialogical.[4]

The images of God associated with the Spirit model dramatically affect how we think of the Christian life. Rather than God as a distant being with whom we might spend eternity, Spirit—the sacred—is right here. Rather than sin and guilt being the central dynamic of the Christian life, the central dynamic becomes relationship—with God, the world, and each other.

The mystics of every religious tradition, following the Spirit model rather than the monarchical model, have always spoken out against specific definitions of God. The Western mystics appear to have assumed that a personal God was only a stage, and an inferior one at that, in human religious development. The mystical portrait of God was first imaginative, and then ineffable. It involved an interior journey, not an exterior one. In the mystical tradition no one can claim objectivity for his or her insight. Each person is called to journey into the mystery of God along the pathway of his or her own expanding personhood. Every person is thus capable of being a theophany, as sign of God's presence; but no one person, institution, or way of life can exhaust this revelation. God, for the mystics, is found at the depths of life, working in and through the being of this world, calling all nature to its deepest potential.

Alfred North Whitehead, who began his professional life as a mathematician, laid out the theological framework for perceiving God not as a divine being external to the universe, but as a divine process coming into being within the life of this world. This conception of God as existing with all of reality, not prior to it, became known as process theology. Dietrich Bonhoeffer called the world to something he named "religionless Christianity," suggesting in his letters, written from prison as he awaited his execution by the Third Reich, that Christians need to live in this world "as if there were no God." His death as a martyr prevented him from conceptualizing further the implications of his hypothesis, but

---

4. Ibid., 75–76.

a religionless—perhaps even a nontheistic or godless—Christianity appeared on the horizon of his thinking.

Paul Tillich, himself a refugee from Nazi Germany, proposed as far back as the 1930s and 1940s that Western Christians should abandon the external height images in which the theistic God had historically been perceived, replacing them with internal depth images of a deity not apart from us but the very core and ground of all that is. This God was not a person, but rather was the mystical presence in which all personhood could flourish. This God was not a being but rather the power that called being forth in all creatures. This God was not an external, personal force that could be invoked but rather an internal reality that, when confronted, opened us to the meaning of life itself.[5] Tillich, who believed that the word "God" had been distorted by the inadequate images of the past, was convinced that those images must die before the word "God" could ever be used again with meaning. He urged a moratorium on the use of the word "God" for at least a hundred years.

Following Tillich, Bishop Spong provides a model that integrates the Christian doctrine of the Trinity with this understanding of God. The meaning of God, according to his conception, is understood as (1) the source of life, (2) the source of love, and (3) the ground of being. He finds in this triune understanding a portrait of God embodied in Jesus of Nazareth, a whole human being who lived fully, loved lavishly, and had the courage to be himself under every circumstance.

So the call of this internal God found in our depths becomes primarily a call into being, a call that is not unique to religion. It is a call that refocuses what has been known as the religious dimension. In this scenario, the task of the church becomes less that of indoctrinating or relating people to an external divine power and more that of providing opportunities for people to touch the infinite center of all things and to fulfill all their potential. This understanding of God places a premium on the church's vocation to oppose anything that prevents us from the fullest expression of our humanity.

Jesus largely communicated through parables, stories, aphorisms, and often obscure riddles. This form of teaching is not pleasing to dualistic or systematic thinkers. One such teaching, found in Luke's Gospel, is particularly relevant, for Jesus is addressing both Pharisees and disciples, outsiders and insiders, simultaneously. In response to their question about when the kingdom would come, he tells them that Ultimate Reality is neither here nor there, but rather is "within you" (Luke 17:21). If people concentrate too much on specific times and seasons and definitive answers, they forget

---

5. Spong, *Christianity Must Change*, 64.

it is always here and now when Ultimate Reality exists and happens. In Luke 17:23, Jesus makes the identical point about place. When people ask, "Where should we look for your coming?" Jesus says, in effect, "Don't look here and don't look there." Once we localize God's action in one place or in one type of event, we can easily miss it in another place or setting, or worse, "that it is not available everywhere and all the time."[6]

In relativizing time and space, Jesus is affirming both the immanence and the transcendence of God, upholding the famous Sanskrit *neti, neti* of ancient Hinduism. "Not this, not that" was taught by ancient sages, not only to safeguard the Mystery of sacred Reality, but to protect human beings from the arrogance of knowing with certainty and finality.

In his interfaith Chautauqua lecture, "God's Limited Effervescence: A Jewish Understanding of Grace," Rabbi Shapiro likened God to grace, by which he meant not simply discernable moments of blessing, but "the whole of life." While people often limit "grace" to goodness, Shapiro views grace as "the whole thing, the stuff we like and the stuff we don't like. And because grace is the whole thing, then God is the whole thing. We want a God who is good, as we define good . . . I am suggesting God isn't good. God is God! God is Reality. God is the aliveness that happens." Looking to scripture, Shapiro cites Isaiah 45:7, which states: "I form the light and create darkness, I make peace and create evil. I the Lord do all these things" (KJV).

The King James translation of Isaiah 45:7, vital to the Perennial Tradition, raises textual and theological questions. To attribute "evil" to God in this context is misleading, for the evil of which the text speaks is the Babylonian exile, an experience Israel's prophets interpreted as God's judgment on God's unfaithful covenant people. Rather than attributing all evil to God—cosmic and existential alike—most translations use terms such as "woe" or "disaster" to convey the nuanced specificity of the text's intended meaning.

In the past, theologians frequently distinguished between God's "active" and "permissive" will, maintaining an equal emphasis on free will and human responsibility. Evil, they taught, is something God allows, not wills. A common explanation for cosmic evil, a favorite of conservative Christians, most of whom affirm the sovereignty of God or some form of supernatural theism, assumes the existence of a realm of evil, engaged in a cosmic struggle with the forces of God. Such a view, however, essentially dualistic, contravenes the biblical doctrine of creation, which maintains the inherent goodness of reality (viewing evil as temporary and ethical rather than eternal or ontological) and upholds the sovereignty of God.

---

6. Rohr, *Naked Now*, 76.

GOD AS TRINITY

Another question concerns the Christian doctrine of God as Trinity. Despite its foundational place in Christian thought, the notion of God as Trinity mystifies Christians, even to the point of embarrassment. For one thing, it seems illogical, overly complex, and hard to comprehend. Furthermore, it makes God excessively personal, accessible, and seemingly less transcendent and divine. Hence, throughout Christian history, the doctrine has been largely ignored. Richard Rohr, trained as a Franciscan priest, recalls learning the *Baltimore Catechism* as a youngster. One of its first questions is, "Where is God?" The correct answer is, "God is everywhere." Despite this teaching, the rest of the catechism—and of Christian teaching, according to Rohr—seemingly proceeded as if such ubiquity is not true, for, according to official Catholicism, God is generally in heaven, and when on earth, primarily with Catholics, in churches, and available to those "good" people who follow the rules.[7]

Internally, the doctrine of the Trinity has been divisive, resulting in schism and splits by groups such as Unitarians, a church movement that grew out of the Protestant Reformation in the 1560s. Opposed to the doctrine of the Trinity, which defines God as three persons in one being, Unitarians focused on the monotheistic belief that God is one person, denying the deity of Jesus and the Holy Spirit as distinct from the one God.

Externally, the doctrine of the Trinity seems contradictory to non-Christians, a stumbling block to Jews, Muslims, and others who adhere to a strictly monotheistic understanding of God and accuse Christianity of polytheism or, at best, of tritheism.

Despite its paradoxical nature, trinitarian theology is vital to Christianity, not only for its distinctive message, but because it serves as a bridge to perennial wisdom. If we are able to get past the Christian distinctives, the doctrine of God as Trinity, at its core, challenges dualistic logic—God cannot be one and more than one at the same time—countering the binary nature of the human brain. For Christian spirituality, God as Trinity makes either/or thinking irrelevant and useless. Trinitarian theology changes human consciousness, particularly when it becomes a lens for viewing reality. If it ceases being something to believe factually, Trinitarian consciousness can provide a wide avenue for interreligious dialogue.

In explaining the Trinity as a doctrine of belief, theologians have used analogies found in nature, such as the yolk, white, and shell of an egg; the root, tree, and fruit of a plant; or water in its three forms of ice, liquid, and

---

7. Ibid., 78–79.

vapor. These analogies point us in the right direction, because they point us to nature rather than to exclusively human logic. However, because these illustrations miss the personal element in the Christian doctrine of the Trinity, the medieval theologian Augustine proposed a psychological analogy. He believed that if humans are created in the image of God, they are created in the image of the Trinity. His psychological analogy for the Trinity came from the human mind: God, he said, is like the memory, intelligence, and will resident within the human mind.

Beginning with the unity of God, a starting point essential to Western Christianity, Augustine proceeded to explore the implications of love for understanding the nature of the Godhead, arguing that the persons of the Trinity are defined by their relation to one another: the Father is the lover, the Son the beloved, and the Spirit the "bond of love" between Father and Son.

These concepts are useful as illustrations, but analogies ultimately fall short when human beings seek to speak of the mystery that is God. When we think metaphysically, even using analogies and metaphors, most of us think dualistically, using paired opposites such as good and evil, light and darkness, male and female, and yin and yang to depict reality. However, this way of seeing places limits on our understanding. To expand our horizons, Christian scholar Cynthia Bourgeault suggests that we replace binary systems with ternary perspectives, adding a third "mediating" or "reconciling" principle to the mix. For instance, instead of focusing on man and woman, emphasizing man, woman, and child, and instead of envisioning black or white, seeing black, white, and gray. This principle is evident in the Christian Trinity, with the incarnated Christ as its culminating expression. According to this perspective, the third force is not a product of the first two, as in the classic Hegelian synthesis, but is independent and coequal with the others. According to Bourgeault, the interweaving of the three produces a fourth force or realm of possibility. In contrast to binary systems, which seek completion in stability, through the balance of opposites, ternary perspectives create a synthesis at a completely new level, seeking completion in newness. In *The Holy Trinity and the Law of Three*, Bourgeault advises that we not limit this metaphysical principle to one triad (Father, Son, and Holy Spirit), but rather that we envision the Holy Trinity as one of many triads, each revealing different facets of the divine wholeness.

This way of thinking is helpful, for it says that God is more a verb than a noun. God is three "relations," more than three persons, which boggles our minds. To understand the Trinity, that is a good place to start, with mystery and newness rather than with certainty and rationality.

Christianity teaches that God the Father is formless, God the Son is form, and God the Holy Spirit is the energy between those two. The three do not cancel each other, nor do they replace one another. Rather, they do exactly the opposite: they are relationship, and known in relationship, not only in the human realm, but also in the realms of biology, cosmology, and physics. The world of science—from molecular biology to astrophysics—now affirms this trinitarian truth, although from different angles. These disciplines see all things as interdependent, reality as a force field of constantly changing forms.

Viewed perennially, the doctrine of the Trinity defeats the dualistic mind and invites human beings into nondual, holistic consciousness. It replaces the argumentative, limiting, binary principle of two with the dynamic, mediating principle of three. It takes us into the wonderfully transformative realm of "not one, but not two either."

The word "person" as we use it today, meaning a separate human individual, is not found in the Hebrew Bible. Instead, we find the concept of "face," as in the well-known priestly benediction in Numbers 6:24–26, "The Lord bless you and keep you; the Lord make his face to shine upon you, and be gracious to you; the Lord lift up his countenance upon you, and give you peace." In the Greek translations, the word for face is *prosopon* (Latin *persona*), a word referring to the stage masks that Greek actors wore, which served as both an enlarged identity and a megaphone. The New Testament also uses *prosopon* to translate "face" as personhood, such as in 2 Corinthians 4:6, which speaks of "the glory of God in the face of Jesus Christ."

This same language is used in the early Christian centuries to communicate how God could be both one and three at the same time. Each member of the Trinity was considered a *persona* or "face" of God. Each person of the Trinity fully communicated its "face" and "glory" to the other, while also maintaining its unique identity. Each person of the Trinity "sounded through" the other, a brilliant way to describe the Trinity, but also how all relationships essentially work.

During the patristic period, when church theologians spoke of God as Trinity, they introduced the term *perichoresis* to explain the relationship between the divine persons. Even as they focused on unity within the Trinity (they spoke of three *hypostases* [persons] in one *ousia* [essence or substance]), they used *perichoresis* to articulate the eternal mutuality within the Godhead. *Perichoresis*, derived from the Greek word *chorein* (meaning "to make room for" or "to contain"), is the theological term that describes the eternal mutual "interrelatedness" and "interpenetration" of the divine persons of the one Being of God.

Originally, *perichoresis* was used by the early church to articulate the coherence of the human and divine natures of Christ. Later, it was used to describe the intrinsic unity and mutual indwelling of the three persons of the Triune God. Trinity was understood as the perichoretic relationship within God's Self, as a "sounding through" of three "persons," each being a mask and megaphone for the larger whole.

To speak of *perichoresis*, however, is not to dismiss the concept of personhood. While the Father, Son, and Holy Spirit are in common with one another, they remain distinctly what they are in themselves. The personal relationships within God's Self are therefore properly understood in terms of their relationship to one another. The Father is the Father only in relation to the Son; the Son is the Son only in relation to the Father; and the Holy Spirit is the Holy Spirit only in relation to the other and the Son. The Father cannot be the Father apart from the Son, and so forth. Consequently, the relationality of the distinctiveness of the persons of the Godhead constitute their unity. The three do not *enter into* relations; they simply *are* relations.

The perichoretic articulation of the Triune God is of vital significance for humanity and of our interrelationship with God, nature, others, and oneself (a topic we examine in chapters 5 and 6), for we, too, are created in God's capacity for love and communion.

From this perspective, when the Christian scriptures teach that "God is love" (1 John 4:3), they are telling us that the whole of life, to use Shapiro's analogy, is love. God is this aliveness that happens, even that which we don't like, what we call bad: all is love. That is how we should experience life, both as gift to be received and as gift to be returned, always in love.

Trinitarian theology, properly understood, should not sequester Christianity from other religions in the Perennial Tradition. Instead, it affirms perennial wisdom's core message that all things are enveloped by and participate in the glorious adventure called Ultimate Reality. The deep sense of the connectedness and oneness of all things within the cosmos was well understood by the nineteenth-century Russian novelist Fyodor Dostoyevsky, who wrote that reality is like an ocean, all things flowing and blending. A touch in one place sets up movement at the other end of the earth; if one sins, something somewhere will suffer. "Love all God's creation," he wrote, "the whole and every grain of sand in it. Love every leaf, every ray of God's light. Love the animals, love the plants, love everything. If you love everything, you will perceive the divine mystery in things. Once you perceive it, you will begin to understand it better every day. And you will come at last to love the whole world with an all-embracing love."[8]

---

8. *The Brothers Karamazov* 6.3.7.

QUESTIONS FOR DISCUSSION AND REFLECTION

1. Which of Borg's two biblical models for God do you find most attractive, the "monarchical" or the "Spirit" model"? Must we choose between them? Is there a better model?

2. How do images associated with the monarchical image affect how we think of the Christian life?

3. How do images associated with the Spirit image affect how we think of the Christian life?

4. In your estimation, what did Bonhoeffer, one of the most courageous Christians of the twentieth century, mean by "religionless Christianity," by suggesting that Christians need to live in this world "as if there were no God"?

5. Assess the advantages and disadvantages of Tillich's reference to God as Ground of Being.

6. In your estimation, what did Jesus mean by speaking of the kingdom of God as being "neither here nor there but within you"?

7. Assess Rabbi Shapiro's likening of God to "grace," meaning "all of life, the stuff we like and the stuff we don't like." Explain and assess his idea that what we call "evil" is a sign of grace.

8. Explain the advantages and disadvantages of the Christian doctrine of the Trinity and how it can serve as a bridge to perennial wisdom.

9. Explain and assess Bourgeault's idea that we need to replace binary systems with ternary perspectives.

10. Explain and assess the concept of *perichoresis*. How helpful is this idea in affirming the unity and plurality within the members of the Trinity? How helpful is this idea in affirming the unity and plurality of all living beings?

11. In your estimation, what is the primary insight gained from this chapter? Does this chapter raise any issues you might need to address in the future?

Chapter 5

Perennial Wisdom and the True Self, Part I

HAVING EXAMINED THE FIRST truth of the Perennial Tradition, namely, the existence and nature of the one Ultimate Reality, this chapter introduces the second corresponding truth taught by the great sages and mystics throughout human history, namely, how human beings relate to that Ultimate Reality.

THE TWO SELVES

In 2019 I came across the book *Perennial Wisdom for the Spiritually Independent* at the Chautauqua bookstore and was immediately intrigued. The writer, Rabbi Rami Shapiro, a professor of comparative religion, is the author of thirty-six books and famously known for his website *Dear Rabbi Rami*, which showcases questions he has been asked in person or on various media outlets.

While the book is organized around five questions central to the spiritual quest, it does not begin with the topic of Ultimate Reality. In fact, the question about Ultimate Reality's existence and nature is never addressed directly in the book. The reason is simple: Rabbi Shapiro is not interested in metaphysical speculation about what is Real, because in his estimation, such talk is misleading and ultimately meaningless. In his view, Ultimate Reality is exclusively Subject, and cannot be made into an object of conversation. Of course, it is easy to fall into the trap of making an object of the eternal

Subject. We do it all the time, for it is dualistic and suits our preferred way of thinking, but it is faulty and deceptive, a trick of consciousness perpetrated by the individual human ego.

The key to Shapiro's philosophy is radical liberation, helping people dissociate from the narratives that define their uniqueness in order to see divinity everywhere and in everyone. In his Chautauqua lecture, he identified two ways to look at the individual self. The preferred method uses the lens of being a character in a story. This approach tends to be static and often misses the opportunity to be grateful for being alive. The second approach is to see one's truer self as part of the larger "aliveness," which has no age and is eternal.

Shapiro emphasized the idea of moving away from seeing a dichotomy between one's individual self and Ultimate Reality. "This is how I understand God," he said. "God is this aliveness." He noted that people often have a limited scope of God when they make use of partnerships with God or see God as dualistic Other. For this reason, his analysis of perennial wisdom begins with the question, "Who Am I?" For Shapiro, this is the necessary starting point, not only because it is practical and personal, but also because the true answer is liberating: to begin with oneself is to begin with Ultimate Reality, for the human "I" is God.

"In a world where many individuals have narrative forced upon them," Shapiro noted, "it is important to see divinity in everyone, because once people see God in others, it is harder to work against them. You are God, and when you know that, you act godly," he concluded.

That concept, of course, is transformative, for it illustrates all four aspects of Agostino Steuco's Perennial Philosophy, particularly the fourth assumption, that when we realize our true nature is a manifestation of Ultimate Reality, we will relate to others less violently and competitively and with greater compassion and respect, replacing anxiety and needless suffering with serenity and grace.

For Shapiro, God cannot be found "out there" until God is first found "in here," within ourselves. In fact, the search for God and for our True Self is essentially the same search, for what we seek is what we are. To acquire this perspective, we must acknowledge that what we are—least in part—is what we seek. Indeed, this identity is what makes us seek in the first place.

While starting with the individual and one's own experience represents a modern intuitive approach, Shapiro's starting point is not my own. To one trained in biblical theology and reared in traditional Christianity, his approach seems tenuous, subjective, and overly humanistic. My Christian conditioning is simply too strong. Christianity starts with the big picture and, working deductively, concludes with the individual. So that's what I am doing here. In my way of thinking, God is Being itself, and therefore distinct, and greater than me. Nevertheless, God is also a Being more me than I am myself. I am never totally absorbed into God, not the same as God, which is pantheism. I am, however, inherently in union with God, and this changes everything. God is a Thou, and not just an energy field. Moreover, I am an I, and not just an object or a statistic.

The connecting path is relationship, and not simply discipline or duty. Authentic contemplation of the Other, through all the necessary stages of personal relationship, calls us beyond our false selves into The Self. We become the One we gaze upon. And, according to the medieval German theologian Meister Eckhart, "the eyes by which we look back at God are the same eyes by which God has first looked at us." This reciprocal gaze is the True Self.

The brilliance of perennial wisdom is that either approach (Shapiro's and mine) works, because in either case, the starting point is the same. Everything is a manifestation of the divine—everything! The notion of divine union was first convincingly expressed in the Hindu Upanishads some twenty-five hundred years ago, and it is the first and foundational insight of the Perennial Tradition: "YOU Are That"—the phrase in Sanskrit is *tat tvam asi*. It can be translated many ways, such as "You ARE what you seek," or "You are IT." You are the Subject that embraces and transcends all objects. You are not other than what you observe, but you are always greater than what you observe. You are nobody and somebody, the eternal and the temporal, the absolute and the finite, God and not God. You are both, simultaneously. Of course, these concepts are words, labels. The true "I" is without labels. It is very difficult if not impossible to speak of the true "I." The problem is not with the Reality, but rather with the language. It is nearly impossible for us to speak without falling into the trap of making an object of the eternal Subject. This is the limitation of language, and we run into it repeatedly when we speak of Ultimate Reality.

At this point, some may think that I am talking about being "personally divine" and easily dismiss this way of talking as pantheism. This, however, is not what I mean. To examine what I have in mind, we must begin with Jesus. For Christians, he is the model and metaphor for this teaching. He is the archetypal True Self offered to history, where matter and spirit operate as one, where divine and human are held in one container. For Christians, Jesus is the starting point. Yet, this is the surprising thing missed by so many. In his birth, life, death, and resurrection, Jesus is a stand-in for all of us. The True Self—my True Self, your True Self—is neither God nor human. The True Self is both at the same time, and both are a gift. That is the good news of the gospel, news most of us never heard, and if we did, were unable to hear or believe. For that reason, as so many sages teach, spirituality tends to be more about unlearning than learning. That was Paul's discovery in writing his letter to the Philippians: "For to me, living is Christ and dying is gain" (Phil. 1:21). While many take Paul literally, the deeper truth is metaphorical: To live in Christ is to live according to one's True Self, and to die to the old and False Self is always gain.

A necessary place to begin, then, in answering the question of how human beings relate to Ultimate Reality, is with the idea that two selves inhabit every person: the temporary False Self and the permanent True Self. Eventually, everyone who embarks on the spiritual quest, Christian or otherwise, necessarily encounters the thorny question: When I act or think, who is acting and reflecting? Is it "my" self? A False Self? A True Self? The God self? If the scenario seems contrived, the question deceptive, or the answer obvious, the chances are good that the "wrong" person is acting, and this is a problem.

To be spiritual, that is, authentically human, is to be on a quest. While sometimes disguised as love, beauty, truth, or happiness, these represent a higher pursuit, the search for transcendence. As Augustine wrote at the start of his *Confessions*, "You have made us for yourself, O Lord, and our hearts are restless until they find their rest in You" (*Confessions* 1.1.1). Later in the book we find this famous prayer, "Late have I loved you, Beauty so ancient and so new . . . You were within me, but I was without" (*Confessions* 10.27.38).

This quest for the divine, this search for the sacred within and without, seems to many so daunting and impossible that they give up eventually—or perhaps do not even try—to seek the truth, retreating instead into the comfort and convenience of individualism and egocentricity. When we back off, it is on account of our ego, because egoism is our common default, even if it is largely unconscious. As we shall see, this retreat into the personal ego is both inevitable and ineffectual, necessary and misguided.

We are right about going inside, but the question is, "Which inside?" It is necessary to center oneself, to pull back into one's True Self, but disastrous to center oneself habitually on one's ego. That there are two selves is a distinct teaching in the Perennial Tradition. We might call the False Self our temporary self or ego, and the True Self our eternal self or soul. The terms "ego" and "soul," helpful in the short term, are ultimately undefinable, since they are human constructs, a way to speak of noumenal realities universally acknowledged yet scientifically unverifiable.

By ego, we normally mean the temporal self, defined by gender, ethnicity, religion, nationality, personality, age, profession, social class, obligations, and anything else that attaches to the "me" I normally take myself to be. This "I," though temporary, mortal, and changing, is self-centered, for it sees itself as "somebody." In this regard, it senses, acts, thinks, and reflects. By soul, we normally mean "our inherent identity." In this regard, the soul has no gender, ethnicity, religion, nationality, personality, age, profession, likes or dislikes, or other identifying characteristics. This view of the self, free from all labels, sees itself as "nobody," for it transcends temporality, mortality, and change. In this sense, we can speak of the soul as eternal.

When we speak popularly of "soul," we rarely communicate precisely or accurately, for we are referring to a concept difficult to conceptualize, hence, to define. In older translations of the Bible, such as the King James Version, the word often meant "person," particularly that part of us that is alive or responsible (see Genesis 2:7, where the newly created Adam, upon receiving the "breath of life," becomes a "living soul"; such usage, common in Elizabethan English, is translated more accurately by newer versions as "living being," NRSV; see also Ezekiel 18:4, where the KJV rendering, "the soul that sinneth, it shall die" is more accurately translated, "the person who sins shall die, NRSV).

Ancient Greeks believed in the doctrine of the "immortality of the soul," meaning they understood the soul to be eternal in the absolute sense of having no beginning and no end. When Christians spoke of the "soul," they took it in the Hebraic rather than the Greek sense, as a reference to the unified human being, dependent for life upon God. Viewing humans as temporal creatures rather than as eternal beings, Christians viewed immortality as a gift conferred upon mortal humans by God, rather than as a quality intrinsic to human nature. Hence, Christians often equate the soul with the "image of God" in a person, the part that transcends death and experiences eternity in the afterlife.

Theologians have written many volumes to clarify the meaning of the message in Genesis 1:26 that human beings are formed in the "image" and "likeness" of God. The theological consensus is that "image" denotes our spiritual DNA, an "original blessing" that objectively marks humans as creatures of God, and that "likeness" refers more to a process, a "personal appropriation and gradual realization of this utterly free gift of the image of God."[1] All humans have the same objective gift (True Self), but how they subjectively realize this gift and say "yes" to it varies greatly from one person to another. What we said earlier about the perichoretic nature of the Trinity is applicable here as well, helping us articulate our interrelatedness to God, nature, others, and our True Self.

The many definitions for "soul" present in popular culture today do not reflect the Hebraic understanding, which viewed humans as unified beings, but rather go back to the ancient Greek language, where *psyche*, the word for soul, literally meant "butterfly." For that reason, many cultures associate

---

1. Rohr, *Diamond*, 122.

butterflies with the human soul. In Native American cultures, for example, the butterfly represents the soul of the dead. The Aztecs believe that happy ancestors visit living relatives to assure them that all is well. One town in Mexico promotes this tradition, and it is to that mountainous region that monarch butterflies migrate every year around the holiday known as the Day of the Dead. Their migration from November until March is viewed as the returned souls of the deceased.

For Christians, the three stages of the butterfly's metamorphosis—as caterpillar, pupa, and then winged insect—represent spiritual transformation. The butterfly's existence in four distinct forms is an apt metaphor for the human self: (1) the fertilized egg represents the True Self in the mother's womb; (2) the caterpillar, which only eats and creeps along, represents the life of the False Self; (3) the dormant pupa in its chrysalis represents the death of the False Self; and (4) the butterfly, symbolic of rebirth after death, represents the risen Christ.[2]

Our False Self does not let go easily. It will hang on at all costs. However, this doesn't mean the False Self should be attacked or eliminated. If you go after it directly, it will only disguise itself further. You might feel better, but like most New Year's resolutions, it will fail in the end, leaving your soul largely unformed. Furthermore, the ego is essential to first-half-of-life tasks: establishing an identity, a home, a career, relationships, friends, community, and security, all foundational for getting started in life.

There has probably never been a culture in human history that did not value law, tradition, custom, authority, boundaries, and a clear sense of morality. Such containers provide humans with the requisite security, continuity, predictability, impulse control, and ego structure needed to confront the challenges of life. Individuals grounded in these foundations tend to grow up more naturally and happily than those who receive little by way of guidance. Without boundaries, but also without pushing against those boundaries, humans cannot develop fully or naturally. Required behavior and beliefs are good and necessary to get us started. However, when we invest in them too heavily, they soon hold us back. As Paul says, they are like a disciplinarian ("custodian," RSV; "tutor," KJV; Gal. 3:24) to help us get started. Like training wheels on a bicycle, they keep us safe and prevent us from falling, but if we rely on them too long, we never "grow up."

Ironically, one needs a strong ego structure to let go of ego; one cannot or should not give up a self that is not well formed. As two-year-olds assert their identity and teenagers their rebellion, so we find in nature that goslings must break their shells and butterflies their cocoons in order to fly.

---

2. The concept of the death and resurrection of the self is explored in chapter 8.

The creature cannot be healthy and whole unless its egg shell is tough and its cocoon resistant. But if one remains in the protected half of life beyond its natural period, one becomes a "well-disguised narcissist or an adult infant (who is also a narcissist)—both of whom are often thought to be successful 'good old boys' by the mainstream culture."[3]

As you can see, your False Self is not your bad self, your clever or inherently deceitful self, the self you shouldn't like. Actually, your False Self is quite good and necessary as far as it goes. It simply doesn't go far enough; and it regularly substitutes for the real thing. Its role is temporary, a warm-up rather than the adventure itself, a preparation rather than a destination. That is why we call it "false," because it pretends to be more than it is. Various false selves, like temporary costumes, are necessary to get us started, but they show their limitations when they stay too long. If a person keeps growing, his or her false selves usually die in exposure to greater light.

The False Self sees everything in parts, in hierarchies and in reference to itself. The True Self, however, sees everything in wholes, and therefore in contrast to the way the world sees things. The True Self is conscious, the False Self largely unconscious. The False Self lies because it is a lie. Hence, it is a house built on sand (Matt. 7:26). The True Self is honest. It can see and speak truth to itself. It is a house, therefore, built on rock (Matt. 7:25). As such, it is a shared and shareable self, faithful and useful to all.

This does not mean that the True Self is morally perfect or psychologically whole. It can make mistakes, but it sees them for what they are—mistakes—and is able to apologize and change. Many saints, prophets, and mystics are eccentric and strange, with serious blind spots. But they know who they are in God, and are able to return there. The True Self does not really "go to heaven" as much as it lives there already.

To this point, it seems appropriate to equate the soul with the True Self. In some ways they are interchangeable, yet they are also different. The soul is who you are in God and who God is in you. You can never really lose your soul; you can only fail to realize it (this is perhaps the best meaning of "forfeiting" one's life in Matthew 16:26, or, as the KJV reads, "losing one's soul"). You are unique: your soul—your essential being—will never appear again.

The task of religion, of education and the liberal arts, is to create an environment that awakens one's soul, that enlivens one's heart, that helps individuals find what electrifies them. If religion doesn't put you in touch with your center, then you have accepted someone else's religion, someone else's center.

The True Self, however, is larger than the soul, because it includes Spirit. In *Forgotten Truth*, the renowned scholar of comparative religions, Huston

---

3. Rohr, *Falling Upward*, 26–27.

Smith, delves into the Perennial Tradition, identifying therein a cosmology based on the idea of an ontological gradation of reality. According to Smith, the many-layered nature of both Reality and the Self can be narrowed to four layers: Reality is composed of the terrestrial, intermediate, celestial, and infinite levels, while the Self is composed of the body, mind, soul, and Spirit.[4]

The highest and deepest tiers, Infinite and Spirit, are, according to Smith, without limitation; while the Infinite is unbounded externally, the human Spirit is unbounded internally. These two (undifferentiated) levels, therefore, are in fact the same. As one moves down the tiers of reality and out the tiers of selfhood, one encounters increasing levels of differentiation and/or materialization. On the levels of reality, God's attributes and personality as well as "archetypes" are on the celestial plane, the psychic reflections of the archetypes on the intermediate plane, and material reality on the terrestrial plane. On the levels of selfhood, one encounters the soul as the source of mind and locus of individuality, then the mind, and finally the corporeal body.

Smith's cosmological image shows the earth, symbolic of the terrestrial sphere, enveloped by the intermediate sphere, which in turn is enclosed by the celestial, the three concentric spheres together superimposed on a background that represents the Infinite. With each higher level, different laws apply, together with a different way of experiencing reality.

In Smith's anthropological image, body and mind are not separate; neither are body and emotions or body and soul. Humans are not spiritual beings trapped in a carnal existence. The self is like a diamond, each part a facet of the same essence. When we view our bodies as base and vulgar and our souls and spirits as pure and distinct, we affirm dualism, the bane of spirituality. If we recognize our bodies to be "materialized spirit," and therefore spiritually based, we are on our way to wholeness and truth. Care of the body, therefore, is the first and most important principle of religion. If we are to make spiritual progress, we must learn to love and care for our bodies. The physical is the doorway to the spiritual. This is the starting premise of all healthy spirituality.

Moving inward from body we come to mind, the seat of consciousness, conceived as distinct from the brain, which is part of the body. The mind is not our thoughts, but rather a container for life's continual creative impulses. According to Smith, there is no convincing materialistic explanation of mind, for mind cannot be measured quantitatively. Furthermore, mind conforms to laws that differ in kind from those that matter exemplifies.

The third level of selfhood is the soul, the final locus of our individuality, its source and yet superior. The soul is closer to our essence than is the mind, with which we usually identify. While the soul is finite, it is the only

---

4. Smith, *Forgotten Truth*, 62.

possible bridge to Spirit, the fourth level of selfhood. If soul is the element in humans that relates to God, Spirit is the element that is identical with God, not with God's personal mode but with God's mode that is infinite. Mystics and theologians speak of identity at this level because here the subject-object dichotomy is transcended. While Spirit is infinite, humans remain finite because they are not Spirit only. Our specifically human overlay—body, mind, and soul—is said to veil the Spirit within us.

QUESTIONS FOR DISCUSSION AND REFLECTION

1. Assess the merits of Rabbi Shapiro's lack of interest in metaphysical speculation about what is Real or the question "Who is God?" and why he begins instead with the notion of the individual self and the question "Who Am I?"
2. In your estimation, what did Meister Eckhart mean by the statement, "the eyes by which we look back at God are the same eyes by which God has first looked at us."
3. Assess the merits of the Sanskrit phrase, *tat tvam asi*.
4. Explain why Christians start with Jesus rather than with themselves as the archetypal model and metaphor for anthropology and ethics.
5. What does the author mean by the True Self? How is the True Self related to God?
6. Explain your understanding of Augustine's statement regarding God, "You were within me, but I was without."
7. Explain the relationship between one's ego and one's False Self.
8. Explain the relationship between one's "soul" and one's True Self.
9. Explain how the False Self sees everything in parts and how the True Self sees everything in wholes.
10. Explain the relationship between one's "spirit" and the True Self.
11. In your estimation, what is the primary insight gained from this chapter? Does this chapter raise any issues you might need to address in the future?

Chapter 6

Perennial Wisdom and the True Self, Part II

HAVING CONSIDERED THE FIRST two truths of the Perennial Tradition, namely (1) the existence and nature of the one Ultimate Reality and (2) the existence and nature of the individual self, this chapter examines the remaining existential truths, namely, how our relationship with Ultimate Reality affects the way we live and think and what we hope for.

Having learned that Ultimate Reality is not external to life but must be discovered in our own depths and imposed on life by an act of our own will, we have to decide how we will live now with this reality.

LIVING WITH AWARENESS

Most of us live with a steady stream of consciousness, with a continual flow of ideas, images, and feelings, clinging to these ideas and feelings as if they were us. They are us, but not our True Self. To ascertain our True Self, we must discover "the face we had before we were born," who we are behind our thoughts and feelings. This is the first goal of contemplation.

As Einstein said, "No problem can be solved from the same level of consciousness that created it." For this reason, a contemplative stance toward life provides an entirely new way of knowing reality, providing the power to help us move beyond mere ideology and dualistic thinking. What religion calls contemplation is the only approach that is broad enough and deep enough to deal with the real and important questions of life. Mature religion will always lead to some form of prayer, meditation, or contemplation to balance our calculating mind. Such a way of seeing gives us the capacity to be comfortable with paradox and mystery. Largely immune to mass consciousness and its false promises, it is called wisdom seeing.

In this respect, I recommend that you practice the "river meditation."[1] Imagine you are sitting on the bank of a river, where boats and ships are sailing past. While the stream flows past your inner eye, name each vessel. For example, one of the boats might be called "my anxiety about tomorrow." Another boat could be called "my inferiority," or "I'm angry with my spouse." Every judgment that you make is one of those boats. Take the time to give each one a name, and then let it move on.

For some people this is a difficult exercise, because they want to jump aboard the boats immediately. However, what we are practicing is un-possessing, letting go. With every idea, with every image that comes into our head, say, "No, I am not that; I don't need that; that's not me." Once may not be enough. Sometimes we have to tell ourselves this repeatedly, for our natural inclination is to jump aboard. That's why some boats head upstream and return.

Some of you will feel the need to torpedo your boats, but that is not helpful. Don't hate or condemn them; if you do, they will fight back. The point is to gain awareness and to say, "That's not necessary; I don't need that." But do it amiably. If we learn to handle our souls tenderly and lovingly, we will be able to carry this same wisdom out into the world.

The great enemy of both mystery and perennial wisdom is dualistic thinking, which uses either/or questions to arrive at truth, generally associated with certainty. The problem with either/or questions is that they promote either/or answers. Such dichotomous forms of thinking set a trap, for the structure of either/or thinking implies that the options presented exhaust all other alternatives: either the Bible is divine or it is human; either one believes there are proofs for God's existence or one is an atheist; if one religion is true, others are false, and so on. Either/or thinking is intolerant of religious pluralism, impatient with both/and resolutions, and dissatisfied with anything less than all-or-nothing answers. It accepts only absolute answers and dismisses uncertainty as a sign of unbelief.

I am fond of the question that has been making the rounds lately: "What is the opposite of faith?" Either/or thinking answers, "Disbelief!" Both/and thinking answers: "Certainty!" The aim of this study is to present alternative responses to rigid, either/or approaches that narrow the possibilities for seekers at all stages of their journey.

---

1. Rohr, *What Mystics Know*, 83–84.

Most people tend to see me as liberal, yet I would say I am conservative regarding values and progressive regarding process. I believe in honesty, justice, follow-through, personal and financial responsibility, justice, committed love, and humility—all deeply traditional values. Yet I also believe one needs to be imaginative and even countercultural to embody these values with depth. Whether in religious life or politics, neither conservatives nor liberals are doing this very well today. Both are stymied by dualistic thought—they are unable to think or see like mystics. For mystics, all speech must be balanced by unsaying, and knowing must be humbled by unknowing. Without this balance, politics and religion invariably become arrogant, exclusionary, and even violent.[2]

Such balance can only be achieved when we acquire new spiritual software, something that takes place primarily through contemplation, a powerful form of prayer accomplished not by willpower but by relinquishment. Learning to be present, what some people call "mindfulness," is living not merely "in the moment," as pop psychology or "group think" might call it, but living in what Eckhart Tolle calls the eternal Now. Such experience is transformative because it is not possessive or selfish. Pure presence lets be what is, as it is. When we can be present in this way, we will know Real Presence.

Such experience is at the heart of Perennial Philosophy, but unfortunately, the world religions have ceased teaching it. Through this negligence, they have stopped doing their job of spiritually transforming people and cultures. When religion becomes preoccupied with belief, and associated with financial and material success, such ideology actually impedes true spirituality, which results in harmony, compassion, generosity, and bliss.

So much of religion involves teaching people an accumulation of facts and imperatives supposed to lead to salvation. The great sages know that for humans to know and experience Ultimate Reality, they need to change how they view the present moment. When Jesus was a guest of Martha and Mary, Martha did what was expected of her gender—fixing, preparing, and serving. Busy and distracted by many things, she did everything right, except being present to herself. Mary, however, simply sat at Jesus' feet; she was present, to himself and, presumably to herself. Presence is primary in life; how you are present is how you do everything. Jesus affirms Mary precisely in this way, for by being present in the moment, she was present to life.

What is true for Mary and Martha is true for us as well. Presence is the prerequisite to divine Presence. Silence, listening—contemplation—are so simple, yet so hard to practice. They remain the best way to experience the

---

2. Rohr, *Naked Now*, 11.

Holy in our midst. I urge the Martha in us all: there is a kind of goodness, a need to be needed, that does little good. If we cannot be present to our True Self, we cannot truly be present to others, certainly not to God.

Perennial wisdom is not another religion, another school of thinking or system of belief. It is not about gathering additional facts and information. Rather, it is the freedom to be present, which produces a different way of seeing and knowing facts and information. Presence is the one thing necessary for transformation, but in many ways, the hardest state to achieve. Why? Because presence is wisdom. Hence, presence is the practical, daily task of all mature religion and all spiritual disciplines. Like us, most of Jesus' contemporaries missed the Presence that was in their midst. Spiritually, they were focused on the afterlife, and he was focused on the Ultimate Reality around him, which he found in birds, lilies, infants, suffering, and the tasks of life. If we learn one thing from the Perennial Tradition, it is that eternity is happening all around us, present all the time. Like Jesus, spiritual sages see continuity between time and eternity. Their assumption is unwavering: "if you have it now, you will have it then." If you examine the great accounts of spiritual breakthrough, the experiences of conversion, you will discover, as John Newton expressed in the famous lyrics of *Amazing Grace*, that they focus on *how* they see rather than on *what* they see: "T'was blind, but now I see."

Early Christian writers tell us that the discovery of our True Self is at the same time a discovery of God. While the two encounters are similar, though not identical, they are largely experienced simultaneously, our awareness of them growing in parallel fashion.

How does one experience this Reality? The answer, I believe, is twofold. To begin with, one must act on the truth, for only then does it become your truth. When Jesus "cured" people, he actually "healed" them, meaning he brought them lasting change. He didn't just give them new physical software, he gave them a new "motherboard." True healing is what Jesus says to the paralytic in Mark 2:11, "Stand up, take your mat, and go home." The real healing for the paralyzed man was to courage to "act as if"—and then his mind and body would follow. This total realignment of the Self is often portrayed in the Gospels as new self-confidence, new capacities for relationship, new joy, and forgiveness of the old self—all made recognizable by the physical cure. Bodies, minds, and souls operate as one. However, we cannot solve the way to a new life in our head; we have to live our way into a new kind of thinking. First we must act.

Paradoxically, we do not really discover the True Self. It gradually appears as we do the work of growing up, just as the Risen One randomly appeared as a friend on the road, was confused with the gardener, showed up in a locked room, and came for breakfast on the beach. As Thomas Merton noted, "a door opens in the center of our being, and we seem to fall through it into immense depths, which although they are infinite—are still accessible to us. All eternity seems to have become ours in this one placid and breathless contact."[3] This door needs to open only once in your lifetime, and you will forever know where home base is.

To experience this Reality, where does one begin? The best way I know is told in the story of the Jewish boy who went to his rabbi, saying he didn't know how to love God.[4] "How can I love God when I've never seen him?" asked the boy. "I think I know how to love my mother, my father, my brother, and my little sister, and even the people in our neighborhood, but I don't know how I'm supposed to love God."

The rabbi looked at the boy and said, "Start with a stone. Try to love a stone. Start with that. Try to be present to the most simple and basic thing in reality until you can see its goodness and beauty. Then let that beauty speak to you. Start with a stone." The boy nodded with understanding.

"When you can love a stone," the rabbi continued, "try a flower. See if you can be present to it and let its beauty come into you. You don't have to pluck it, possess it, or destroy it. You can love it right there in the garden." The boy nodded again.

The boy seemed to understand, but just in case he didn't, the rabbi chose the boy's pet dog as the next object of loving and listening. "Then, after that, try to love the sky and the mountains, the beauty of all creation. Try to be present to it in its many forms. Let it speak to you and let it come into you." The boy sensed the rabbi wanted to say more, so he nodded again, as if he understood. "Then," the rabbi said, "try to love a woman. Try to be faithful to a woman and sacrifice yourself for her. After you have loved a stone, a flower, your dog, the mountain, the sky, and a woman, they you'll be ready to love God."

People with little or no patience for communing with stones, flowers, pets, or human beings will probably not have patience communing directly with God. Of course, the rabbi knew that by loving each item of creation, one by one, he was loving God. In loving God, where do we begin? Begin with a stone. The fragmented person seems to fragment everything else. The reconnected person sees rightly and, not surprisingly, sees God as well.

As soon as we distance ourselves from the control center of our brains, as soon as we free ourselves from the convenient principles of our preconceived theology, as soon as we are no longer caught in the myth

---

3. Merton, *New Seeds of Contemplation*, 227.
4. The story about loving a stone is adapted from Rohr, *What Mystics Know*, 85–87.

of reason, then the transcendent can reach us. Then we can open to the nonrational as well, to grace, to the transcendent, to the burning bush. It's all a matter of seeing.

WHOLENESS AND HOLINESS

As contemplatives have always known and modern-day ecology and quantum physics is only now discovering, all things in nature are both metaphysically distinct and one at the same time. As discoveries of holons[5] and fractals[6] demonstrate, the part contains the whole or replicates the whole, and yet each part still has wholeness within. Such wholeness is true physically and biologically, but also spiritually. Such union implies interrelationship between God and all things. Thus, each human replicates the whole while containing wholeness individually, uniquely. Hence, humans are never entirely whole apart from connection with the larger whole.

Holons and fractals provide a natural way of speaking about wholeness and holiness. Biblically speaking, holiness refers to that which makes individuals and communities unique and distinct, and wholeness refers to the mystery of participation. Holons and fractals help us understand how holiness participates in the whole. From this perspective, if one is "holy" alone, one is not holy.

Salvation, then, is not a divine transaction that occurs because someone is morally perfect, but much more an organic unfolding, a becoming of who someone already is, a capacity for one's Creator. Thus, individual believers can be said to abide in the whole, while also contributing to the whole, as Paul teaches in his analogy of the body (see 1 Cor. 12:12–30). Modern society seems to have lost this sense of wholeness, and therefore also the sense of holiness. When Christians think with their secular mind, they think dualistically. Failing to recognize their inherent belonging in this natural world, they think they have to "buy" their way in or acquire a "ticket" or "key" in order to gain salvation. This tragic spiritual loss takes many forms today. The reality is, many live outside the gates of paradise—excluded by angels of their own making (Gen. 3:24).[7]

---

5. A holon is something in nature that functions simultaneously as a whole and a part, such as a whole atom being part of a molecule, a whole molecule being part of a cell, and a whole cell being part of an organism.

6. A fractal is a repetitive pattern found in nature—as well as in mathematics and art—such as a snowflake, a crystal growth, or a galaxy formation.

7. Rohr, *Eager to Love*, 178–79.

One of Jesus' greatest teachings is "rejoice that your name is written in heaven" (Luke 10:20). If we could trust this, it would change our life agenda. This discovery will not create egoistic individualism, as religion often fears, but instead makes all posturing and pretending unnecessary. Our core anxiety that we are not good enough is resolved from the beginning, and we can stop all our striving, contending, criticizing, and competing. Most of Christian history has largely put the cart of requirements before the "horsepower" itself. The horsepower is precisely our experience of primal union with God. Find God, the primary source, and the fresh water will forever flow naturally (John 7:38). Once you know that, the problem of inferiority, unworthiness, or low self-esteem is resolved at the core. You can then spend your time calmly and happily on the road. Teresa of Avila used a similar metaphor when she described how we either keep digging the channel or find the actual spring and let it simply flow toward us, in us, and from us. Her entire mystical theology is about finding the Inner Flow and not wasting time digging trenches.

"Presence," for the contemplative practitioner, is the word for this encounter, this way of knowing. Most of us call it awareness, as opposed to judgment or thinking. Whatever we call it, this nondualistic way of seeing the moment refuses to be pulled into the emotional and mental tugs of war essential to dualistic life. A vulnerable approach, lacking all sense of control, sitting in silent meditation, is necessary to experience joy and truth simultaneously in this world.

Prayer, contemplation, nondualistic thinking, or "third-eye" seeing, is not, however, a technique for acquiring things, a pious exercise that makes God happy, or a requirement for entry into heaven. It is more like practicing heaven now. Such experience is invariably the same—relinquishing particularity, one's sense of separate self, to an egoless awareness that leaves one with an unshakeable sense that all is God.

Once we are ready to acknowledge Ultimate Reality as it is, and are able to set aside dualistic frames of reference, we need further clarifications to live holistically with nature, others, and ourselves. In this respect, process theologians often appeal to some form of the mind-body analogy as a model for the God-world relation. This position can be expressed by saying, as does Charles Hartshorne, that God is essentially "the soul of the universe," related to the universe like the human soul is related to its body. Feminist theologian Sallie McFague, applying this approach to ecological issues, introduces models of God as mother, lover, and friend of the world, writing extensively on care for the earth as if it were God's "body."

Another approach, more direct and intuitive, examines the body's relationship to its natural surroundings. While accepting the uniqueness of one's individual body, it seems obvious that the body cannot function effectively in isolation. While we can agree, for example, that the lungs are part of the human body, what would happen if they were removed from the body? Of course, one would die, for their function—taking in oxygen and eliminating carbon dioxide—is essential to one's survival. And where is oxygen produced? Not by the body, certainly, but rather by trees and plants and the ocean. If we humans cannot survive without trees, plants, and the ocean, why not recognize them as part of our body? If we do that, why stop there? Trees, plants, and oceans don't exist in isolation either; they need the earth and sun to live and produce oxygen, so why not see them as part of our body as well? Perhaps they should be understood as part of our bodies no less than lungs, heart, and brain.

The sun doesn't exist in isolation either. It is in relation to the earth because of our solar system, and our solar system is the way it is because our galaxy is the way it is, and so on. If this is true, the entire universe is one's body. That's the position of perennial wisdom: if all this is you, and all is God, then you are God. In Sanskrit, this is summed up in the phrase, *tat tvam asi*; in English, You are That! You and I are the entirety of being and becoming. Each of us is an expression of the universe as the universe is an expression of God.[8]

According to traditional Hindu teaching, one's self or soul is called Atman, and this Atman is actually Brahman (the world soul), only the Atman is ignorant of the fact, due to temporary and material separation from its source and destiny. The Atman is like a drop of rain, flowing into a stream, then into a river, and ultimately into the ocean (Brahman). When the drop reaches the stream, it ceases being a drop; when the river reaches the ocean, it ceases being a river. In popular Hinduism, Atman is the flowing stream that, over many lifetimes, comes closer to the ocean and eventually merges with it. At that point Atman becomes Brahman, but not before.

This view, however, is still dualistic. Another Hindu view, the Advaita nondual view, is that God is the world, and that while reincarnation is real, it isn't you who returns, but God. The first view, the river-ocean metaphor, views the Self as separate from the Ocean. The unity of river and ocean happens only once, at that point in time and space where the river flows into the ocean. The second view, the wave-ocean metaphor, views the Self as a wave of a vast shoreless sea. You are still you—a wave—and yet so much more than you—the sea itself. According to this view, the unity of wave and ocean is always real, and is independent of time and place. The wave-ocean metaphor is most in line with perennial wisdom.[9]

8. Shapiro, *Perennial Wisdom*, 59–60.
9. Ibid., 6, 121–22.

Of course, knowing yourself as a wave is a way of knowing the relative world, the world of seemingly separate things. Knowing yourself as the sea is knowing the absolute world, the world of the One who is all these seemingly separate waves. However, there is yet another level of knowing, best labeled "unknowing." This "knowing" and the knower who "knows" it cannot be known. It is the eternal Subject, the Knower that cannot be known, the Subject that cannot be made an object of knowing.

There is no name for this Knower or this knowing. This is where human language breaks down. Even the word "silence" is insufficient to describe what we are talking about, because what we are talking about cannot be described: "The tao that can be named is not the eternal Tao." Yet it is the truest Self, the truest you.

Western Judeo-Christians are often uncomfortable with the word "nonduality." They often associate it with Eastern religions. In some cases, of course, this is true. But in other respects, it is central to the teachings of Jesus. The reason we so often miss it in Jesus is because "Jesus was the first nondual religious teacher of the West,[10] and one reason we have failed to understand so much of his teaching, much less follow it, is because we tried to understand it with a dualistic [a Platonic or Greek philosophical] mind."[11]

Even after two thousand years, it is hard to realize what a revolutionary teacher Jesus was. He turned theology upside down. He said, in effect, "Who you think God is, God isn't." He learned this not only through the crucible of his life, but primarily in his death and resurrection. This may explain why people who encounter the risen Christ are humble people. In Christ they find a humble God, a God who is not triumphant and overwhelming, with all the answers and all perfection, but a God who is somehow in this with us; a God who is infinite, yet somehow finite; who is in charge, yet chooses not to be in control at all.[12]

The nondual (contemplative) mind holds truth humbly, knowing that if it is true, it is its own best argument, and any formulation is still partial and incomplete, as Paul states in 1 Corinthians 13:12, "Now I know only in part." Non-polarity thinking teaches us how to hold creative tensions, how to live with paradox and contradiction, how not to run away from mystery,

---

10. See, for example, Matthew 5:45 ("[God] sends rain on the righteous and on the unrighteous") and 13:30 ("Let [the weeds and the wheat] grow together"). However, Jesus is dualistic about wealth, caring for the poor, and allegiance to God (see Luke 4:18; 6:24; 14:13–14; and 16:13), for he knows we are wired to care for ourselves and to focus on profit and personal gain.

11. Rohr, *Naked Now*, 34–35.

12. Rohr, *What Mystics Know*, 65.

and therefore how to actually practice what all religions teach as necessary: compassion, mercy, patience, forgiveness, and humility.[13]

In nondual spirituality, acting precedes understanding: first, we must act, and then we will understand, meaning we will understand intuitively. However, we will never truly know *why* we know, nor will we be able to prove it to others. The mysterious wisdom of faith is not learned in abstraction, or by reflection, but only when one is on the way. It is not a lesson anyone else can teach us; we must go down this road ourselves. This is the place of the soul, the place of wisdom, toward which we must move. And as Jesus so often told his followers, "don't be afraid!" Fear comes from a need to control; however, we are not in control anyway.

Once you let go of control, we will come to the inner place of compassion. In this place, we will notice how much the suffering of the world is our suffering, and how committed we are to this pain. At this inner place of compassion, we will find the peace that the world cannot give. We won't need to win anymore; we just do what we need to do as simply and joyfully as possible. That is why Augustine could make such an outrageous statement as "love God and do what you want." People who are living from a God-centered place instead of a self-centered place are dangerously free precisely because they are tethered at the center.

When one lives in this manner, from this center, all is possible, because all is permitted. If it is true that "with God all things are permitted," how do we decide right from wrong? The answer is simple: by focusing on the biblical command to love God, self, and neighbor equally. That is our sole priority. Perennial wisdom is a call to engagement, not passivity. We may not be able to change the present, but we are free to engage it differently. Only the False Self is conditioned, locked into the habits of the past. The True Self is unconditioned, free to engage the present creatively and the future hopefully.

The spiritual question, of course, is this: Does one's life give any evidence of an encounter with God? Does this encounter bring about in you any of the things that Paul describes as the "fruit" of the Spirit: "love, joy, peace, patience, kindness, generosity, faithfulness, gentleness, and self-control" (Gal. 5:22–23)? Is the person or the group after this encounter different from its surroundings, or does it reflect typical cultural values, biases, and norms? Even worse, does your religious group spend much of its time defining and deciding who can and who cannot participate, who can and who cannot belong? Why, if God is for you a tyrant, an eternal torturer, or with

---

13. Ibid., 129.

a smaller heart than most people you know, would you want to be intimate with or reflect such a God?

The brilliant word, nonduality (*advaita* in Sanskrit), is used by many different traditions, both Eastern and Western, to distinguish from total and perfect absorption or enmeshment. Nondualism is not monism. Monism reduces all things to the same thing, erasing all diversity and difference. Nondualism celebrates difference and affirms diversity. It simply refuses to see this diversity as anything other than the greater unity of a singular Reality.

ULTIMATE REALITY AND HOPE

We come to the fourth and final question posed by the Perennial Tradition: "How does my relationship with Ultimate Reality affect what I hope for"? We begin with some questions and concerns.

Many people, when they hear about relinquishing the ego and affirming oneness with the universal Self, respond defensively, fearful they are being asked to give up their uniqueness and individuality. What is the purpose of living, they wonder, if it is not to "make something" of oneself, to improve one's lot and get ahead, to make things better and leave a legacy?

Traditional Christians, particularly, find the premises of perennial wisdom incompatible with traditional theology, threatening belief in free will and responsible living. "The world is the way it is," they argue, "so that we can choose between good and evil, truth and error, and then gain the benefits or suffer the consequences of our choices. Doesn't the perennial teaching negate biblical revelation? Aren't we responsible for our action and choices? Isn't there cosmic judgment, and eternal punishment and reward? Doesn't this teaching contradict the doctrine of creation and belief in a personal God? Doesn't it eliminate the uniqueness of humanity and the purpose of life?"

To answer these questions, we go to the book of Job, a text in the Bible that represents the heart of the biblical wisdom tradition. Job, arguing his innocence in the face of underserved suffering, demands that God explain the "why" of life's tragedies. Job's plight is universal, and his demand of God requires an answer. Like Job, we all want to know why things are the way they are, and we all imagine that only God—through scripture and the wisdom of our faith traditions—can answer this for us.

While Job and his friends argue about sin and its connection to punishment, the reader of the book knows that this is irrelevant to the truth. Job is being tortured (and his servants and children murdered) just to see whether

Job will, as his wife urges him to do, curse God and die (Job 2:9). Job refuses both to confess the sins he didn't commit and to curse a God he doesn't blame, and he clings mightily to the hope that God will appear and make known to him why it is that he—and by extension all the innocent—suffer.

When God appears, however, the fact of a wager God had made with Satan is dropped in favor of something more profound. God doesn't fall into the trap of answering Job's questions. The liberation that Job seeks, the book of Job seems to tell us, is not found in answering the question "why?" but in dropping it altogether. Instead, God seems to be saying, "The universe is wild and wonderful and terrifying all at the same time. You can't pick and choose what happens to you, and in time all of it will happen to you, bad and good, blessing and curse, joy and sorrow. That's life! Your task is not to avoid or eliminate suffering, but to embrace it and make the most of it. The key to living well is radical acceptance, not control and avoidance."

Job seems to accept this, coming to a realization that is wise and comforting. Unfortunately, most English translations of Job miss this and end the book with Job despising himself and repenting in "dust and ashes" (Job 42:6). The Jewish Publication Society's Tanakh Translation reads differently, telling us that in the end, Job recants and relents, "being but dust and ashes." While this verse is essential for understanding the book's meaning, the passage is notoriously difficult to translate. Ambiguity is caused, in part, by the verbs translated as "despise" and "repent." Neither verb has a direct object, meaning we are not told what Job despises or from what he recants. Does he despise himself, or his mortality? Is he recanting the presumptuous words he has uttered, or rejecting his angry complaints against God? Further, what does the author mean by "dust and ashes"? Do they represent the religious ritual surrounding repentance, or are they a reference to Job's human condition? Assuming the reference is to the ritual of repentance, biblical scholar Richard Clifford translates the verse: "Therefore I retract and give up my dust and ashes."[14] Seen from this perspective, Job repents of repentance, taking religious action (42:5) to renounce religious ritual.

These possibilities, while intriguing, miss the point. Rather than despise himself in dust and ash or as dust and ash, Job finds comfort in being dust and ash (see 30:19), knowing that dust and ash are the very stuff of Ultimate Reality. "Job isn't made small by God's revelation of the enormity and wildness of the universe; he is made larger through the realization that he too is this enormity and wildness."[15]

---

14. Clifford, *Wisdom Literature*, 95.
15. Shapiro, *Perennial Wisdom*, 260.

Once we accept reality as encompassing all things, we cease needing to be other than what we already are. Once we accept our True Self as it is, the only thing we need to change is to avoid being less than we are. The essential religious experience is that you are being "known through" more than knowing anything in particular yourself. Yet despite this difference, it will seem like true knowing. This is what we call nondualistic thinking, third-eye-seeing, or true prayer. Such seeing takes away our anxiety about figuring things out, or needing to be right in our beliefs, ideologies, or perspectives. "At this point, God becomes more a verb than a noun, more a process than a conclusion, more an experience than a dogma, more a personal relationship than an idea."[16]

To live in such a way is to possess an unexplainable hope, because your life will seem more expansive than your own. In fact, it is not your own life, and yet, paradoxically, you are closer to your True Self than ever before. Such is the consistent realization of the mystics—a vision that can also be ours. Like Jacob at Bethel, we, too, can awake from our sleep and say, "Surely the Lord is in this place—and I did not know it!" (Gen. 28:16). The Bethel narrative concludes with Jacob's exclamation, "How awesome is this place! This is none other than the house of God, and this is the gate of heaven" (Gen. 28:17).

The Fourth Gospel alludes to Jacob's vision at Bethel, in which he saw a ladder with angels ascending to heaven and descending to earth (John 1:51). Here, however, the angels are said to be ascending and descending upon Jesus. The meaning is that Jesus is the new Bethel, the place where heaven and earth, God and humanity, meet. If this is true for Christianity, Jacob and John's revelation become a prelude to an ever greater unveiling, that you and I—as children of God, as image bearers of the divine—are the gate of heaven, our identity and awareness connecting heaven and earth, God and humanity.

Much of religion is a search for order, group cohesion, personal worthiness, or a way of escaping into the next world, which unfortunately destroys much of its transformative power. For many traditional people of faith, hope is centered on the afterlife—going to heaven and not to hell. However, as many theologians are discovering, heaven and hell are primarily "states of consciousness," and the "kingdom of God" is the Reality we experience when we have moved through duality to nonduality. Heaven is now and forever for those who are willing to keep changing, for those who practice "letting go" into love. Those who are in communion with Ultimate

---

16. Rohr, *Naked Now*, 23.

Reality are already in heaven. As Catherine of Siena put it, "It is heaven all the way to heaven, and it is hell all the way to hell."

True spirituality is not a search for perfection or control or the door to the next world; it is a search for divine union now. Union and perfection are two different journeys with very different strategies. Common religion seeks private perfection; mystics seek the foundation itself—divine union. Personal perfection insists on private knowing and certitude. Surprisingly, union is a much better way of knowing.

The most amazing fact about Jesus, unlike almost any other religious founder, is that he found God in disorder and imperfection—and told us that we must do the same or we would never be content on this earth. This is what makes Jesus so counterintuitive to most eras and cultures, and why most never perceive the good news in this shift of consciousness. That failure to understand his core message is at the center of our religious problem today. We look for hope where it was never promised, and no one gave us the proper software so that we could know hope for ourselves, least of all in disorder and imperfection. Worst of all, we did not know that hope and union are the same thing, that real hope has nothing to do with mental certitudes.

If you surrender to the fear of uncertainty, religious life can become a set of insurance policies. Your short time on earth becomes small and self-protective, circling around what you can be sure of and what you think you can control—even God. A second group tries a different approach. They choose to look the other way, or just keep busy, building "bigger barns." For them, life becomes a series of manufactured dramas, entertainment, and diversionary tactics intended to help them avoid the substantial questions. This avoidance is symbolized by what we call the consumer culture.

A third group seeks transcendence and spirituality, but often in immature ways. This characterizes so much religious seeking today, people dualistically split from any objective experience of union with God, self, others, or nature. Christianity, authentically experienced, is the overcoming of the split. How this takes place is the subject of the second half of this study.

QUESTIONS FOR DISCUSSION AND REFLECTION

1. In your estimation, how is the practice of contemplation an antidote to dualistic thinking?
2. Can one be conservative and liberal (progressive) simultaneously? Explain your answer. How would you describe yourself on this spectrum?

3. In your estimation, what is the difference between being "mindful" and living with "Presence"?
4. Explain and assess the meaning of the statement, "to discover the truth, we must become the truth."
5. According to the author, if one wishes to experience Ultimate Reality, where does one begin?
6. What did Teresa of Avila mean that in one's quest for fresh water, one should "not waste time digging trenches"?
7. How does viewing nature as "God's body" change one's way of living and thinking?
8. Explain the difference between the river-ocean metaphor and the wave-ocean metaphor.
9. Explain the merits of nondual spirituality.
10. Explain Augustine's statement that with God all things are permitted.
11. Explain why the question, "How do I get to heaven?" is no longer relevant in nondual spirituality.
12. In your estimation, what is the primary insight gained from this chapter? Does this chapter raise any issues you might need to address in the future?

Metaphor

Chapter 7

The Power of Metaphor

SINCE THE EIGHTEENTH CENTURY, people have developed a scientific view of history, meaning they are concerned primarily with facts, with what actually happened. However, in the pre-modern world, when people thought of the past, they were more concerned with what an event meant. In this respect, they were aided by mythology, an art form that points beyond history to what is timeless in human existence. Today, the word "myth" is often used to describe something that is simply not true. That, however, is not what we are discussing here. Mythologist Joseph Campbell tells of a time he was interviewed by a radio talk show host who introduced himself to Campbell with the words, "I'm tough; I've studied law." In his mind, and according to his training, myths were lies. When Campbell responded that a myth is a metaphor, he turned the tables on his host, asking him to define a metaphor. After some hesitation, the host provided as an example of a metaphor the idea that "a person who runs fast is said to run like a deer."

"That," Campbell replied, "is not a metaphor. The metaphor is, 'That person *is* a deer.'"

"That idea is not true," replied the host. "It's a lie!"

"No," Campbell responded. "It's a metaphor."[1]

A great many people in the world today think metaphors are facts. These we call theists. Many others think that metaphors are not facts. Those we call atheists. When we use the word "God," we are using a metaphor for

---

1. Campbell, *Hero's Journey*, 134–35.

a mystery that transcends all categories of thought, even the categories of being and nonbeing. The best things, mystics tells us, cannot be spoken; the second best are misunderstood; third best is conversation. If words are necessary but inferior forms of communicating truth, then mythology is more effective, yet limited, penultimate rather than final truth—penultimate because the ultimate cannot be put into words. Ultimate truth is beyond words, beyond images. Hence, it is important to live life fully, but not arrogantly or with finality, taking risks and recognizing the positive value in what appear to be negative moments and aspects of one's life. The big question in spirituality is whether one is able to embrace uncertainty and adventure.

Modern Christians spend a great deal of time trying to connect the dots, attempting intellectually to penetrate the core of reality to see what is good, beautiful, true, lasting, and transcendent. While most early Christians sought the same things, they did not approach life and faith analytically, as we do today. Rather, they applied what they believed mystically, spiritually, and intuitively. As a result, they lived kindly, in harmony with nature and others. Although they did not use the word "nondual," the idea was consistently assumed, implied, and even taught for at least sixteen hundred years.

Religion knew the truth of metaphor and symbol for almost all of history until the past few hundred years. Since the Enlightenment, however, modern believers have approached reality in a more detached and scientific way, looking to facts, evidence, and objective truth for hope and truth, content with shadow over reality, doctrine over direct experience. In trying to defend its ground in the face of rationalism and scientism, modern religion tried to become "rational" and lost its alternative consciousness. Losing access to the higher levels of consciousness—the transrational, transpersonal, and transcendent—many Christians settled for finality and conformity, content to rest in shallow waters rather than plumbing the depths. Tragically, many lost the inner experience that underlies the outer belief system. That is the heart of religion's problem today, taking the symbols too literally, and now the emerging generation is throwing them out as useless. Without searching, nothing will be found, but how one searches will determine what one finds or even expects to find.

If we wish to discover the Center—and experience life in the Center—I suggest that we search primarily in the universal and wise depths of recurring symbols, metaphors, and sacred stories, which is where humans can find deep and lasting meaning—or personal truth. This is what we mean by the Perennial Tradition, and why George Bernard Shaw declared, "There is only one religion, and there are then a thousand forms of it." As we shall discover, the best religious metaphors, like resurrection, assert not just a truth held by Christians, but a universal truth as well.

Why metaphor? Because it is a common device, used globally, whereby human beings describe one thing in terms of another. Used in literature and art, but also in all fields of human endeavor, from economics and advertising to business and science, metaphor is a way of seeing, imagining, and understanding. In advertisement, it influences purchasing decision; in politics, it nudges public opinion; in art, it spurs creativity and innovation; in science, it announces new theories and discoveries; in psychology, it is the natural language of human relationship and emotion. As bestselling author James Geary summarizes in *I Is an Other*, his fascinating book on metaphor, "metaphorical thinking—our instinct not just for describing but for comprehending one thing in terms of another—shapes our view of the world and is essential to how we communicate, learn, discover, and invent."[2] In fact, there is no aspect of human experience not influenced in some way by metaphor's perennial presence.

Our understanding of metaphor is changing. For centuries, metaphor was seen as a cognitive ornament, an elegant but useless embellishment to ordinary thought. This approach is no longer tenable. Current research in the social and cognitive sciences make it increasingly apparent that metaphorical thinking influences our attitudes, beliefs, and actions in surprising and often undetected ways. In fact, metaphor is a way of thought long before it is expressed with words. "Metaphor," says Geary, "has finally leapt off the page and landed with a mighty splash right in the middle of our stream of consciousness."[3]

If you are skeptical about metaphor's ubiquity, listen carefully the next time you or anyone else speaks. You will find yourself in a metaphorical blizzard. Think of the common expressions we use every day to convey our feelings: I'm down in the dumps; I'm on the straight and narrow; I'm at a crossroads; I'm cool as a cucumber; I'm hot under the collar. Or think of the visual metaphors we see, such as the lightbulb that appears above someone's head to signify a bright idea, or the "thumbs-up" gesture we use to indicate general well-being. Experts estimate that in common speech, humans utter about one metaphor for every ten to twenty-five words of speech, or about six metaphors a minute. If this is true of ordinary speech, it more accurately describes literature—prose as well as poetry, and historical narrative as well as fiction.

---

2. Geary, *I Is an Other*, 3.
3. Ibid, 3–4.

Ordinary conversation is rife with figurative phrases because metaphor is about more than just words. Human beings think metaphorically. Metaphorical thinking is how we humans make sense of the world, and every individual metaphor is a specific instance of this imaginative process at work. Understanding a metaphor, however, like listening to a speech or a sermon, reading a book or a poem, examining a painting or sculpture, or watching a ballet or movie, is a seemingly random walk through a deep, dark forest of associations. The path is full of unexpected twists and turns, veering off into a thicket one minute and abruptly disappearing down a rabbit hole the next. Then suddenly, somehow, you step into a clearing. In this respect, a metaphor is both detour and destination, a paradox in that it tells us as much about what a person, place, or thing is as by telling us what it is not.

As we noticed in speaking about nondualism, during the Enlightenment, scholars began considering metaphor as a devious use of language, as a literary trick employed chiefly by charlatans, faith healers, and poets. Some philosophers regarded metaphorical language as political obfuscation. In *Leviathan*, Thomas Hobbes classified metaphor as an "abuse of speech" and accused people of lying when they used words metaphorically, that is, in a sense other than what "they are ordained for." Ironically, Hobbes, in his denunciation, repeatedly abused speech by using words in senses other than that for which they were ordained. The meaning of the word "ordain," for example, comes from roots that mean "to set in order," not "to designate," "to decree," or even "to admit to the Christian ministry." Likewise, John Locke spoke against the art of rhetoric in *An Essay Concerning Human Understanding*, urging people to "speak of things as they are" rather than rhetorically, for "all the artificial and figurative application of words eloquence hath invented are for nothing else but to insinuate wrong ideas, move the passions, and thereby mislead the judgment; and so indeed are perfect cheats" (Book 3.10).

Despite being accused of seeming imprecise, however, metaphor is astonishingly precise. Nothing is as exact as an apt metaphor. The ancient philosopher Aristotle identified the mastery of metaphorical thinking as "a sign of genius, since a good metaphor implies an intuitive perception of the similarity in dissimilars."[4] The English literary critic and etymologist Owen Barfield picked up Aristotle's insight when he writes, "When a new thing or a new idea comes into the consciousness of the community, it is described, not by a new word, but by the name of the pre-existing object which most closely resembles it."[5] Such use happens regularly. "What ac-

---

4. Aristotle, *Rhetoric and Poetics*, 255.
5. Barfield, *History in English Words*, 20.

counts for the acceleration of a sports car? Horsepower. What happens to an economy when growth drops and unemployment rises? A depression. What do you see when you turn on a computer? A desktop. These are all metaphors, names taken from one thing and applied to a completely different thing because someone at a key moment noticed a resemblance."[6]

Etymologies make perfect sense. The word "emotion," for example, comes from the Latin verb *movere*, "to move." How do we describe the emotional state occasioned by a meaningful encounter, an evocative film, or a stirring piece of music? We are "moved." Movement is implied in the word "emotion." Even the word "literal," derived from the Latin *litera*, meaning "letter," is a metaphor. "Literal" means "according to the letter," that is, accurate or factual. But literal is, in turn, also a metaphor, for it is derived from the verb *linire*, meaning "to smear," and it was associated with *litera* when authors began smearing words on parchment instead of carving them into wood or stone. The roots of *linire* are also evident in the word "liniment," which denotes a salve or ointment. Thus, the literal meaning of "literal" is "to smear or spread," a fitting metaphor for the way metaphor oozes over rigid definitional borders.[7]

In his essay, "The Poet," Ralph Waldo Emerson described language as a kind of etymological artifact or "fossil poetry." However, before language was fossil poetry, it was fossil metaphor, as Emerson wrote:

> The poets made all the words, and therefore language is the archives of history, and, if we must say it, a sort of tomb of the muses. For though the origin of most of our words is forgotten, each word was at first a stroke of genius, and obtained currency because for the moment it symbolized the world to the first speaker and the hearer. The etymologist finds the deadest word to have been once a brilliant picture. Language is a fossil poetry. As the limestone of the continent consists of infinite masses of the shells of animalcules, so language is made up of images or tropes, which now, in their secondary use, have long ceased to remind us of their poetic origin.[8]

As neuroscience indicates, the human brain repeatedly prospects for patterns. The brain is so fanatical about pattern that it generates patterns even when none exist. Where patterns are incomplete, or even nonexistent, the brain naturally fills in the blanks. Some researchers suggest that there is a specific brain module, called the "interpreter," that is tasked with

---

6. Geary, *I Is An Other*, 20.
7. Ibid., 21.
8. Emerson, "The Poet," 12.

sifting out patterns from the random information continuously flowing through our brain.

From an evolutionary perspective, pattern recognition is essential for survival and well-being. The brain's pattern recognition circuits take raw data from the senses, sort through them for apparent patterns, and use those patterns to determine response, behavior, and even belief. Once a pattern repeats consistently, it starts to influence behavior. Neurobiologist Gerald Edelman theorizes that the human brain's astonishing interconnectivity produces consciousness and, because of the astronomical number of associations our brains are capable of making, pattern recognition is the basis not just for metaphorical thinking but for all thinking. "It is likely," he argues, "that early human thought proceeded by metaphor, which, even with the late acquisition of precise means such as logic and mathematical thought, continues to be a major source of imagination and creativity in adult life."[9]

Metaphor grounds even the most abstract ideas as physiological facts in our brains. Through a process known as "priming" (the power of suggestion), clusters of neurons respond together, shaping our beliefs and behavior. The more often neurons respond together, the stronger the connections among them become. If specific neuronal groups respond repeatedly over time to the same stimulus (including such religious stimuli as prayers, creeds, doctrines, scripture passages, theological terminology), the connections between them become fixed. In neuroscience, this is known as the "neurons that fire together wire together" axiom. In priming, the physical fuses with the psychological. Once this rewiring takes place, traffic flows both ways: from mind to matter and from matter to mind. Priming helps explain the lasting power and sometimes stubborn and inflexible influence of repetitive patterns in domestic and religious attitudes, values, and behavior, usually without our conscious knowledge. Priming can even influence judgments intended to be objective, unbiased, and completely independent.

What, then, is truth? According to the skeptical German philosopher Friedrich Nietzsche, truth is "a mobile army of metaphors, metonymies, and anthropomorphisms; in short, a sum of human relations which become poetically and rhetorically intensified, metamorphosed, adorned, and after long usage seem to a people fixed, canonic, and binding; truths are illusions of which one has forgotten that they are illusions; worn-out metaphors which have become powerless to affect the senses."[10] This view, while

---

9. Edelman, *Second Nature*, 58.
10. Nietzsche, *Complete Works*, 183–84.

overly cynical, nevertheless confirms the function and power of metaphor in moral and religious realms.

According to Geary, metaphor is an indispensable tool for informed decision-making. When faced with complex issues like cosmology, human origins and destiny, and the human condition, metaphor puts things on a manageable scale. Of course, all metaphor are distortions, but some are more constructive than others. The challenge is to find metaphors that produce good results. The surest sign of a successful metaphor is its ability to reproduce. Research shows that people not only remember metaphors better than the actual wording of texts, but that they also continue to use those metaphors when thinking further about the same topic.

In *New Science*, Giambattista Vico, an eighteenth-century professor of rhetoric, took on the task of explaining all of human history, emphasizing the evolution of speech and writing. Interested in language, he believe that metaphor played a formative role not just in the evolution of language, but also in the advance of civilization. Vico identified three historical ages: the age of gods, of heroes, and of humans. Each age had a specific form of language adapted to its specific stage of human development:

- Age of gods; this earliest language, dated from a time "when pagan peoples had just embraced civilization," was a mute and wordless language that used gestures or physical objects bearing a natural relationship to the ideas they wanted to signify.
- Age of heroes; this second phase of language used emblems such as similes, comparisons, images, metaphors, and descriptions of nature as the principal lexicon.
- Age of humans; this third phase was the civilized language that used vocabulary agreed upon by popular convention.

Keenly sensitive to how ordinary speech is filled with figuration, Vico wrote that "In all language expressions for inanimate subjects, everyday metaphors derived from the human body and its parts, or from human senses and emotions," listing common examples such as the "neck" of a bottle or the "mouth" of a river.[11] Vico was convinced that he had discovered the "universal principle of etymology . . . Words are transferred from physical objects and their properties to signify what is conceptual and spiritual." His views anticipate much of the conceptual metaphor and embodied cognition theories prevalent today.

---

11. Vico, *New Science*, 159–60.

This explanation also helps explain the descriptions of God in the Hebrew scriptures, whereby human physical and emotional attributes are ascribed to God. Scholars name such attributes anthropomorphisms and anthropopathisms. In all biblical cases, whether speaking of the "wrath" of God, the "arm" of the Lord, or of God's lovingkindness, the biblical writers were using human language, which, when ascribed to deity, is limited, unreliable, and defective. The same holds true for all creedal and dogmatic formulations about God, Jesus, the Holy Spirit, and the Trinity. All such language is metaphorical and hence not to be taken literally.

In "Education by Poetry," a lecture poet Robert Frost delivered in 1930, Frost said, "I have wanted in late years to go further and further in making metaphor the whole of thinking." He argued that without proper training in metaphor, individual students could not examine and evaluate the claims made by historians or scientists, editorialists or campaigners.

In his 1939 essay, "Bluspels and Falansferes," the medieval scholar and Christian apologist C. S. Lewis described a thought experiment in which the world had four dimensions instead of the three we can perceive. A four-dimensional world seems inconceivable, but he likened the task of imagining it to explaining to Flatlanders—a race of people who only know two dimensions: back and front, and left and right—that the world is round.

The Flatlanders think they live on an edgeless plane extending indefinitely in all directions. They have no concept of, much less words for, height and depth. So how can anyone get across to them the idea of up and down? "As these Flatlanders are to you, so you might be to a creature who intuited four dimensions, "Lewis wrote.[12] Thanks to this analogy, what before was impossible to conceive—a four-dimensional world—acquires some semblance of meaning. The point of Lewis's thought experiment is that the unknown can only be made known through metaphor and analogy.

The analogical form of metaphor is particularly useful when science communicates new discoveries, such as when Robert Hooke discovered in 1665 that plants contain small compartments, which he called "cells" because of their resemblance to the room in which monks lived in monasteries; or when French mathematician Jean-Baptiste-Joseph Fourier discovered that trapped heat in the earth's atmosphere increased the surface temperature of the earth, a phenomenon he called the "greenhouse effect;" or when German physicist Max Planck, a gifted pianist and cellist, spoke of "string theory," imagining electron orbits as the vibrating strings of a musical instrument and likening the universe to an eleven-dimensional oscillating string. Try explaining that to Flatlanders!

---

12. Lewis, "Bluespels and Falansferes," 139.

What is true of metaphor also applies to analogy. Lewis called metaphorical analogy—the type that compares the unknown with the known—a "master's metaphor," a teaching tool essential to communicating any kind of innovative, original thinking. Likewise, philosopher Suzanne Langer wrote, "Language, in its literal capacity, is a stiff and conventional medium, unadapted to the expression of genuinely new ideas, which usually have to break in upon the mind through some great and bewildering metaphor."[13]

John Stuart Mill, one of the nineteenth century's few philosophical advocates of metaphorical thinking, said that a metaphor "is not to be considered as an argument, but as an assertion that an argument exists."[14] Lewis would have agreed. Metaphor and analogy prove nothing; yet they point to what reality must be like if religious or scientific arguments are true. For Lewis, that meant we must never lose sight of the fact that metaphors are metaphors, models of things rather than the things themselves. "If your thinking is ever true," Lewis wrote, "then the metaphors by which we think must have been good metaphors."[15]

We all live in community, and human experience, such as birth, suffering, and death, and natural symbols, like trees, water, animals, are means of understanding and communicating, even if in different ways. Such metaphors "carry us across," which is the exact Greek meaning of the word (*meta* means "over, across, or beyond," and *phor* means "to carry").

Metaphor is the most suitable language for religion, for it alone is honest about Mystery. "Metaphors only seem to describe the outer world of time and place," wrote scholar of world mythology Joseph Campbell. "Their real universe is the spiritual realm of the inner life."[16] Good religion should be a master at metaphor, carrying us across and beyond. When we realize that different religions and denominations use culturally conditioned images to communicate universal experiences of God, we can detect possible agreement underlying those images. However, when metaphors become dogma and images are equated with truth, the container is mistaken for the content, the husk for the kernel.

Wallace Stevens, a successful businessman, was also one of the greatest poets of the twentieth century. He described metaphor as "the creation of resemblance by the imagination."[17] Metaphor is the imagination at work, and "its singularity," he wrote, "is that in the act of satisfying the desire for

---

13. Langer, *Philosophy in a New Key*, 201.
14. Cited in Johnson, *Philosophical Perspectives on Metaphor*, 13.
15. Lewis, "Bluspels and Falansferes," 158.
16. Campbell, *Thou Art That*, 7.
17. Stevens, "Three Academic Pieces," 72.

resemblance it touches the sense of reality, it enhances the sense of reality, heightens it, intensifies it."[18] Elsewhere, Stevens expressed the same thought more concisely, "Metaphor creates a new reality from which the original appears to be unreal."

Hart Crane, author of two books of poetry, regarded the poet as a professional visionary and poetry as an alternative logic, calling it the "logic of metaphor." Such logic, writes James Geary, "is the logic of our lives. Metaphor impinges on everything, allowing us—poets and non-poets alike—to experience and think about the world in fluid, unusual ways. Metaphor is the bridge we fling between the utterly strange and the utterly familiar."[19]

In the city of Pittsburgh, near my home, two rivers join to form the Ohio River, namely, the Allegheny and the Monongahela rivers. Beneath the city, however, flows a fourth river, indispensable to the city's ecosystem, an unseen subterranean aquifer called the Wisconsin Glacial Flow. Some city buildings make use of this water, and during heavy rains, the water in the aquifer adds to the flooding. This is how the Fourth River, like a long-forgotten metaphor, reminds us that it is still there, even though we cannot see it; that it is still felt, still flowing, and knows exactly where it is going.

Jesus regularly used metaphors, such as when he declared, "I have other sheep that do not belong to this fold. I must bring them also, and they will listen to my voice. So there will be one flock, one shepherd" (John 10:16). There are many metaphors in that single verse, all of which need to be mined for the crucial truths they teach. Jesus used clever metaphors to teach unclear spiritual truths. He called them parables.

A parable is a metaphor in story form. Narrated metaphors, parables use a fictional story to describe a fact of life. Religious parables are object lessons that place spiritual truth side by side with natural truth. Parables are teaching tales, the most compressed and concentrated forms of story. They are compact metaphorical thought experiments that help solve not only religious problems but also essential psychological and social problems in the real world. They are common to every country and culture. They make difficult concepts easier to grasp, as exemplified in the moral and spiritual tales of teachers as diverse as the Buddha, Jesus, and Muhammad. The educational and existential aspects of parables also account for their perennial popularity. Probably no collection of tales is more popular than *Aesop's Fables*. Parables are often appended to Aesop's fables as a way to sum up and reinforce the story's import.

---

18. Ibid., 77.
19. Geary, *I Is an Other*, 224–25.

Jesus used parables to subvert our unconscious worldview, unlocking it from within and thereby exposing its illusions. All religions have tried to do the same with riddles and koans and mythic stories. Our entire universe has to be rearranged truthfully before individual teachings can be heard correctly. Unfortunately, what religion has been doing in the West is give people new moral and doctrinal teaching without rearranging their mythic worldview. This approach does not work, for it leads nowhere new. It only creates legalists, specialists, ritualists, minimalists, and literalists, who always kill the spirit of a thing.

A parable confronts our world and subverts it. It doesn't call for discussion, debate, or question. Rather, it calls us to insight and decision. Parables are intended to make us uncomfortable, because they enable us to see and hear reality correctly. If we fit them nicely into our business-as-usual world, parables have not served their purpose. Like a joke, it leads up to the punch line. Either you get it or you don't.

Like metaphors, parables have multiple meaning. Parables come in a variety of forms. For example, an allegory, such as Bunyan's *Pilgrim's Progress* or Dante's *Divine Comedy*, is a dramatic parable with different characters. A fable is a parable featuring animals, and a myth, such as *The Quest for the Grail* we examine in chapters 10 and 11, is but an epic parable.

If parables are metaphors in story form, then proverbs are parables in miniature. Like parables, proverbs often feature animals ("You can lead a horse to water, but you can't make it drink"), and always contain hidden moral lessons. They are, in essence, one-sentence stories, which nineteenth-century British prime minister John Russell succinctly defined as "the wit of one, the wisdom of many."

The proverb and its close relation, the aphorism, are the world's oldest written art forms. They are also the oldest written examples of metaphor. In ancient Sumer, where writing was invented around 3500 BCE, proverb collections were used as textbooks. Despite their antiquity, they still ring true. The Sumerian saying, "Wealth is hard to come by, but poverty is always at hand," anticipates "The poor are always with us."

It is impossible to understand Jesus' strong and important message if we do not honor metaphor. Perhaps that is why we have missed so much of his core message. Metaphor produces invariably more—not less, as fundamentalists fear. Literalism is the lowest and least level of meaning. Surely Paul had this larger concept in mind when he penned his famous principle, "the letter (legalism, literalism) kills, but the Spirit (metaphor, symbol, story) gives life" (2 Cor. 3:6).

While we need metaphors to go deep, we must never be so tied to our own metaphors as if they alone speak the truth. That is the inherent tension and conflict: only the right symbol at the right time produces results, allowing us to move beyond complexity and illusion. Often only that which looks like mere symbol becomes the doorway to all we really need to know.

Ancient peoples seem to have understood this better than we have, for they lived with a greater sense of wonder, gratitude, and inherent belonging than we do. Our individualism and autonomy often stymy such spiritual skills as listening, allowing, trusting, and belonging. These are the trustworthy guides into the good, the true, and the beautiful.

Modern atheists and fundamentalists are invariably linked to a narrowed-down and literal view of reality and seldom understand metaphor. Being literalist, religious fundamentalists often miss the symbolic in scripture. They view symbols as shallow, preferring sermons and creedal statements to sacraments, meditation, and silence. Atheists simply dismiss religious symbols as superficial, untrue, unscientific, or "just a symbol."

As mystics and all spiritual masters teach, we live in an entirely symbolic universe. Symbols are in fact the only solid way to experience substance. True symbols, by nature, bring things together, in new and startling ways (*sym bolon* in Greek means "throwing together"). They do so not only by putting us in touch with reality, but by actually becoming reality itself. Poets, artists, and storytellers have always known this, and now scientists realize that they too need metaphors to point to reality (for example, black holes, string theory, and the big bang). Without symbols, unconscious meanings never break through to consciousness, and the invisible has no way of becoming visible.

Many have called our postmodern world "a crisis of meaning," a world where things lack objective meaning.[20] It is very lonely in such a universe. Humans cannot live happily without meaning, and ever-deeper meaning. Symbols have the power to give meaning, and religion should help us mine for meaning. Why else do we read novels, have belabored conversations, or go to movies. Surely not for their entertainment value alone. Is it not to seek answers to that most existential of questions, "What does it mean to be human?"

Most meaning is largely preconceptual and not subject to words, and in that sense is nonrational, but meaning lies beneath the surface, waiting for the right symbol in the right moment. Our sense of wonder can be triggered by a sunset, and one look at Picasso's *Guernica* makes us feel the terror and absurdity of war. At such a moment, we normally feel more alive, connected, and authentic, even if it is sadness that we feel. The inner self is expressed, the inner breath is exhaled, and the inner and outer worlds meet. The Greeks call it catharsis, or emotional cleansing; Christians call it sacrament.

---

20. See the chart on postmodern consciousness in appendix B.

QUESTIONS FOR DISCUSSION AND REFLECTION

1. When you use the word "God," do you associate it with metaphor, fact, or somehow as both metaphor and fact?
2. Explain and assess the author's statement that mythology represents penultimate rather than final truth.
3. When thinking biblically or theologically, how comfortable are you with ambiguity and uncertainty? Explain your answer.
4. Explain and assess George Bernard Shaw's statement, "there is only one religion, and there are then a thousand forms of it."
5. In speaking of ultimate truths, should we pursue or avoid deliberate usage of metaphor?
6. What did Ralph Waldo Emerson mean when he called language "fossil poetry"?
7. What do neuroscientists mean by neural priming? Can you think of any examples of this common phenomenon?
8. After reading this chapter, what did you learn about the meaning and use of theological language?
9. After reading this chapter, what did you learn about truth?
10. After reading this chapter, what did you learn about Jesus' use of parables?
11. In your estimation, what is the primary insight gained from this chapter? Does this chapter raise any issues you might need to address in the future?

Chapter 8

Death and Resurrection as Metaphor[1]

IN AMERICA TODAY, as in most global economies, there is a mutual contract between personal egos and egoic cultures. This is the meaning of the phrase "the world" in the New Testament (see John 1:10; 8:23; 12:31; 1 John 2:15–17). In this sense, the word "world" is a way of speaking of the corporate False Self, what we might call "the system" or "the way the world works." Jesus said, "Take courage; I have conquered the world" (John 16:33).

The False Self fears change, even creating moral disguises to achieve its selfish ends. Hence, the New Testament often personifies the ego—whether personal or corporate—as the devil or Satan. The devil's secrets are always disguised, as we see with the snake in Genesis 3:1. Satan's temptations are not always blatant and offensive, but often subtle and self-centered.

Like Jesus, the ego is tempted economically (to be successful), politically (to be powerful), and spiritually (to be right). The ego regularly acquiesces, finding such temptations seductive. When the corporate ego succumbs, the results can be disastrous. Temptations to dominate others or to remain isolated and self-sufficient seem obvious to us, unlike the third temptation, which fuels the ego with high octane. The True Self, rooted in Ultimate Reality, has little need for limited answers and temporary certitudes. It has found its certainty elsewhere and lives inside a "Yes" so eternal that it can absorb life's disappointments and fractures. The False Self, however, fears and denies all paradox and uncertainty, probably because it unconsciously knows it is itself a mass of contradiction and uncertainty.

1. Ideas in this chapter are adapted from Rohr, *Diamond*, 43–102, 139–58.

The True Self, symbolized by the Risen Christ, has already overcome the contradictions and paradoxes of life.

In speaking of the Christian life, pastoral theologian Andrew Purves distinguishes between imitating Christ (*imitatio Christi*) and participating *in* Christ (*participatio Christi*). While many believers today strive to "be like Jesus," early Christians though differently, emphasizing the importance of participating in Jesus Christ through the power of the Holy Spirit. Trying harder was not the solution. Rather, they understood that God was the primary actor, and the Christian life a response to Christ's "vicarious humanity," experienced through the Holy Spirit.[2]

Jesus confronted the False Self's seductive lies by living within an entirely different frame of reference, the eternal "kingdom of God." The False Self is no longer a threat or an enduring attraction when viewed from the vantage of the True Self. This is what Christians mean at Easter when they proclaim that Jesus destroyed death. Perhaps it would be more accurate to say, "Jesus exposed the lie," because there is clearly plenty of "death" in our society that has not died.

DEATH AND THE FALSE SELF

Mature religion talks about the death of any notion of a separate, False Self, while recognizing that only a deep security in a larger love will give you the courage to do that. The True Self can let go because it is secure at its core. Our False Self, however, does not let go easily. Unwilling to die to the old, it resists all such change.

As Jesus and other great spiritual teachers made clear, there is a self that must be found and another that must be renounced. This teaching is found in each Gospel (see Matt. 10:39; 16:25; Mark 8:35; Luke 9:24), but is central to John's Gospel, where it is coupled with "dying to the self": "unless a grain of wheat falls into the earth and dies, it remains just a single grain; but if it dies, it bears much fruit" (John 12:24). Hence, "those who love their life lose it [that is, their False Self], and those who hate their life [their False Self] in this world will keep it [their True Self] for eternal life" (John 12:25; see also 1 Cor. 15:36–37, 42).

In one way or another, almost all religions say that you must die before you die—and then you will know what dying means, and what it does not mean. What it does mean, of course, is the relinquishment of selfish, possessive living, of egoic existence. This includes the death or renunciation of easy opinions, forced certitudes, intellectual or moral superiority, futile

---

2. Purves, *Reconstructing Pastoral Theology*, 152.

attempts at perfect control, and eventually any belief in our separateness from God.³ The ego self is the self before death; some form of death—psychological, spiritual, relational, or physical—is the way we will loosen our ties to our small and separate False Self. Only then does it return in a new shape, which we call the soul, the True Self, or the Risen Christ.

There are four major splits from reality that we have all made in varying degrees to create our False Self:

- We split from our shadow self⁴ and pretend to be our idealized self.
- We split our mind from our body and soul, and live in our minds.
- We split life from death and try to live without any "death."
- We split ourselves from other selves and try to live apart, superior, and separate.⁵

Each of these illusions must be overcome, either in this world or at the moment of physical death. Spirituality, pure and simple, is overcoming these splits from Reality.

Anything less than the death of the False Self is inadequate religion. The False Self must die for the True Self to live, or, as Jesus put it, "if I do not go, the Advocate [the Holy Spirit] will not come to you" (John 16:7). Theologically speaking, what this verse is telling us is that Jesus (a good person) still had to die for the Christ (the universal presence) to arise. This is the pattern of transformation, where the letting go of the original indispensable self results in the arrival of a better reality. This pattern of death and rebirth—of cross and resurrection—is both spiritual and natural. As we know from science, the death and birth of every star and atom is this same pattern of loss and renewal.

Your True Self sees truthfully and will live forever. Your False Self is constantly changing and will eventually die. Your False Self is your necessary warm-up, the ego part of you that establishes your separate identity, especially in the first half of life. It is your incomplete self trying to pass for your whole self. The role of true spirituality, of mature religion, is to help

---

3. Rohr, *Eager to Love*, 26.

4. The shadow self, something everyone possesses, represents the least-developed part of one's personality. The shadow uses relatively childish and primitive forms of judgment and perception, often as an escape from the conscious personality and in defiance of conscious standards. One's shadow includes "good" qualities as well as "bad" or "shameful" qualities that one denies. As one makes room for one's polarities, one becomes healthier and more open to transforming grace. The shadow self is described more fully in chapter 11, in the segment titled "The Wasteland."

5. Rohr, *Diamond*, 29.

speed up this process of dying to the False Self. Whatever one calls it, true spirituality is the form of living embodied by Jesus and taught by the Buddha. Such calm, egoless approach to life is invariably characteristic of people at the highest levels of doing and loving in all cultures and religions. These are the ones we call sages or holy ones.

Without what Jesus called "the sign of Jonah" (see Matt. 12:39–40)—the pattern of new life only through death—Christianity remains a largely impotent ideology, another way to "win" instead of the "way of the cross" characterized by Jonah, Jeremiah, Job, John the Baptist, and Jesus. Viewed this way, Jesus become the teacher of the path rather than the cosmic problem-solver. The Jonah-Job-Jesus pattern has been hard for Westerners to recognize and accept, but it is taught by what we call Eastern religions. The sign of Jonah is at the heart of the matter.

Psychologically, the large fish (whale?) represents "the power of life locked in the unconscious. Metaphorically, water is the unconscious, and this creature in the water is the life or energy of the unconscious, which has overwhelmed the conscious personality and must be disempowered, overcome, and controlled. . . . In the story of Jonah, the hero is swallowed and taken into the abyss to be later resurrected—a variant of the death-and-resurrection theme."[6]

The egoic self is real, precious, unique, but temporary, for your False Self is what changes, passes, and ends when you die. There is no escape from death when the "you" is the egoic self. It is a manifestation of the True Self, but it tends to forget this and imagines itself to be apart from God rather than a part of God. However, such thinking is in error. There is no "you" separate from God, just as there is no wave separate from the ocean. When you die—psychologically and spiritually but also physically—you are still what you were and are: holy, sacred, and immortal.

To not let go of your False Self at the right time and in the right way is what it means to be trapped, addicted to yourself. This, I believe, is the meaning of Jesus' words to Mary Magdalene after his resurrection, "Do not hold on to me" (John 20:17). What Jesus is saying is, "Don't cling to the past, Mary, to your needy False Self. You and I are heading for something far better." Great love is both attachment and detachment. There is a spiritual art to attachment and detachment. Such art is love, but not addiction.

If all you have at the end of your life is your False Self, there will not be much to eternalize. However, there is no death when the "you" is the divine Self, for the True Self lives forever. When you are connected to the Whole, you no longer need to defend or protect the isolated part. You are

6. Campbell, *Power of Myth*, 146.

now connected to something Real, eternal. When you are able to move beyond your False Self—at the right time and in the right way—it will feel like freedom and liberation, as if you had lost nothing.

It is no surprise that we humans would deny death's certain coming, fight it, and seek to avoid the demise of the only self we have known. This process of transformation is something we both deeply desire and desperately fear. It is the phenomenon Rudolph Otto termed the *mysterium tremendum*, an experience both alluring and frightful at the same time. Originally described in the language of symbol and myth, this experience has been acted out in ritual and other kinds of human activity long before it became a topic of philosophical and theological discussion. It is the union that will liberate us, yet we resist and flee.

The path of dying and rising is exactly what in-depth spiritual teaching must address. It is the letting go of all you think you are, moving into a world without any experienced context, and becoming the person you always were at depth and yet did not know on the surface. The surrender of our False Self in the final days and hours in any conscious dying have been called "enlightenment at gunpoint" by Kathleen Dowling Singh, a woman who spent her life in hospice work.

We put off enlightenment by decades if we are not present at deaths—and births. Remember, salvation is not so much a matter of *if* as *when* you get it, and maybe how much we can handle.[7] It makes us wonder why we have turned the spiritual journey into a forced march or into a game of *Survivor*, instead of a joyous proclamation of this necessary but good process of surrender into love. The reason seems obvious; it is because the False Self prefers win-lose over win-win, even, strangely enough, when it ends up defining itself as a loser. The ego will always choose trumped-up competition over calm cooperation. Such a mindset—more "hell" than "heaven," seems almost the American way.

Once you know you are sharing in "the force field of resurrection," you can always live within it, drawing from its power.[8] Nevertheless, the price of such momentous realization is that you must first go into the tomb with Jesus, "so that, just as Christ was raised from the dead by the glory of the Father, so we too might walk in newness of life" (Rom. 6:4).

---

7. Rohr, *Diamond*, 141.
8. Ibid., 144.

RESURRECTION AND THE TRUE SELF

Religion (*re-ligio* meaning re-binding) is not doing its job if it only reminds us of our distance, our unworthiness, our sinfulness, and our inadequacy before God's greatness. Whenever religion increases the gap, it becomes antireligion instead. Such gap creating between God and creation is actually diabolical (*dia balein*, Greek for "to throw apart"). What we need, of course, are adequate symbols (*sym bolon*, "throwing together"), and that, precisely, is what the New Testament provides: an entirely symbolic way of understanding Reality.

Let us be clear; in his human mind, Jesus was limited. It seems likely, as modern biblical scholarship indicates, that Jesus did not fully know his True Self as the "Son of God" until after the Resurrection. Before his transformation, Jesus lived by faith and was like us in every respect except sin (Heb. 4:15). This means he never accepted the "lie of separation," which is the core meaning of sin. He could affirm, without hesitation, "The Father and I are one" (John 10:30). That affirmation, and other equally remarkable affirmations attributed to Jesus, such as "before Abraham was, I am" (John 8:58), are not so much declarations of uniqueness as indications that in Jesus we have the ultimate model and trustworthy leader for all humanity.

When we examine other well-known biblical passages in this light, they come alive in new ways. For instance, when Jesus says, "I am the vine, you are the branches" (John 15:5), there really isn't a division between vine and branches, even though we can tell the difference between them. And when Jesus says, "I am in my Father, and you in me, and I in you" (John 14:20), there is no implied separation of the Self and God. The same holds true in Acts, when Paul defines God as that in which "we live and move and have our being" (Acts 17:28). This realization that God is living in us and through us is how we plug into the much larger heart and mind beyond our own.

Thus, when I use the word Resurrection in this segment, it is for its symbolic value. Despite its uniqueness in Jesus, Resurrection is not about psychological optimism, religious miracle, theological proof that Christianity is the true religion, or even an affirmation that there is life after death. Rather, I am referring to something more constant and universal than any of these, something intrinsic to almost everything in life, even things we fear or dislike.

The False Self is energized by problems, challenges, and self-created goals. The True Self, however, is energized by a different fuel: union, contentment, and particularly, deep resonance (meaning) of any kind. Once you know that life and death are not separate but part of a whole, you will begin to view reality in a holistic way, and that will change everything. For one thing, it is the initial birth of nondual consciousness. No one can teach you this. It can only be modeled. Interestingly, the only person Jesus ever called "Satan" or "devil" is Peter, when he tried to oppose this central message of death and resurrection (Matt. 16:23).

The eminent Swiss psychiatrist Carl Jung spoke of Jesus as "the Archetype of the Self," meaning that what happens in the life of Jesus happens always and everywhere.[9] Discovering in the Jesus story a map of the unconscious human journey, he feared that Western civilization could lose this pattern, and that the results would be disastrous. Jesus is our "Savior," then, because he is the one who charts and guides us on the necessary path. The contours of that path can be summed up in the twin concepts of death and resurrection, for they serve as the template for full and authentic human life, what Jesus called "abundant life" (John 10:10).

As resurrected Lord, the risen Christ is not being rewarded for a job well done as much as he is modeling the full, completed journey and goal of life. The New Testament depicts Jesus as the "pioneer and perfecter" of the entire human journey, as Hebrews 12:2 poetically states, the guarantee (Heb. 7:22) and pledge (Eph. 1:14) that life is stronger than death, that love is everlasting. Furthermore, this guarantee has been implanted in every heart by God's Holy Spirit.

When Jesus called his disciples, he was not asking others to join a new security system, a religious club, denomination, or order. He did not invite them to a belief system, but rather to a lifestyle: "Follow me." Where faith was elicited, it was in the form of trust, not belief. When he called his first disciples, Jesus was talking about further journeys to people who were already settled, socially and religiously.

The Gospels are essentially resurrection accounts, written after the fact. Their purpose is to unify Christian believers by evoking faith in Christ. The Gospels can be misleading, particularly for those who view faith systematically, as a set of doctrines and beliefs. They were not intended to be read doctrinally or dogmatically. It took Christians several centuries to create a systematic understanding of Jesus and his mission, one that, in my estimation, they got wrong. When I think of Jesus, it is not about how he is dissimilar from other human beings but rather how he serves as the model and metaphor for all humanity that I seek to understand. In my estimation, the historical Jesus embodies the universal Christ, the True Self that gives all humans final meaning and definition. In that respect, Jesus' story is the universe story.

---

9. Jung, *AION*, 5.70, 115–16, 124; 12.283.

Longing for God and longing for our True Self are the same longing. Religion has only one job description: making one out of two. For Christians, that is the "Christ Mystery," the belief that God overcame the gap from God's side, doing "the heavy lifting," initiating the longing. What God is saying in the incarnation of Jesus is, "I am not totally Other. I have planted some of me in all things." Christians would say that it is God who is doing the longing in us and through us, by means of the divine indwelling we call the Holy Spirit. The core meaning of the Christian doctrine of the Holy Spirit is simply this, that God implanted a natural affinity and allurement between Godself and all God's creatures. Otherwise, the limited and the limitless would be incapable of union. Apart from God's Spirit, the finite and infinite could never be reconciled.

THE THIRD INCARNATION OF GOD

What we call Resurrection is one of the greatest and most compelling symbols available to human beings, for it discloses the universal pattern of the undoing of death. The three Abrahamic religions saw God as the one "who gives life to the dead and calls into existence the things that do not exist" (Rom. 4:17). For Christians, this pattern of incarnation, death, and resurrection revealed in "the Christ" was true long before Jesus of Nazareth, from the very birth and death of the stars to the entire circle of life on this planet.

When we speak of Jesus, we also have in mind the eternal or Cosmic Christ. Christ is simply another word for "the body of God," another name for "God-as-materialized" (what scientists call the "Big Bang," which apparently happened about 13.8 billion years ago). This Cosmic Christ is God as revealed through every aspect of creation, as the New Testament makes clear (John 1:1–10; 1 Cor. 8:6; Col. 1:15–20; Eph. 1:3–14; Heb. 1:1–3; 1 John 1:1–3).

When ordinary people become Christians, that is, "little Christ's," they embody or enact in their lives the "third incarnation" of God, or the "second coming" of Christ.[10] Let me explain what I mean. The first incarnation is the moment described in Genesis 1 as "the first day," when God became the Universal Christ, joining in unity with the physical universe and becoming the light inside of everything. This is described in Genesis 1:3–4 by the statement, "Then God said, 'Let there be light'; and there was light. . .and God separated the light from the darkness." This teaching is affirmed in the prologue of John's Gospel, by the relationship between God and Christ (the

---

10. The concept of three incarnations, exemplified in what Richard Rohr calls an incarnational worldview, is articulated in his book *The Universal Christ*, 12–21.

Word/Logos): "In the beginning was the Word, and the Word was with God, and the Word was God. . . in him was life, and the life was the light of all people. The light shines in the darkness, and the darkness did not overcome it" (John 1:1, 4–5). The first incarnation—what we are calling the Cosmic Christ—is the divine presence pervading creation since the beginning. From this perspective, wherever the material and the spiritual coincide, we have the Christ.

The second incarnation of God and the "first coming" of Christ represent what Christians believe about the historical incarnation we call Jesus. Let us be clear: Christ is not Jesus' last name. The word Christ is a title, meaning Anointed One. When Christians speak of Jesus Christ, they include the entire sweep of the meaning of the Christ, which includes all the divine activity since the beginning of time (see Rom. 1:20). Of this activity, Jesus is the visible map, the one who brings this eternal message home personally.

The third incarnation of God (the "second coming of Christ") occurs whenever true discipleship occurs, when Jesus Christ is born in us. For Christians, evidence for the third incarnation appears in the Eucharist: "Eat it and know who you are," Augustine said. As any nutritionist knows, we are what we eat and drink. Christians are part of the Christ Mystery. No longer alienated from God, others, or the universe—at least in principle—Christians embody cosmic belonging, oneness with Christ, the name we give to everything purposeful and harmonious in the universe. Paul affirmed this truth when he declared, "It is no longer I who live, but it is Christ who lives in me" (Gal. 2:20).

Exhorting believers to adopt the mind of Jesus (Phil. 2:5), Paul also confirms that Christians incarnate Christ, since they possess "the mind of Christ" (1 Cor. 2:16). When individuals become Jesus people—incarnations of Christ—they exchange one mindset for another, their "monkey mind" (the obsessive, noisy chattering we observe during silent meditation) for the mind of Christ. This is likely what Paul meant when he called believers God's "new creation" (2 Cor. 5:17): "If anyone is in Christ, there is a new creation: everything old has passed away; see, everything has become new." For Paul, when the minds of believers are transformed into the mind of Christ, their bodies become temples, dwelling places of God's Spirit (1 Cor. 3:16–17; see Rom. 12:1–2).

As we travel inward, into the interior depth of soul, we discover that each believer is a chip off the old block, a miniature word of the Word of God, a mini-incarnation of divine love. This entails allowing God's grace to heal, hold, and empower us. It means entering the unknowns of our lives, and learning to trust the darkness, for the transformative power of divine love is already there.

The full Christ Mystery serves as a pattern for the entire journey of the True Self, from divine conception, to beloved status, through crucifixion, and unto resurrection. This whole process of living, dying, and then living again starts with God breathing life into the "dust of the ground" and calling this living being *adam* ("of the earth"). The point is that a drama was forever set in motion between breath and what appears to be humus (human, *adamah*, from the soil). Matter and spirit are forever bound together, divine and mortal endlessly intermingled. The changing of forms is called resurrection, and the return is called ascension, although it appears as death.

As scholars point out, taking the concept of the ascension of Christ literally is nonsensical and counterintuitive in a scientific age. The idea of an eternal heaven somewhere above us is the product of an antiquated cosmology often described as the "three-story universe." We know there is no known place in the universe where Jesus literally went. Even ascending at the speed of light, Jesus would still be traversing our galaxy today. Astronomy and physics have eliminated ascension to heaven as a literal, physical possibility. However, if we understand ascension metaphorically, meaning Jesus has gone inward—not into outer space but into inward space, into the kingdom within, into the consciousness that is the source of all things—this we can imagine. The images are outward, but their reflection is inward. The point is that one can ascend with Jesus by going inward. This is a metaphor of returning to the body's dynamic source.[11]

This process of life, death, resurrection, and ascension is called incarnation. Because it is about Christ, it is also about creation, and that includes all humans, coming forth as individuals and then returning unto God, the Ground of all Being. As Jesus indicated, to God all people are alive (Luke 20:38); those who are deceased are simply in different stages of aliveness. This is the staggering change of perspective that the gospel was meant to achieve. This realization is the heart of all religious transformation (*transformare* is Latin for "to change form"). The Risen Christ represents the final perspective of every True Self: a human-divine perspective that looks out from God and sees all things as ultimately good and as united.

Resurrection is incarnation come to its logical and full conclusion. It fully demonstrates that this world, this physicality that includes our human flesh, is part of the eternal truth and forever matters to God. Resurrection is not a miracle to be proven, but a manifestation of the wholeness that we are all meant to experience, even in this world. The Risen Christ is the standing

---

11. Campbell, *Power of Myth*, 56–57.

icon of humanity in its final and full destiny. Resurrection is about Jesus, but it also says something essential about us, namely, that we too are larger than life. Finally, we can live meaningfully, filled with hope. Our code word for this is heaven.

When we take the Resurrection metaphor absolutely seriously, it moves us far beyond the stripped-down literal meaning where so many flounder. It does not have to mean "an eternally enduring life" as much as "a present life of eternal significance." Science strongly confirms this principle, only with different metaphors and symbols, like condensation, evaporation, hibernation, sublimation, the recurring seasons, and even the constant death and birth of stars from the same stardust. God appears to be resurrecting everything all the time. It is not something we need to "believe" as much as something to observe and ponder.

We all want to know that life on earth has both temporal and eternal meaning. We can be assured it is going someplace good because it came from someplace good—a place of "original blessing" instead of a place of "original sin." For Christians, the model and exemplar is Jesus: "I know where I have come from, and where I am going, but you do not know," he states in John 8:14. If the original incarnation is true, then resurrection is inevitable and irreversible. The only difficulty is that transformation and "crucifixion" must intervene between life and Life. Loss always precedes renewal.

The great unfolding of God's Mystery involves all the events and stages of our life; nothing is wasted or discarded—not even evil, sin, or death (this is why the Bible includes those seemingly extraneous stories of murder, rape, deceit, and war). God is going somewhere with this whole thing called life. Why else would the Creator take the great risk in fashioning a universe where the parts evolve and develop but not the whole? Humans are preoccupied with stability, efficiency, and control; God, by contrast is clearly into freedom, imagination, and creativity.

The Risen Christ affirms everything with a big "Yes" (2 Cor. 1:19), even its own earlier imperfect stages. The final astonishing gift is that our False Self has now become our True Self; the one and the many have become the One. That is precisely the metamorphosis we call resurrection. The raw material of every aspect of life is not ended but merely changed: "this perishable body must put on imperishability, and this mortal body must put on immortality" (1 Cor. 15:53).

According to John's Gospel, the Risen Christ appeared first to Mary Magdalene, not to one of the Twelve (John 20:1–18). At first, this seems surprising, until we realize that she is the symbolic stand-in for all longing humanity, all who have experienced sorrow, rejection, and pain. She is the

Gospel personage who most needs love to be stronger than death, and so she is the first to know it—and perhaps at the deepest level. She is the first one who symbolically comes to awareness, the first real knower, and thus is the clear "witness to the witnesses" (20:18). It is not surprising, then, that she is named as standing at the foot of the cross (John 19:25), with two other Marys—who walked through the mystery with Jesus. And they were also the first ones at the tomb on Sunday. Mary is the archetypal name for all those who live out of their True Selves and know its Source. This True Self cannot find or know God without wanting to bring everybody else to the same awareness.

The True Self has already overcome the contradictions and paradoxes of life, which is symbolized by the Risen Christ, who presents the full tension of death and life, earth and spirit, human and divine—precisely as overcome. Once we know that there is an implanted and positive direction to creation, we can go with the primary flow (faith); eventually we will learn to rest there (hope), and finally to actually live there in peace and joy (love). We are home at last in an inherently sacred universe.

We North Americans really don't know how to live in peace or without enemies. Our economy, our self-image, our very psyche have thrived in a triumphalistic and paranoid stance for so long that it will be hard to change to a positive and creative mode. What we can and must do, however, is to live and to announce the alternative: a new way of living based on faith instead of fear, peacemaking instead of moneymaking, community instead of competition, for this is what Resurrection life looks like.

The Risen Christ knows that good is more powerful than evil, love stronger than hatred, life more durable than death. Until we know that in our bones, until we risk it in our actions, until we base our life's choices on such awesome trust, all our preaching is useless and our believing in vain (1 Cor. 15:14). The mystery of the death and resurrection of Christ tells us that we live in a benevolent universe. God is on our side, we belong here, and there is no basis for existential fear. We no longer need to control or live in fear, because something far better is taking place. Resurrection says that the true apocalyptic message is not "The end is near!" but "The beginning is always happening!"[12]

As the mystics and sages teach, the path of dying and rising is one continuous movement. It begins with learning to love one's life, and then with allowing oneself to die into it—and never to die away from it. Once death is joyfully incorporated into life, you are already in heaven, and there is no

---

12. For a practical sense of the Resurrection message and its implementation in our lives, see appendix A: "Twelve Ways to Practice Resurrection Now."

possibility or fear of hell. This is the Way, modeled by Jesus and enacted by his followers. "The Gospel is not a fire insurance policy for the next world, but a life assurance policy for this world."[13]

QUESTIONS FOR DISCUSSION AND REFLECTION

1. Explain and assess the merits of equating the imperial ego with Satan or the devil.
2. In your own words, explain the difference between *imitatio Christi* and *participatio Christi*.
3. After reading this chapter, explain the meaning of Jesus' statement in John 12:25, "those who love this life will lose it and those who hate their life in this world will keep it."
4. Explain and assess the four shifts from reality that create one's False Self.
5. Assess the merits of the statement, "Anything less than the death of the False Self is useless religion."
6. Explain the meaning of "the sign of Jonah" in Matthew 12:39–40.
7. Assess the meaning of the statement, "If all you have at the end of your life is your False Self, there will not be much to eternalize."
8. Explain and assess the meaning of Kathleen Dowling Singh's phrase "enlightenment at gunpoint."
9. In your estimation, what did Jesus mean by "the Father and I are one"? (see John 10:30).
10. After reading this chapter, what did you learn about Resurrection?
11. Explain and assess the concept of the three incarnations of God.
12. In your estimation, what is the primary insight gained from this chapter? Does this chapter raise any issues you might need to address in the future?

---

13. Rohr, *Eager to Love*, xxii.

Myth

Chapter 9

The Power of Myth[1]

PSYCHOLOGISTS TODAY RECOGNIZE UP to nine different forms of intelligence, building on a theory of multiple intelligence proposed by Howard Gardner in 1983. The original list included seven cognitive abilities: spatial, linguistic, logical-mathematical, bodily-kinesthetic, musical, interpersonal, and intrapersonal. In 1999 he added another category, which he called "naturalist intelligence," and later suggested yet another, "existential and moral intelligence." This last category is viewed as a spiritual or religious capacity, for it involves the ability to contemplate phenomena or to pursue questions that go beyond sense data.

Just as there are many forms of intelligence, so there are various ways of thinking, speaking, and acquiring knowledge. The ancient Greeks affirmed two modes of thought, calling them *logos* and *mythos*.[2] Both were essential and neither was considered superior to the other. While they were complementary, each having its own sphere of competence, it was considered unwise to mix the two. Both were pragmatic. *Logos* ("reason") helped people organize their societies, control the environment, and invent new technology. Although *logos* was essential to the survival of the species, it had limitations. It could not provide ultimate meaning or help cope with tragedy or with death. For help people turned to *mythos* ("myth").

Today, because we live in a society of scientific *logos*, myth has fallen into disrepute. But in the past, myth, like *logos*, helped people to live

---

1. Portions of this chapter are adapted from the writings of Joseph Campbell, a leading figure in the field of comparative mythology until his death in 1987.
2. Armstrong, *Case for God*, xi–xiii.

effectively in a confusing and uncertain world. Ancient myths have been called a primitive form of psychology, for these stories were therapeutic, designed to help people negotiate the obscure regions of the psyche, areas that influence our thoughts and behavior but are difficult to access. Myths were never intended to be taken literally, as though they were accurate accounts of historical events. A myth was "something that had in some sense happened once but that also happens all the time."[3] In other words, myths spoke to existential conditions.

A myth would not be effective if someone simply believed in it, for myths were not designed to provide factual information. A myth was essentially a program of action. Although it could put individuals in the correct spiritual or psychological posture, it was up to them to take the next step and make the truth of the myth a reality in their own life. Myths showed people how to live more fully, how to cope with their mortality, and how to embrace life's suffering creatively. If one failed to act upon myth or to apply it to specific situations, it would remain abstract and incredible.

From an early date, myths were enacted in stylized ceremonies (rituals) that worked aesthetically upon participants and, like any work of art, introduced them to a deeper dimension of existence. Myth and ritual were thus inseparable. Without ritual, myths made no sense.

Religion, which builds upon myth (scripture) and ritual (ceremony), was never intended to provide answers that lie within the competence of human reason. That was the role of *logos*. The task of religion was to enable followers to find wisdom, the sort of wisdom that helps them live creatively, peacefully, and even joyously with realities for which there are no easy explanations.

Of course, religion does not work automatically. It is a practical discipline that teaches humans to discover new capacities of mind and heart. Religion, which connects myth with ritual, is not, like *logos*, something that people believe or think, but something people do. Its truth is acquired by practical action, by translating the teachings of religion into ritual or ethical action.

Like any skill, religion requires perseverance, hard work, and discipline. Some people will be better at it than others, some will be inept, and others will miss the point altogether. But those who do not apply themselves will get nowhere at all. Early Daoists, practitioners of one of China's indigenous religious traditions, considered religion as a knack acquired by constant practice. People who acquired this knack discovered a transcendent dimension of life that was not simply an external reality "out there"

---

3. Ibid., xi.

but was identical with the deepest level of their being. This reality, called by many names and understood in different ways by different religious traditions, has been understood as a fact of human life, though it is impossible to explain solely in terms of *logos*.

According to the Perennial Tradition, everything that happens in this world has its counterpart in the divine or transcendent realm, which is deeper, stronger, and more enduring than our own. Every earthly reality, therefore, is but a pale shadow of its archetype. It is only by participating in this sacred life that fragile, mortal human beings fulfil their potential. The ancient myths give explicit shape and form to Ultimate Reality, something primal peoples sensed intuitively.

Religion has created the world's most lasting narratives, stories that help people make sense of birth, death, and everything in between. These ancient stories have guided and consoled people for thousands of years. The holy texts assign meaning and purpose to the human condition, provide a set of moral codes, and tell us how to live. They do this through metaphor and imagery, character and conflict, rhythm and poetry. However, the real power of religious stories stems from the depths of the questions they raise and the topics they cover, matters of the human heart. Spiritual cultures come together around these powerful tales, and hand them down to younger generations as a way of explaining life. Religions established themselves in the imagination through story.

When myths speak of heroes, of gods and sacred things, the intent is not to satisfy idle curiosity or provide entertainment, but rather to offer models for human behavior. In the ancient world, mythology was not about theology, in the modern sense, but about human experience, a way to help individuals cope with the problematic human predicament. In addition, myths provide hope for the future by expanding our sense of wonder, helping us glimpse new possibilities by asking "what if?"—a question that has provoked some of our most important discoveries in philosophy, science, and technology. Like poetry and music, mythology should awaken us to rapture. If a myth ceases to do that, it has died and outlived its usefulness.

A myth, therefore, is true because it is effective, not because it gives us factual information. If it works, that is, if it forces us to change our minds and hearts, gives us hope, and compels us to live more fully, it is a valid myth. A myth is essentially a guide; it tells us what we must do in order to live more fully. However, mythology will only transform us if we follow its directives.

In the field of religious studies there are two kinds of truths: *literal truth* (natural, factual, or scientific in nature) and *mythological truth* (religious or symbolic in nature). Religious myths are not fables but rather sacred stories that hold sacred truths within the worldview of a believer. These stories are often recorded in sacred texts but sometimes in oral tradition. They set forth fundamental knowledge regarding the nature of things and the proper way to live. In religion, myths provide answers to boundary questions. They may not be provable historically or logically, but nevertheless they are real in that they guide the behavior of believers.

Biblical religion begins with a sense of wonder and awe, told in story form. Then, in the Greco-Roman world, these stories were reduced to theological codes and creeds. Reducing mythology to theology is a violation of intent. Mythology is poetry, and poetic language is flexible. Religious authorities, thinking theologically, turned poetry into prose, historicizing symbol and literalizing metaphor.

Myths, based on stories of great religious leaders like Abraham, the Buddha, Jesus, or Muhammad, provide models that guide human behavior within a given faith community and that serve as important links between belief, believer, and behavior. Myths are infinite in meaning; when metaphor is discarded, meaning is highjacked.

THE FUNCTIONS OF MYTH

There is a famous line at the end of Goethe's *Faust*, "Everything phenomenal or temporal is but a reference, a metaphor." Upping the ante, Friedrich Nietzsche remarked, "Everything eternal is but a reference, but a metaphor."[4] In this context, the function of mythology is to help us experience all realities, temporal and eternal, as references. This poetic imagery is the language of religion because it is the language of the soul. Mythology opens spaces within us, and is a language we must try to rediscover, for it makes transparent that which lies beyond words and thoughts—in short, to what we call transcendence.

In an age of global warming and environmental degradation, the first field to be transcendentalized this way is the realm of nature, the world in which we live. A mythological perspective views the world as a gateway to a dimension of wonder and mystery. Every object in the world speaks of this mystery, and consciousness pours in through every body and being around us. Each one of us is similarly transparent to transcendence.

Without myth, people disintegrate psychologically. This can be validated in culture after culture, tribe after tribe. Destroy the mythic universe, and the psyche begins to deteriorate. All the social indices today point to

---

4. These quotes are cited in Campbell, *Hero's Journey*, 161.

a rapidly deteriorating society: sickness, addiction, neuroses, desperation, fear, suspicion, and suicide are everywhere.

In a mythologically organized society, rituals help participants to experience themselves, the world, and their social order in mystical ways. In such societies, mythology serves four functions:

1. *Mystical function.* Mythology opens the mind to wonder and the heart to transcendence, pointing out the ultimate mystery in which all things participate.
2. *Cosmological function.* Mythology presents the world as an icon, radiant to life's transcendent energy.
3. *Sociological function.* Mythology supports and validates social order. Here the myths vary enormously from place to place. In modern society, characterized by mobility and widespread change, this function is inadequate, outdated, or nonexistent.
4. *Pedagogical function.* Mythology guides individuals through the stages and transitions of life. It provides harmonious ways through the inevitable crises of life, linking human beings to society and to one another.[5]

In the past several centuries, modernity has encouraged us to do an end run around the soul and the body to get to the spirit. But it doesn't work that way. Soul and spirit are not the same thing; they are not even the same realm. End runs around soul and body only lead to cheap religion or cheap spirituality, which is what we have now, where soul-work is not taken seriously, where the body and the psyche are not integrated.

Fundamentalist religious movements, for example, represent the concretization of the myths, taking symbolic statements as historical fact, reading mythology as prose rather than as poetry. The Virgin Birth, for example, has nothing to do with biology but rather points to spiritual rebirth and newness, and the concept of the Promised Land has little to do with real estate and more to do with our harmonious relationship to the land and the world of nature. The biblical concept of chosenness—of election—has also been distorted. The doctrine, symbolically understood, does not validate one group's status over another, but rather every group's status. The truth is that everyone is chosen; everyone belongs. All beings are Buddha beings; all atmans are Brahman: *tat tvam asi*: you are that mystery you seek to know. This reference, however, is not to one's ego, the False Self in the phenomenal world that is acting, but rather to the Ground of Being that is present and will always be present. The role of mythology is to link all things to

---

5. Campbell, *Power of Myth*, 31.

something bigger, to make all things "transparent to transcendence," to cite German psychotherapist Karlfried Graf Dürkheim.[6]

One of the great problems of our day is the enormous accent on sociology rather than biology. Economics and politics are the governing powers of life today, and that helps explain why things are out of balance. Myths and rites were never intended to control nature, but rather to control society, putting it in accord with nature.

In the biblical Garden of Eden, for example, there are two trees. The Garden represents timelessness in the natural realm, and humans are there as creatures of nature. They are about to enter into the realm of time. In the realm of time, everything is dual—past and future. When humans move into the realm of opposites, the Tree of Knowledge represents the way out, the exit from the Garden. Adam and Eve, representatives of humankind, are not expelled from the Garden by God; they had already expelled themselves. Their shame and wearing of clothes come from recognizing differentiated consciousness, expressed by maleness and femaleness. To return to the Garden, they must overcome duality in nature, recognizing that all is one Ultimate Reality. The second tree, the Tree of Life, is the tree of the return. An angel guards the Garden, drawing a sword "to guard the way to the tree of life" (Gen. 3:24). The guardian is a symbol of human fear, but more importantly, of clinging to ego identity. That is what keeps humans out.[7]

The monotheistic religions are religions of exile. In the Christian tradition, Jesus has gone through the gate, eaten of the fruit of the tree of life, and in his crucifixion, become the tree. That's the meaning of the cross. It beckons us to let go of our individuality, our separation, our exile, and gain eternity, which is in us and in all things. Thus, Jesus hanging on the tree—which is the second tree in the Garden—is like the Buddha seated under the Bodhi tree. Bodhi means "one who has awakened to the fact that one is what one seeks to know," namely, the Buddha.

What Buddhism declares openly—you are the Buddha already—Christianity hints at—you are the Christ, only you don't know it. Despite their similarities, one of the major differences between Buddhism and Christianity is that in traditional Buddhism, one is the Buddha child already, only you just don't know it, whereas for many traditional Christians, to say one is the Christ—a child of God—appears blasphemous.

There is a beautiful line in the writings of the eighteenth-century German poet Novalis: "The seat of the soul is where the inner and the outer

---

6. Transcendence means to "transcend," that is, to go past duality; Campbell, *Hero's Journey*, 166–67.

7. This interpretation of the biblical account of the Garden of Eden is taken from Campbell, ibid, 168–70.

worlds meet."[8] The outer world is what we get in literature and theology, the inner world is our response. Where these two worlds come together is the realm of myth. As Irish novelist James Joyce affirmed, "Any object [or text and story] properly regarded can be the gateway to the gods [the divine]." This is one way to interpret the Grail romances, that the best way to transcend the ego system is through compassion.[9]

Because we have lost the great mythic universe, we find ourselves in a post-Christian era dominated by rationalism, with its desire to understand and control. Mythic language is nature-based and mystery-filled, always pointing inward and upward. As Richard Rohr indicates, "when you don't mythologize, you pathologize."[10] When we don't mythologize, all we have left is our own little story. When it goes awry, we get therapy and recover. After that, what then? Recovery alone is not the point. We need a mythology for a bigger, better world to which we can "recover." A mythic universe holds the individual and the group soul together, by giving it purpose and meaning. It operates in our unconscious for the most part, but when it breaks down, desperation prevails.

THE QUEST FOR ADVENTURE

In *The Hero with a Thousand Faces*, Joseph Campbell dwells on a particular type of myth from all times and found across the globe: the myth of the human quest. This classical endeavor, titled "The Hero's Adventure," symbolically addresses the stages of human realization, the trials of the transition from childhood to maturity, and the meaning of maturity. The various mythologies, whether they depict the hero as going in quest of a boon or in quest of a vision, present the same essential undertaking: individuals leave their everyday lives and travel a distance, sometimes into a depth, and sometimes up to a height. The hero leaves the ordinary world, sometimes by choice and other times by force, and undertakes a journey to the center, into a region of supernatural wonder, where he[11] encounters fabulous forces and wins a decisive victory. Then comes a greater challenge: should the protagonist remain in his enchanted setting, thereby forsaking his former world, or should he return with a boon to benefit others? The hero does come back

---

8. Cited by Campbell, ibid., 181.
9. This topic is the subject of chapters 10 and 11.
10. Rohr, *Quest for the Grail*, 23.
11. In traditional quests, the hero is typically male. Today, heroes are equally male and female.

from this mysterious adventure, returning with the power to bestow blessings on fellow humans.

The hero's adventure, we are told, is about one's character and its potential for transformation. The path of the mythological adventure, and of all successful quests, involves a twofold venture: an inward journey to a spiritual center—a place of healing, vision, and transformation—and an outward journey toward others.

The messages of the world's great teachers—Moses, the Buddha, Jesus, Muhammad—differ greatly. But their visionary journeys are much the same. All are heroes, for they leave the predictable in search of the unknown, resisting temptation to find a liberating truth. Moses is such a hero, for he ascends the mountain, meets with Yahweh on the summit of the mountain, and comes back with Torah, a constitution for the formation of a new society. That's a typical hero act—departure, illumination (fulfillment), and return.

One might also declare that the founding of a life—your life or mine, if we live authentically instead of imitating the lives of those around us—comes from a quest as well. At birth, a lifetime of adventure beckons. A hero lies dormant within each person, awaiting a spiritual awakening, a call to departure. In order to affirm something new, one must leave the old and go in quest of the germinal idea, a seed that contains the potentiality of bringing forth that new thing.

Opportunities for transformation are present all around us. When they arise at critical moments in our lives, they are called rites of passage, conversions, revivals, or moments of awakening. What we call them is not important, but how we envision them. Not all transformational opportunities arise dramatically. Some are manifested subtly, through solitary endeavors such as meditation, fasting, confession, prayer, and Bible reading; others emerge publicly and corporately, through disciplines like worship, receiving a sacrament, or through sacrificial service to the poor and needy. The deepest opportunities arise unexpectedly, however, through the twists and turns of everyday life, including suffering, loss, and events that we think of as accidents and tragedies. Such experiences can rob us of our vitality or they can fuel the growth of our spirit and provide a powerful transformative impetus for our character.

THE QUEST FOR MEANING

Humans quest for meaning. Meaning, understood as vitality of purpose, leads to fulfillment, and the prospect of fulfillment makes life worth living. When Abraham Maslow outlined his hierarchy of needs, represented as a pyramid consisting of five levels, he placed "self-actualization" (by which he meant working toward fulfilling one's fullest potential) at the top. In Maslow's scheme, the final stage of psychological development comes when the individual feels assured that lower levels of needs—both physiological and emotional—have been satisfied. Once these are met, self-actualization drives the personality.

Mythology and ritual traditionally supplied the symbols that carry the human spirit forward, energizing individuals to navigate successfully the necessary passages of their adulthood. Think of the rites of passage, those rituals associated with the vital transitions of human life, especially birth, puberty, marriage, and death. Each of these passage points frames the individual within the context of the community, serving to transform the person into the new stage of life and to integrate her or him into the community at that new spiritual level. Because passages of life are liminal—that is, they involve crossing a threshold from one state of existence to another—they are critical to the full human development of the person and to the welfare of the community.

In the past, people quested for meaning through rites of passage; their quest was intentional, predictable, and patterned. Society demanded it, clans promoted it, and families made it happen. Although similar rites are enacted today, particularly in traditional families, modern (and postmodern) people tend to quest spontaneously, often doing so unintentionally.

To find meaning, or to connect with something deeper, some people quest through adventure, visiting exotic locations or engaging in enterprising ventures. Others quest through careers of service and devotion to others. Some apply for the Peace Corps; others participate in humanitarian efforts or campaigns to eradicate poverty or disease. Some quest through lifestyle choices such as fasting, celibacy, or vegetarianism. Others quest hedonistically, seeking meaning through pleasure, drugs, power, wealth, and materialism. Some seek meaning through disciplined acts of devotion such as prayer, Bible study, and inspirational reading. All such quests reenact aspects of some ancient rite of passage. When human beings stop questing, they abdicate their identity.

THE QUEST FOR WHOLENESS

Humans—indeed most living creatures—desire good health, safety, and security; taken together, these vital qualities contribute to the wholeness and wellbeing that make life supremely special. In traditional societies, the ability to apprehend the sacred was regarded as of crucial importance to health, wholeness, and wellbeing. Indeed, without this sense of the divine, people often felt that life was not worth living. Like other aesthetic experiences, the sense of the sacred needs to be cultivated. In our modern secular society, the sacred has diminished in value and in priority; left unused, it has tended to wither away.

In the past, when people tried to speak about the sacred or about their inner life, they did not express their experience in logical, discursive terms. Rather they had recourse to symbols and myths. Freud and Jung, who were the first to chart the so-called scientific quest for the soul, turned to the myths of the classical world or of religion when they tried to describe interior events. Mythology, they realized, was never designed to describe historically verifiable events. Mythology was an attempt to express inner significance or to draw attention to realities that were too elusive to be discussed in logically coherent ways. Mythology, religion scholar Karen Armstrong indicates, was an ancient form of psychology.

Western religions are often focused on the past, on what happened long ago. The accent is on the historical understanding of images. By contrast, the focus on Eastern religions is on what is happening to you now, how the symbol is affecting you now. Eschatology works for those who think in historical terms. Those who see eternity in all the forms of time think mythologically—living and thinking in ways that transcend time. Mythologically speaking, the Christ idea and the Buddha idea are equivalent symbolically. To live out of that center, out of that immanence, becomes the way of salvation—to do so is to accept nature as beneficent and harmonious, not as fallen or corrupted.

THE MYTH OF THE LABYRINTH

Western civilization was shaped by Greek, Roman, Jewish, and Christian stories. These myths are at the heart of how we see ourselves. One of the most significant of these is the myth of the labyrinth or maze. The most famous labyrinth story is of the Minotaur, the beast that Theseus fights in the labyrinth.

The labyrinth is an apt description of the modern ethos, in which we do not know where the enemy is, what the path is, or how to enter or exit. Moreover, we do not know whether the Minotaur is within our selves or separate from us. In the end, Theseus does kill the Minotaur, but only after using a string to find his path. The string is given to him by a woman—"symbol for the soul-wisdom that tells us how to make it through the maze."[12]

12. Rohr, *Quest for the Grail*, 35.

Western civilization does not want to view life as a labyrinth or maze. However, in Chartres Cathedral in France, one can see that Christianity once did understand the appropriateness of the myth. In the center aisle of the cathedral, directly before the altar, is a labyrinth. In the Middle Ages, people would come to worship early and "walk the labyrinth" as a devotion.

We, by contrast, have grown up with a post-Christian mythology of progress that is linear. As children, we are indoctrinated into the progress myth, which says that the goal of life is to get from one place to another as quickly as possible, in lines as straight as possible. This may work in football, but it has nothing in common with the spiritual life. The spiritual dynamic is two steps forward, then perhaps three steps back. The important thing is that the pilgrim stay on the path, and learn from the path. The pilgrim sees that three steps backward have as much to teach as the two forward—perhaps more!

The Abraham story exemplifies the true knight of faith. Abraham responded to a deeper truth, an alternative voice, as opposed to the conventional wisdom that others followed. He was willing to forsake possessions, even reputation, to follow the voice of God. There is in Abraham's call not one aspect that would make sense to a modern Western person. However, three of the world's great religions call Abraham father of their faith. He is the symbol, in one mythic story, for what faith means. He moved from security to insecurity, from the known to the unknown, from having answers to having no answers. He left all, hearing that he would be given children as numerous as the sands by the sea. He died not seeing the promise fulfilled, tempted even to sacrifice the child of promise. His life provides an unparalleled example of what it means to walk the labyrinth.

In spiritual life, myths are more than images, stories, or references. Ultimately, they must be lived. This brings us to the Grail myth.

QUESTIONS FOR DISCUSSION AND REFLECTION

1. Assess Howard Gardner's theory of multiple intelligence. According to this theory, if some people are gifted artistically, musically, or athletically, is it possible that some people are naturally inclined to think literally and others naturally inclined to think symbolically and metaphorically? Explain your answer.

2. Should science and religion be kept separate from one another, or is it prudent to find overlap, seeking ways they cooperate and interrelate? Explain your answer.

3. In your estimation, how are literal and mythological "truths" similar and how are they dissimilar?
4. Compare and contrast metaphor and myth. How are they similar and how are they dissimilar?
5. After reading this chapter, what did you learn about the function of myth?
6. What is the relationship between myth and transcendence?
7. Explain and assess the merits of the statement, "Destroy the mythic universe, and the psyche begins to deteriorate."
8. Assess the merits of viewing concepts such as the Virgin Birth and the Promised Land as metaphors (or myths) rather than as factual concepts.
9. Explain what people mean when they say that myths, while not meant to be understood literally, nevertheless convey truth.
10. Explain and assess the meaning of Richard Rohr's statement, "When you don't mythologize, you pathologize."
11. Can you identify a classical myth that provides transformative power, meaning, and wholeness to your life?
12. In your estimation, what is the primary insight gained from this chapter? Does this chapter raise any issues you might need to address in the future?

Chapter 10

The Quest for the Grail, Part I

THE WORD "QUEST" COMES from the same root as the word "question." In other words, we cannot go on a quest until we know the right questions. The journey or search for the Grail is fundamentally a clarifying of the question, "What is the purpose or goal of life?" At first the pilgrim (knight)[1] thinks the object of his quest is to meet the wonderful, secure, eternal, feminine ideal that will complement him and care for him. As he progresses on the journey, the question is clarified. "Whom does the Grail serve?" That is the question to which the knight slowly learns the answer.

The quest forces all of us to ask life's existential questions: Why are we living? Why are we experiencing the anguish of life? Unless we feel the pain, unless we go down "into the depths, into the great unconscious, into the labyrinth, normally we won't know the deepest answers. We will have stayed on the level of life's superficial questions, which is precisely not to go on the quest."[2] The Grail quest is symbolic of authentic existence, representing a life lived fully, authentically, and volitionally. What it tells us is that we must live our own life and determine our own values, and not simply allow the system to dictate how we should live. People who tend to settle for formulas, clichés, and prevailing opinions haven't asked the right questions, haven't lived without answers for a while, which is necessary. Perhaps that is why

---

1. In the Grail romances, the person questing is invariably male, which made sense in the twelfth and thirteenth centuries. Today, at least in the West, males and females are encouraged and expected to quest equally.

2. Rohr, *Quest for the Grail*, 79.

our current public discourse is so dualistic, angry, and unhelpful. We must do better, but we will not do so without questing.

The guide on the quest—the journey of spirituality and psychological wholeness—has two tasks to fulfill, which can be described by the titles "prophet" ("seer") and "pastor" ("priest"). The prophet guides us through the "path of departure" (how to fail, let go, separate, and withdraw from the status quo), and the pastor guides us in the "path of return" (how to see, what to see, how to channel desire, and union with the sacred). First, the prophet must teach the would-be hero to enter the maze. Today we do not have many who are willing and able to do this. Instead, we have glib clergy and slick televangelists who declare solutions apart from the labyrinth. They jump immediately to spirit, leap-frogging over body, mind, and soul.

Biblical anthropology can be confusing. In the Hebrew scriptures, the human being is divided into body, mind, soul, and spirit (see Mark 12:30/Luke 10:27 and 1 Thess. 5:23). In Galatians and Romans, the paradigm shifts to flesh and spirit, and it is the one most familiar to Christians: "spirit" meaning "good" and "flesh" meaning "bad." Paul, however, was making a different point: "flesh" (the False Self) is what is trapped in the temporal, and "spirit" (the True Self) is what is open to the transcendent, the universal, and totality. Those who are not open to the unconscious, to totality, are therefore not open to God. Ego consciousness is limited to what one knows. The spirit part of individuals is what keeps us open to the new, the transcendent, which we call God.

Throughout much of church history, particularly in the Western church, "soul" was understood to be the eternal part of human beings, the part that goes to heaven or hell. And the job of pastors, priests, and evangelists was to save that soul. That, however, is not the historic meaning of soul, which referred to that part of individuals that represents depth. Depicted spatially, "spirit" is that part that connects us to the transcendent, and "soul" descends into the depths of things, into the unconscious and the symbolism of things. Soul expresses itself in dreams, poetry, metaphor, and myth. If one is not doing "soul work," there is little room for "spirit."

Few legends of the Middle Ages have had so strong an evocative power as those that developed about the Grail. Thanks to Tennyson and Wagner,[3]

---

3. Alfred Lord Tennyson was the most important poet of the Victorian period, and his works include some of the finest poetry in the English language. The *Idylls of the King*, one of his best-known compositions, deals with an exciting age in English history, and with such fascinating characters as King Arthur, Guinevere, Sir Lancelot, and the other Knights of the Round Table. Perceval, another Grail hero, was the main inspiration of Wagner's *Parsifal*.

Galahad and Perceval have become knights of virtue, and the quest of the Grail has come to mean either a vain following after "wandering fires" or the arduous search for supreme mystical experience.

The stories of the Grail—and there are many of them—have fascinated leading literary figures of our time, with varying results. They inspired T. S. Eliot's poem *The Waste Land*, Charles Williams's fantasy novels on the struggle between the forces of evil and good, and films such as *The Da Vinci Code, Indiana Jones and the Last Crusade, Excalibur*, and the irreverent *Monty Python and the Holy Grail*.

Whence came this fantastic development of the Arthurian legend—a development of which the first record is found in a French poem dated about 1180, and which in the next fifty years produced so many varying forms? How did it come to be linked with relics of Christ's Passion?

The concept of the Grail developed from the tales of King Arthur and the Knights of the Round Table, an extensive body of medieval literature. The Arthurian legends have always had a firm hold on British and Continental literature, due to the heroic and evocative picture of the past that they present. There is, however, little historical evidence about the real King Arthur. He seems to have been a minor king or warlord of the Celtic Britons who, in the confused and violent period following the withdrawal of the Roman legions from Britain around 410 AD, led his people in temporary resistance against the Anglo-Saxon invasion. Despite Arthur's legendary twelve battles, the Anglo-Saxons were ultimately triumphant and drove the defeated Britons into the remote regions of Scotland and Wales. It was in these areas that the Arthurian legends first arose.

A great number of these derive from the Welsh tradition. The most considerable collection of these Welsh legendary tales is known as the *Mabinogion*. The oldest poems in this collection have been dated to the sixth century AD. Whoever Arthur was, and whatever his real achievement, there is no question that he rapidly became the most important hero and the central figure of British legendary history. Over time, many ancient Celtic myths and traditions became attached to his name, including such legendary figures as Gawain, Lancelot, and Tristram (Tristan), all originally independent characters. By the end of the Middle Ages, Arthur was the hero of romances composed in France, Germany, Italy, and Spain.

Were these tales written to extol courtly life (particularly the art of chivalry), religious life (particularly monastic life), or life in general (particularly the qualities of honor and virtue)? The approach one takes depends on how one answers the question that Perceval is reproached for not having asked, not "What is the Grail?" but "Who is served by the Grail?"

Since the stories of the Grail belong to the Arthurian cycle, the most likely region in which to look for their origin and primary meaning are Ireland and Wales. It is in the early literature of those Celtic lands, so long and so closely linked by cultural ties, that we must go to find perspective.[4] The adaptation of these stories to a new cultural milieu is, of course, one of the inevitable changes that took place in their passage from the Irish and Welsh to the French and other non-Celtic people, and it would take many forms. Like *The Iliad* and *The Odyssey*, the Grail legend originated with Irish and Welsh poets and was developed orally by itinerant *conteurs* (storytellers). Hence, they were secular in origin and universal in application.

The principal texts concerned with the Grail fall into two classes: (1) Those that relate the adventures of knights of King Arthur's time who visit the castle in Britain where the vessel is kept, and (2) those that relate the history of the vessel from the time of Christ to the time of Merlin[5] and that account for its removal from the Holy Land to Britain. The most important romances of the first group are:

1. The *Conte del Graal* or *Perceval*, composed by Chrétien de Troyes, a poet of French Champagne. The poem ends with the adventures of King Arthur's nephew and best knight, Gawain. This tale breaks off unfinished. Over the following fifty years, four different poets took up the challenge begun by Chrétien, continuing the adventures of Perceval and Gawain.

2. Four long continuations of Chrétien's *Conte*, two anonymous, one by Manessier, and one by Gerbert de Montreuil.

3. The *Parzival* of Wolfram von Eschenbach, a Bavarian knight, which was the main inspiration of Wagner's *Parsifal*.

4. The Welsh prose romance, *Peredur*, included in the collection called the *Mabinogion*.

5. The *Didot Perceval*, a French prose romance, so called from the name of a former owner of a manuscript.

6. *Perlesvaus*, a prose romance from northern France or Belgium, translated into English as the *High History of the Holy Grail*.

7. *Lancelot*, a prose romance that forms the third member of a vast compilation known as the Vulgate cycle.

---

4. The development of the Grail legend from Celtic myth to Christian symbol is pursued convincingly by Roger Loomis in his 1963 volume, *The Grail*.

5. This legendary wizard, featured in Arthurian legend and medieval Welsh poetry, is said to have been the king's advisor until his untimely demise.

8. The *Queste del Saint Graal*, the fourth member of the same cycle. Sir Thomas Malory, the fifteenth-century author of *Le Morte D'Arthur*, made use of much of this material in his *Tale of the Sankgreal* (translated as *The Quest of the Holy Grail*).

Two romances dealing with the early history of the Grail are:

1. *Joseph d'Arimathie*, by the French Burgundian poet, Robert de Boron.
2. The *Estoire del Saint Graal*, the first member of the Vulgate cycle, but probably composed after the *Lancelot* and the *Queste*.

The earliest surviving version of the Grail legend is *Perceval, le Conte del Graal* of Chrétien de Troyes, who declared that he adapted the tale from a book given to him by his benefactor Count Philip of Flanders, shortly before the departure of Count Philip for the Holy Land in 1190. We do not know why Chrétien left the tale unfinished, or how he would have carried it to conclusion. Many themes are left unfinished.

THE BEST OF TIMES, THE WORST OF TIMES

Often, when a new historical era begins, a myth for that era arises simultaneously. The myth is a preview of what is to come, and it contains sage advice for coping with the psychological elements of that period. The myth of Perceval's search for the Grail provides a prescription for our modern day. The Grail myth arose in the twelfth century, a time when some scholars believe that our modern age began. Asserting that the defining ideas, attitudes, and concepts by which we live today had their beginnings when the Grail myth took form, the Jungian psychotherapist Robert A. Johnson wryly proposes that the winds of the twelfth century have become the whirlwinds of our time.[6]

It is noteworthy that the basic texts of the Grail myth listed above were composed within a period of about fifty years. The earliest, Chrétien's poem, was written about 1180, Wolfram's *Parzival* is dated between 1200 and 1210, and the dates of the other versions are uncertain but probably precede 1230. During this period there were three Crusades: one against the Albigensians in southern France, which had the notable effect of crushing the joyous world of the troubadours; another was diverted to Constantinople and resulted in increased hostility between Western and Eastern Christendom and in flooding the West with relics; a third expedition by Frederick II secured temporarily the passage of pilgrims to the city of Jerusalem. Furthermore, during this period, Richard the Lionhearted nearly succeeded in winning back the Holy Sepulcher

6. Johnson, *He*, ix.

from Saladin. During the thirty years after 1200, King John lost most of his continental possessions to Philip, was worsted in his struggle with Pope Innocent III, and was compelled by his barons to sign the Magna Charta.

Notably, during this period St. Francis and St. Dominic revitalized the church by founding the mendicant order of friars. This half-century also saw the building of numerous cathedrals, including Notre Dame at Paris, as well as the growth of the universities of Paris, Bologna, and Oxford. At no period in the history of Western Europe did the arts and the zest for knowledge attain a higher level. The Grail romances belong to a great experimental and creative epoch.

At this time in the Christian tradition two ideals of love coexisted in opposition: *eros* (erotic passion) and *agape* (spiritual love, of the love-thy-neighbor sort). Both types of love are impersonal. A third ideal, *amor*, emerged in the twelfth century. The Provençal troubadour Giraut de Bornelh (c. 1138–1215), who flourished in the middle and end of the twelfth-century, epitomized the troubadour ideal. Troubadour poetry of courtly love was a protest against supernaturally justified violation of life's joy. Giraut's approach synthesized the two existing traditions in the following way. Love, he declared, is born of the eyes and the heart. When these three, the two eyes and the heart, are in accord, and result from personal choice, love is born. This protest against tradition and arranged love lies at the heart of the Tristan legend and of at least one of the great versions of the legend of the Grail, that of Wolfram von Eschenbach.

The problem of the Grail arises out of medieval society, when people were required to profess beliefs they did not hold, profess love for mates they married by arrangement, hold positions they had inherited and not earned, and profess allegiance to rulers and kingdoms they did not admire or respect. Significantly, the idea of passionate love arose around the world at this time:

- In India, Krishna falls in love with Radha (a symbol of the union of the individual and the universal self). The great poem celebrating their love is the *Gita Govinda* of Jayadeva, written about 1172.
- In Japan, Lady Murasaki writes a novel of true love in *The Tale of Genji*.
- In the Middle East, the *Arabian Nights* contain stories of falling in love.
- In France, the Provençal troubadour tradition.
- In Germany, the Minnesinger (singer of love) tradition.
- In France and Germany, the fully developed Tristan and Iseult (Isolde) romance tradition.[7]

7. Campbell, *Hero's Journey*, 110–11.

The concept of *amor* arose precisely at the right time. Representing natural and spiritual virtues such as sincerity, honesty, respect, and personal choice, it challenged vices such as vanity, greed, duplicity, privilege, and deceit.

These preliminaries convey a sense of the changes occurring theologically as well. A new understanding of God as Father and Christ as Savior is emerging, associated with two leading figures of that era, Archbishop Anselm of Canterbury (1033–1109), a Benedictine monk originally from Italy, and Peter Abelard (1079–1142), a leading French philosopher. For centuries, the prevailing view of Christ's death was tied to the doctrine of original sin. According to this doctrine, the devil, through his deception of Adam and Eve, had gained legal power over their souls. And the only way he could be relieved of that power was by being deceived himself. Therefore, God the Father made a kind of contract with the devil, promising to exchange Christ's soul for that of humankind.

The devil, mistaking shadow for substance, thought he should make the swap. As a result, God uses Christ on the cross as bait on a hook. The image of God using Christ as bait to hook Leviathan (a mythical sea monster regularly associated with Satan) appeared frequently in the twelfth century, notably in a short work written by Herrad of Landsberg called *Hortus Delicarum* (The Garden of Delights), a handbook nuns used to teach children. The devil was caught on the hook, but Christ, through his resurrection, escaped. The Ransom Theory was one notion of the atonement: Christ redeeming us, in the sense of redeeming a bank loan or a debt.

However, a new Christian view of the crucifixion appeared in the eleventh century, notably in *Cur Deus Homo* ("Why God Became Man"), a book by Anselm of Canterbury. In his view, no one owes the devil anything. Rather, it was God the Father who was owed something, because of the offense to him, for which humans were responsible, because of their disobedience in the Garden. Because of God's infinite virtue, no human could pay God the redemption. Therefore, out of love for humanity, Christ assumed the role of being human—he was both human and divine—and therefore eligible to make atonement, a substitution he made voluntarily, through his death.

In Abelard's view, both views—the Ransom Theory and Anselm's Satisfaction Theory—were deficient and erroneous. His view, known later as the Moral Influence or Example Theory, was that Christ came to win humanity through love, not to make restitution or to pay back what was taken. Abelard focused on changing human views of God, not as harsh and judgmental, but as loving. According to Abelard, Jesus died as a demonstration of God's love, a demonstration that can change the hearts and minds of errant children back to God. Christ came to earth simply to prove God's love for us and to invoke our love for God. Abelard's view sets the stage for the Grail romances.

THE GRAIL MYTH: OVERVIEW AND SETTING

Though the Grail stories originated from various levels of society, they became popular in the Christian West as a way for lay people to describe or understand the metaphysical, epistemological, anthropological, and moral quest—in other words, the spiritual path—in a secular way. Placed in a medieval setting, the imagery is patriarchal and feudal. However, it represents Christian lay spirituality at its best.

Since the story was neither canonized nor condemned in any particular way, it grew unfettered and uncensored. The myth expressed the deep wisdom of the Christian "collective unconscious," although in a style that was neither religious nor clerical. Neither did it waste time being anti-church or anti-clerical. Instead, these stories plumbed the depths of mystery and metaphor.

The themes of the Grail myth were prominent in Christian Europe in the twelfth, thirteenth, and fourteenth centuries. We will be using the French version, which is the earliest written account, taken from the poem by Chrétien de Troyes, although on occasion I will include elements from the broader tradition. The French version is simpler, more direct and nearer to the unconscious than the others, and therefore more helpful for our purposes.

Keep in mind, as you read further, that a myth is a living entity, and exists within each person. The most rewarding mythological experience you can have is to see how it lives in your own psychological structure. The Grail myth addresses masculine psychology, but this does not mean that it is confined to the male, for a woman participates in her own inner masculinity. We must take everything that goes into the myth, including the dazzling array of damsels, seeing them as part of our psyche. Understanding male masculinity is also essential for daughters, wives, and mothers of male children. In addition, as modern women take greater part in the masculine world by embracing a profession, the development of masculinity becomes important to her.

Our story begins with the Grail Castle, which is in serious trouble. The Fisher King, the king of the castle, has been wounded. His wounds are so severe that he cannot live, yet he is incapable of dying. He suffers constantly. As a result, the entire land is in desolation, for a land mirrors the condition of its ruler, inwardly (mythologically) as well as outwardly (sociologically).[8]

The theology of the Middle Ages viewed nature as corrupt, based on a literal reading of the biblical story of the Fall in the Garden. Society's view of nature profoundly influences what it means to be a citizen. When myth

---

8. Johnson, *He.*, 1.

presents nature as a manifestation of divinity, life is lived more fully and harmoniously. Conversely, when nature is viewed as cursed, every spontaneous impulse becomes sinful, something to be avoided. That is what T. S. Eliot described in the *Waste Land*, the sociological stagnation of inauthentic living, when society is bereft of spiritual values, people working only to make a living, and living only to stay alive.

Underlying the Grail romance is this wasteland. It is what life looks like when reality is viewed dualistically, the spiritual superseding the natural. This concept took hold during the Middle Ages, turning society into a realm where people lived inauthentic lives, never doing things they truly wanted because religious laws controlled human behavior.

As far as it goes, the Quest is a tale of the type known as the Great Fool: a youth, Perceval, of noble heart, brought up in ignorance of the rules of knighthood, nevertheless sets forth to become a knight, and though in the beginning he is ill-mannered and clumsy, he becomes in time the very model of a knightly champion. By what appears to him to be mere chance, he enters, without knowing, upon the adventure of the enchanted Castle of the Grail.[9]

There he encounters the Fisher King, "wounded by a javelin through his thighs," and in the great hall observes a procession of squires and damsels bearing tokens of unknown significance: a sword in its sheath; a white lance bleeding from its point; the golden Grail, set with precious stones, carried by a damsel of great beauty; and a silver carving dish, carried by another young woman. Perceval fails, however, to ask a certain expected question ("Who is served by the Grail?") that would have healed the king and broken the enchantment of his ailing kingdom. The poem ends with the hero receiving religious instruction from a hermit.

---

9. The tarot deck of playing cards, created during the fifteenth century, shortly after the Arthurian legend was put into writing, contains numerous archetypal parallels to the Grail quest. For example, the Fool tarot card is both the lowest and highest card in the deck. This card symbolizes new beginnings, and consequently, an end to a phase in one's life. The Fool is not viewed as being ignorant, however, but rather as one who lacks experience. The Fool card in the tarot deck depicts the Fool or the Jester in colorful clothes, carrying nothing but a staff and a small sack. A dog is at his heels, and the Fool faces a cliff. Being naïve, he embarks on the Fool's Journey recklessly, undaunted by the future and its unknown risks. Incidentally, the original purpose of tarot cards was to play games. If the symbols had arcane connotation, they seem to have been rooted in Renaissance concepts and value, rather than in occultic ones. The eighteenth century saw tarot's greatest revival, when it became one of the most popular card games in Europe. Only in the late eighteenth century did tarot cards begin to be used for divinations, at which time custom packs were developed for such occultic purposes. The association of tarot decks with the occult seems not to have been their original purpose, intent, or use.

The setting reflects the primitive, magical notion that the health and well-being of the ruler influence the welfare of the realm. The idea of enchantment and disenchantment is that people at a certain time and place come to perceive the world in a way that is inadequate or improper. In Christian legends, Christ comes as Savior to disenchant the world ruled by Satan and bring grace and truth to lost humanity. The kingdom of God, Jesus taught, is present here and now, only we fail to see it because of an enchantment. In the tradition of Buddhism, the Buddha releases humans from the enchantment of *maya*. This enchantment, in psychological terms, is the image of the world we have as a consequence of our fears and desires. If we could break away from our ego limitations, we would behold the world of paradise (nirvana) here and now. In both cases, what must be corrected is not the world, but our own perspective. Thus, we find in the Grail legend that everything needed is present, only it is not being seen. What the hero must do is to clarify the situation.

It was Wolfram von Eschenbach who picked up the theme of enchantment and developed it fully in his *Parzival*, declaring in his preface and conclusion that Chrétien had misrepresented it. According to Wolfram, the reason for the enchantment was that the Fisher King had been severely wounded by a pagan lance. The character of the Fisher King is the crux of the matter. This young man inherited his role; he had not earned it. He was simply appointed as king. The problem in the Middle Ages was that the religious life was under the control of the nobility and their appointees. The salvation of humans transpired through the sacraments, which were handed down through handpicked clergy. The point is that the sacraments were simply ritualistic, available to anyone who went through the paces, while the Grail Castle is to be entered only by one who is worthy of it. Wolfram shows the Grail Castle entered not only by the Grail hero but also by his Muslim half-brother. In Wolfram's context, one doesn't even have to be a baptized Christian to get to the Grail Castle. What counts is the nobility of one's character.

One of the characteristics of enchantment is that there are people who know the rules of enchantment. These are the people of the Grail Castle community. They know what the curse is and how it works, but they are unable to dispel it. The only way the enchantment can be broken is by some naïve person doing what has to be done unintentionally, out of his or her true nature. To do something intentionally will not break the spell. In other words, the rescue of the world occurs through an intrinsic nobility of nature expressed by the hero. In this tradition, the hero is called the Great Fool, one who is uninstructed in the secret of the enchantment. Nevertheless, because of integrity, honesty, courage, and forthrightness, the hero is able to restore the proper natural order, as against the enforced social order of the status quo.

The Fisher King, named Anfortas, was not selected due to competence or character, but rather received his position by inheritance. As a young man, like all young men, he became interested in the adventure of love. As he rode forth, he encountered a Muslim knight in quest of the Grail, the words "The Grail" written on his spear. These two—the one a Christian and the other a Muslim—go into combat. The Moor wounds Anfortas, piercing him through the genitals, emasculating him with his spear. Anfortas kills the "heathen," yet loses his biological virility. The warriors represent a pair of opposites, nature and spirit, in collision with one another. Because Anfortas (the lord of the spirit) is inadequate to his function, his realm is laid waste by this blow; both the world of the spirit and of nature are rendered impotent. A pall falls over the Grail Castle. The king, in terrific anguish, is carried back to his castle, where he is able to behold the Grail, which keeps people alive.

When the head of the lance is extracted from the wound, the words "The Grail" are seen written upon it. The Muslim had been in quest of the Grail. What we have here is spirit in quest of nature, and nature in quest of spirit. However, neither is helping the other; both are in collision with the other. The hero's task is to unite the two.

There is one final aspect to the Grail. When the proper question is finally asked, the king will be healed, but he will lose his position. The position of the Fisher King will go to the hero, the one who asks the question. You might say that the secret problem of the quest is to heal the Fisher King and to achieve his role, but without incurring his wound—that is, to embrace the spiritual principles without losing the natural ones. They are the same. To separate them is to experience the emasculating, sterilizing wound. Heroes must disenchant themselves before they are able to disenchant the Waste Land.

A later version of our story has it that the young Fisher King, early in his adolescence, was wandering around in the woods when he came to a camp.[10] The people of the camp were gone, but there was a salmon roasting on a spit. He was hungry, so he took a bit of it to eat. The salmon was very hot, and so he dropped it. After burning his fingers, he put them into his mouth to assuage the burn, but in so doing, got a bit of the salmon into his mouth. This is the Fisher King wound, which gives its name not only to this ruler but also to much modern psychology.[11]

---

10. The concluding material in this chapter is adapted from Johnson, *He*, 2–10.
11. Salmon are an important food source in many northern cultures, including

We can learn a great deal from the symbol of the wounded Fisher King. The salmon or, more generally, the fish, is one of the many symbols of Christ. As in the story of the Fisher King coming upon the roasting salmon, adolescents touch something of the Christ nature within their psyche, but touch it too soon. They become unexpectedly wounded by it and drop it as being too hot. But a bit gets into their mouth, and they cannot forget their experience. This first contact with what will be redemption later in life is a wounding. This is what turns us into a wounded Fisher King. The first touch of consciousness in a youth appears as a wound or as suffering.

Every adolescent receives a Fisher King wound. We would never proceed into consciousness if it were not the case. This is the expulsion from the Garden of Eden, the graduation from naïve consciousness into self-consciousness. The Fisher King wound may coincide with a specific event, such as an injustice, a grievous accident or mistake, or a moment of awakening to adulthood. But it must happen, else there would be no transformation—or redemption.

According to tradition, there are potentially three stages of psychological development. The archetypal pattern is that one goes from the unconscious perfection of childhood, to the conscious imperfection of middle life, to conscious perfection of old age. In other words, one moves from an innocent wholeness, in which the inner world and the outer world are united, to a separation and differentiation between the inner and outer world, with an accompanying sense of life's duality, and then, at last, to enlightenment—a conscious reconciliation of the inner and outer in harmonious wholeness.

In the Quest, we are witnessing the Fisher King's development from stage one to stage two. We have no right to talk about the final stage until we have accomplished the second one. Likewise, we have no right to talk about the oneness of the universe until we are aware of its separateness and duality. We have to leave the Garden before we can start on the quest for the Grail. It is ironic that the two are the same, but the journey must be made.

Scotland, Ireland, and Wales. In Celtic mythology, the salmon represents wisdom. In Irish myth, salmon swam in the Well of Nechtan (an Irish water god), eating the magic hazel nuts that fell into the water. According to prophecy, Finegas would catch and eat the salmon, thereby gaining all knowledge. However, his apprentice Finn MacCool (Fionn) roasted the salmon and burnt his thumb. Finn put his thumb in his mouth to cool it, and so received the salmon's power. From that point on, he only had to suck his thumb to gain knowledge of the future. So great was his prowess as a warrior that he was appointed to lead the Fenians (the Fianna), the band of warriors responsible for the safety of the High King of Ireland. This Welsh tale became an early Arthurian legend, hence its connection with the Fisher King. Many of the adventures of the Knights of the Round Table recall the exploits of the Fenians.

A man's first step out of the Garden into the world of duality is his Fisher King wound: the experience of alienation and suffering that ushers him into the beginning of consciousness. The myth tells us that the Fisher King wound is in the thigh. A wound in the thigh means that a person is wounded in their generative ability, in their capacity for relationship. The ultimate wound, for all of us, is the wound of anything transpersonal. The implication is that if there is a wound to our inner nobility, the entire personality will be troubled. The Fisher King is described as being too ill to live but unable to die. Much of modernity revolves around the lostness and alienation of the individual; the Fisher King wound is the hallmark of modern personhood.

The Fisher King is carried about in his litter, groaning. There is no respite for him—except when he is fishing. That is to say that the wound, which represents consciousness, is bearable only when the wound is doing inner work, proceeding with the task of consciousness that inadvertently began with the wound in one's youth.

The Fisher King presides over his court in the Grail Castle where the golden Grail is kept. Mythology teaches that the king who rules our innermost court sets the tone and character for that court and thus our whole life. If the king is well, we are well; if things are right inside, they will go well outside. With the wounded Fisher King presiding at the inner court of modern life, we can expect much outward suffering and alienation. And so it is.

The court fool had prophesied long before that the Fisher King would be healed when an innocent fool arrived in the court and asked a specific question. It may shock us that a fool should have to undertake such a crucial role. However, what the myth is telling us is that only the naïve part of our being will heal and cure our Fisher King wound. It also tells us why the Fisher King cannot heal himself, and why, when he goes fishing, his pain is eased though not cured. For people to be truly healed, they must allow something entirely different from themselves to enter their consciousness and change them. They cannot be healed if they remain in the old Fisher King mentality. That is why the young fool part of ourselves must enter our life if we are to be cured. We must look to a foolish, innocent, part of ourselves for our cure. The inner fool—someone or something most unlikely to carry healing power—is the only one who can touch our Fisher King wound. Many legends put our cure in the hands of a fool or someone most unlikely to carry healing power.

QUESTIONS FOR DISCUSSION AND REFLECTION

1. In your estimation, what is the central meaning of the Grail quest? Explain your answer.
2. If the "prophet" guides us on the "path of departure" and the pastor or priest guides us on the "path of return," can you identify figures who have performed this function in your life? Explain your answer.
3. After reading this chapter, what have you learned about the difference between one's "soul" and one's "spirit"?
4. Explain and assess the meaning of the statement, "If one is not doing 'soul work,' there is little room for 'spirit.'"
5. After reading this chapter, what have you learned about the origin of the Grail concept?
6. How were the twelfth and thirteenth centuries instrumental in the development of the Grail myth?
7. Compare and contrast the terms *eros*, *agape*, and *amor*. How is *amor* similar and dissimilar from *eros* and *agape*?
8. Compare and contrast the three main theories of Christ's atonement—the Ransom Theory, the Satisfaction Theory, and the Moral Influence Theory. Assess the strengths and weaknesses of each theory. Which view do you prefer? Why?
9. Explain why the protagonist of the Grail quest is called the Great Fool.
10. If every adolescent receives a "Fisher King wound," what wound in your experience would you say coincides with this concept (keep in mind that such failure or suffering, understood spiritually, is a "grace" that carries healing power).
11. In your estimation, what is the primary insight gained from this chapter? Does this chapter raise any issues you might need to address in the future?

Chapter 11

The Quest for the Grail, Part II

CHRÉTIEN'S POEM BEGINS WITH Perceval, whose father has died before, or shortly after, his birth, and who has been brought up in the woods by his widowed mother, far from society and in ignorance of all knightly accomplishments. He is a child solely of nature rather than of culture. He is born in Wales, during that time a country on the fringe of the known world and a cultural backwater, the least likely place for a hero to appear. He has no siblings, his father is dead, and he knows nothing of him. Ironically, it is the innocent fool from Wales who will heal the Fisher King.

Fearing that her son would suffer a fate similar to her husband, Perceval's mother raised him to know nothing of knighthood or of his heritage. Perceval's father was allegedly a young knight who decided to journey to the Middle East to seek his glory and fortune. A blow from a lance pierced his head and he was killed in action. Perceval grew up in primitive, peasant ways, wearing homespun clothes. He is handsome, strong, and athletic. He has no name, though he is later called Perceval, which means "simple" or "innocent fool," not because he lacked intelligence, but for his guileless innocence, his unpretentious perceptions, and his simple faith.

No sooner has Perceval "come of age" when he encounters knights riding through the forest. He is so taken by their striking appearance that he immediately wishes to become one of them. He leaves his mother, against her will (thereby in some versions causing her death), and asks everyone he finds how he may become a knight. He is informed that he should go to Arthur's court, where he will be knighted if he is strong and brave enough.

FIRST- AND SECOND-HALF-OF-LIFE TASKS

The foundation of life—what we call the "first-half-of-life" task—involves building one's tower, establishing one's identity.[1] That's what Perceval's mother helped him to do. He had been under her protection, taking seriously her advice to respect fair damsels and not to ask many questions. She had clothed and fed him. These were her legacies. Were they enough? Young Perceval lacked a prophet in his life, someone to tell him about the maze and provide the rules to enter. Such youthful formation requires the language of courage, wisdom, persistence, and patience—foundational to the building of one's tower. These are the rules for the first third—or first half—of life. After one builds a tower—one's ego, career, and personal boundaries—the prophet encourages the hero to jump off, to let go, or at least to slowly descend. The sole point of the tower, and of the ladder to the top, is to jump off.[2]

Discipline, order, and law are necessary for eighteen-year-olds. That's building the tower. Ego-morality, the world of logic and discipline, that's how one succeeds in the system. If you don't build the tower, you are in trouble. However, when the eighteen-year-old becomes sixty and is still focused on law, order, and control, there is no spiritual freedom, no soul making to inspire and motivate others.

To jump off is called faith. The rules change at that point. It is no longer law but paradox and mystery, ecstasy and agony, freedom and darkness. We need a different set of rules at that point—not ego morality but soul morality, which asks much more. The quest may seem risky and dangerous, but it will lead to God.

There are two paths to the quest; the first is the *path of departure*, symbolized in Genesis by the expulsion from the Garden. This is designed to lead people into the maze, which involves a willingness to be broken, and then to struggle with the consequences. Society must teach the young how to fall, and give them the courage and support to fall gracefully. Departure calls forth restoration; being cast out of the Garden teaches us to long for the Garden.

At the beginning of the quest, the Grail is veiled, only partially seen, but enough for the seeker to realize what it is. This is the first religious experience of the young hero—just enough to know the real, to know there is something more, something eternal. The second path is the *path of return*. It

---

1. The material in this segment is adapted from Rohr, *Quest for the Grail*, 36–47.
2. Curiously, the tarot deck of playing cards contains the Tower card, symbolizing loss and new starts. The card depicts a tower on a rocky outcrop, set ablaze by a lightning bolt. Flames appear in the windows and people are jumping out. The Tower card represents chaos and distress, which make room for something new as their replacement.

is about escaping from the labyrinth when you are tired of the rat race, when you know life is phony and hypocritical and you are ready to share your true thoughts and feelings with others. How does one escape? How does one find at-one-ment? That is the pastoral (priestly) question. The answers, simply put, are faith, hope, love, grace, freedom, longing for the transcendent, and reconciliation with one's dark (shadow) side, with the sins of others, and even with the sin of the world.

However, society is teaching the need to build towers without departure. The church is teaching people the language of return before they have been taught the language of departure. Adults, parents, and those in authority must help young people leave the Garden, get into the maze, into the mystery, supporting them when they challenge parental rules and life's commandments. Youth rebel because they must. There has to be some loss of faith, some struggle with the status quo, if there is to be a quest for the Grail.

Departure is risky—and scary. It is easier to conform, to play it safe, to play by the rules. However, if your intention is to look good, and be good, no one will ever follow you, and nothing will be transformed. The safe way is sterile, literalized, secularized faith. Sometimes the best disguise for authentic, transforming faith is organized religion. Look at Jesus, and what killed him; it was conventional wisdom, the status quo, fear of the labyrinth, that killed him. The Romans were simply playing by the authoritarian rules they had inherited and perfected. The Jewish scribes, Pharisees, and lawyers were in fact good people—according to conventional wisdom. They were following the rules.

Most people will not set out on the quest unless the Grail is unveiled to them. It may be at an early age—and suddenly they know. Perhaps it is at fourteen, when they first fall in love. The transforming event might be trauma, some accidental or shameful failure that propels them into the maze. However it happens, those fortunate enough to experience the unveiling of the Grail know they can embark on the search, know it is okay to stay in the maze.

Sadly, in our day, the warriors[3] and lovers[4] are going nowhere positive with their energy. Violent young men are aimless in their destruction and lovers have become mostly addicts—if not to substance abuse, then to consumerism. The warriors and lovers are going to join the Quest when

---

3. I am using this term in the mythological sense, as a reference to that part of a person that can say "No" to oneself and to others for the sake of a more important and more enduring goal.

4. I am using this term in reference to that part of a person that tastes, enjoys, appreciates, and creates beauty and connectedness. The lover legitimates ultimate joy by participating in it now.

they sense they are needed as kings and magicians.[5] Today, there are simply not enough wise parents to hold the net together, to be there when their children fall. And there are not enough good kings to encourage young adults to err, to make mistakes, to accept them when they fail.

People in the know suggest one cannot be a king or queen, with full access to royal energy, before one is fifty years old. By that time, one has seen the pattern enough, has been through the labyrinth enough, so that one can encourage young lovers and warriors down that path. Sin is not the worst thing in the world; neither is failure. That does not mean there are no consequences, however. But when we don't have wise "kings," dark warriors and immature heroes dominate.

Heroic societal rules apply only at the beginning. It feels good at twenty-five to be a hero, conquering one task or another, building the tower. But such heroism doesn't work. It is only when the knight is naked, bleeding, condemned, rejected, that true heroism arises. The image of Jesus on the cross is not society's idea of a hero. But this is true heroism, because it serves a just cause.

Whom does the Grail serve? In the beginning, just you. To follow convention, to please authority figures in our lives, may bring rewards, but this is not love of God. Rather, it is love of self, of one's own reputation and power. Such heroism works in the system. But it is false heroism—infantile living. Sanctity is something bigger than conformity. Such heroism is honed in darkness, in the agony of faith. You might not know if you are right, and others might criticize you. But it is the quest, the spiritual story of loss, detachment, discovery, and renewal. In my experience, renewal occurs best in community, with others in recovery. Twelve Step groups are doing this probably better than any other groups right now, providing the net for people in the labyrinth of failure. This is much closer to gospel spirituality than we find in the more fundamentalist-oriented approaches, which insist there is no labyrinth and that there is no need to fall.

THE RED KNIGHT

Perceval finds his way to Arthur's court, where he presents himself, with the most primitive equipment and the roughest of garb, before the king,

---

5. In mythology, the "king" is that part of a person that holds all other parts together in unity and wholeness. The king directs and legitimates the big picture, what is real and enduring. The magician is that part of a person that understands the inner world of mystery, metaphor, paradox, and growth. The magician directs and legitimates the work of the soul—issues of darkness, light, and shadow.

demanding knighthood at his hands. He is told that knighthood is an honor won only after much valor and noble work. There is in Arthur's court a damsel who has not smiled or laughed for six years. The legend in the Court is that when the best knight in the world appears, the damsel who has not smiled will burst into laughter. The instant this damsel sees Parsifal in his naiveté and homespun garments, she laughs loudly. The court is both perplexed and impressed that this naïve youth, this untutored oaf, could be the long-awaited knight.

Perceval's arrival coincides with an insult inflicted on King Arthur and Queen Guinevere by Ither, an invincible foe known as the Red Knight. When Perceval requests the Red Knight's horse and armor, everyone laughs, because there has not been a knight in Arthur's court strong enough to stand up to the Red Knight. As Perceval leaves Arthur's court, he is met by the Red Knight, dressed in bright red armor with the king's golden goblet in his hand.

When the Red Knight sees the young boy riding on his nag, coming as the avenger of Arthur's court, he turns his lance sideways and gives Perceval a blow that knocks the boy to the ground. But Perceval takes his dagger and throws it at the Red Knight, killing him by a wound in the eye. This is his first great deed, but it is not a knightly act. One can say this is the moment when Perceval leaves adolescence and becomes a man.

The Red Knight represents the negative side of masculinity, the potentially destructive power of egocentricity. To truly become a man, masculinity must be mastered, but it cannot be repressed. The lad must not repress his aggressiveness, since he needs the manly power of his Red Knight masculinity to make his way through the mature world.

Perceval now owns the Red Knight's armor and his horse, for in those days to conquer was to own. This is to say that the Red Knight energy is now under Perceval's control and is his to use. He struggles with the Red Knight's armor, but he has never seen anything so complicated. A page helps him get the armor off the Red Knight and puts it on him. However, Perceval won't take off the clothes that his mother gave him. He remains thus, clothed as a knight, yet underneath is his fool's costume. The page teaches him how to hold the lance and sword, but when he gets on the Red Knight's horse, he discovers he does not know how to stop it. He rides all day, the horse leading the way, until the two stop in sheer exhaustion. That happens when masculinity lacks control.

GORNEMANT

The horse brings Perceval to the small castle of a knight named Gornemant. The knight brings Perceval inside, and when Gornemant helps him remove his armor, the clothing he finds underneath mortifies everyone in the castle. However, Perceval is such an attractive youth that Gornemant decides to train him in knightly conduct.

In the quest for the Grail, Perceval finds his mentor. The castle is a place of initiation by a guide, particularly necessary if the child had an abusive or overly indulgent parent. Gornemant coaches Perceval in handling himself on a horse and in jousting and in other knightly forms of combat, so that in a few weeks this gifted youth becomes a full knight under his supervision. Gornemant teaches Perceval information vital to attaining manhood: he must never seduce or be seduced by a fair maiden, and he must search for the Grail Castle with all his might. He also instructs him in knightly rules, including not asking too many questions. His mother had told him to ask no questions, and now his primary male guide agrees, adding only that Perceval ask the right question. The right question is, "Whom does the Grail serve?" In other words, "What is the purpose of life's journey?" It is also the question the Twelve Step program asks, "What is the purpose of recovery?"

Like the Native American Vision Quest,[6] the young brave must return not only with an individual identity, but also with a word of promise for the tribe as a whole. During our recovery or return, we too must ask this question, not only of our own efforts and accomplishments, but also of our society: What is the goal of efficiency and productivity? What is the goal of worship? Of course, there is no one answer. The question, however, must be asked, its intention to keep us in perpetual dissatisfaction. For it leads to what the Gospels call "the kingdom question," the question of the absolute.

BLANCHE FLEUR

After these instructions Perceval remembers his mother and goes in search of her again. Perhaps males can stand only so much of masculinity before they need to be in contact with feminine mother energy again. As Perceval hunts for his mother, he finds that soon after he left her, she died of a broken heart. Naturally, he feels dreadfully guilty about his mother's death, but leaving home and her influence is part of his masculine development. No son ever develops fully without, in some way, being disloyal to his mother. If he remains with her, to comfort and console her, he remains trapped in his

---

6. This topic is discussed in chapter 12, in the segment titled, "The Vision Quest."

mother complex. The son must ride off and leave his mother, even if it appears disloyal, and the mother must bear this pain. Later, the son may return and they may find a new relationship, on a new level. However, this can only be done after the son has achieved his independence and transferred his affection to a woman, in an "interior" way with his own inner feminine side or in an "exterior" way with a real female companion of his own age.

In his search for his mother, Perceval finds, instead, another castle, the castle of Blanche Fleur (White Flower), and comes into awareness of the highest motivation of his life before the Grail encounter. Blanche Fleur, Gornemant's niece, is in distress and her castle is under siege. She implores Perceval to rescue her kingdom. He agrees, dueling heroically with the officers in command of the besieging army, sending them in fealty to the court of King Arthur. This becomes the first in a long series of encounters that will send knights to the Order of the Round Table.

This episode in the story is a poetic way of describing what depth psychologists call the "*anima* encounter," the female qualities in the male. According to Jungian analysis, the opposite side of the *anima* is the *animus*, the male qualities in the female. These qualities are always in need of reinforcement and maturing, in order that individuals might be more balanced and relationships between the sexes may deepen. Viewed as elements of the theory of the collective unconscious, the *anima* and *animus* are said to be the two primary anthropomorphic archetypes of the unconscious mind.

Failure to accept polarities within the self often leads to projection of one's despised or shameful qualities onto the "other." This is happening today in Europe and the United States, targeting Muslims with our fear and blaming immigrants (aliens) for our woes. Such blaming happened before, with drastic consequences. Males, for example, often viewed their dark side as feminine, projecting their darkness onto the "witch." This rejection element surfaced between 1450 and 1750, during the European witch-age, when as many as four million women were burned at the stake. The *Malleus Maleficarum*, a Latin book published in the German city of Speyer in 1487 by a discredited Catholic priest, is the best known and most thorough treatise on witchcraft. The book appeared at a peak point in European accusation and execution.

For males, spiritual growth requires replacing an image of perfection with an image of wholeness. Perfection suggests purity, eliminating moral blemishes and questionable traits. This, it seems, is the ideal so often sought by hierarchical and patriarchal religions such as Christianity and Islam. Wholeness, however, includes darkness but combines it with light elements into a totality more real and whole than any ideal. This is the dimension Christianity and Islam must embrace if they are to remain relevant. This is the sort of spirituality Jesus embodied, and it is our task to recover this holistic outlook.

In the castle of Blanche Fleur, Perceval is lured, attracted, and entrapped. Before him is his other side, his twin, the image of the beloved. It is in the service of Blanche Fleur that Perceval performs his heroic task; she is his fair lady, the carrier of inspiration for everything he accomplishes. It is not by accident that it was the mother-search that led the blundering Perceval to she-who-will-inspire, truly the animating principle of life. Her conduct in the rest of the story would be disappointing if she were only a woman; for all she does is remain in her castle as a symbol of inspiration or perhaps a talisman of affection. But taken as the interior feminine, deep in the heart of a man, she is the source of inspiration.

Believing he has found his wholeness, he goes to bed with her. As he does, he remembers the advice of his mentor, who told him he must respect and protect all women. Under no condition is he to seduce a woman or be seduced by her. So Parsifal lies with her in the most intimate embrace—head to head, shoulder to shoulder, hip to hip, knee to knee, toe to toe—but they remain chaste. The knight's vow must be kept if he is to win a vision of the Grail.

The quest still has power to beckon Perceval. As we read his story, we realize we are watching a person become whole. He can go to the castle of his mentor, he can go to the castle of his beloved, or he can leave both. He is discovering his inner power, finding his authentic maleness and femaleness within. He does not need to remain in either castle.

In *Fire in the Belly*, Sam Keene's remarkable book on masculine spirituality, he tells of his longtime friendship with the African-American theologian Howard Thurman. Keene had first met Thurman when the former was a student at Harvard Divinity School. Thurman was teaching a course at Boston University called "Spiritual Resources and Disciplines," and Keen crossed the Charles River to enroll. Many years later, after Keene's divorce, he met with his mentor once again, telling him about the pain of divorce and of a disintegrating new romance. Thurman, digging deeper, responded with several stories. The last advice Thurman gave before Keen left was later described by Keen as the single most important piece of advice he ever go about being a man.

"Sam," Thurman said," a man must ask himself two questions. The first is "Where am I going?" and the second is "Who will go with me?" If you ever get these questions in the wrong order, you are in trouble.[7] Such wisdom also guided Perceval in his quest.

---

7. Keen, *Fire in the Belly*, 12.

THE GRAIL CASTLE

The quest calls, and Perceval leaves the second castle. He wanders through the woods and comes across two men fishing in a boat on a river. One is the Fisher King, who invites Perceval to stay at his castle. The fisherman points him toward a hidden castle, surrounded by a moat and drawbridge. "But be careful," he adds. "The roads here lead astray; no one knows whereto. If you arrive, I shall be your host." The Grail Castle is an apparition that has appeared to Perceval because he is ready for it. People have ridden through that wilderness repeatedly and never encountered the castle. Perceval sees the castle; it is his castle, his destiny. And he enters.

In the Grail Castle, the hero is in the realm of eternal, life-giving images. In the great hall, tables are spread for a feast, and a procession takes place, with the king lying there wounded. There are many knights on couches, witnessing the strange procession in which squires and damsels carry magnificent objects from one chamber to another. First comes a young man carrying a sword in its sheath, then another carrying a bleeding lance, then two boys carrying candelabra of fine gold. Finally, a beautiful damsel enters, "holding between her hands a grail," followed by another bearing a carving-dish of silver.[8] The grail was "of refined gold; and it was set with precious stones of many kinds, the richest and the costliest that exist in the sea or in the earth. Without question, those set in the grail surpassed all other jewels."[9]

This image from the Grail Castle is what Jesus would call the kingdom of God. It is the New Jerusalem descending to earth in the book of Revelation. It is Jesus in the temple at twelve, in his father's house, where he knows he is secure. Whatever word we choose to describe it, the Grail Castle

---

8. According to ancient Greek thought, matter is composed of four elements—earth, water, air, and fire. For two thousand years, this idea served as the cornerstone of philosophy, science, and medicine. Hence, it should come as no surprise that the objects carried in the strange Grail procession are themselves elemental symbols: the sword represents fire; the lance, air; the grail, water; and the carving-dish, earth. These objects have also been associated with the treasures of the Tuatha De Danann (the Shining Gods) of Irish legend, including the Stone of Fal, which screamed aloud when the rightful king of Ireland placed his foot upon it; the magic sword of Nuada, which could only inflict fatal blows; the spear or slingshot of the sun god Lugh; and the cauldron of Dagda, an inexhaustible pot capable of satisfying every appetite. Celtic scholar Jessie Weston has drawn attention to the relationship between the processional symbols and the four suits of cards in a tarot deck: Cups, Wands, Swords, and Dishes (or Pentacles). As the Grail quest became Christianized, the lance became associated with the spear that pierced the side of Jesus at his crucifixion, the carving dish and grail with the paten and chalice that held the bread and wine at the Last Supper.

9. This translation from Chrétien's *Conte del Graal* is reprinted in Loomis, *Grail*, 33.

represents the ultimate spiritual experience, that time in our lives when we know radically that no matter what is going wrong, everything is going to be okay. This experience can happen to young children, four and five years old, and it can reoccur in teenage years, sometimes associated with one's first falling in love. There is passion and joy, even anguish; yet life finally makes sense.

This is the first numinous experience that opens our eyes to the transcendent. It only needs to happen once, as it did to Julian of Norwich, the English mystic, or to Blaise Pascal, the French mathematician, but they lived out of that experience for the rest of their lives. Some people have religious experiences as teenagers that tell them what they will be, though the fulfillment is postponed until much later in life. When that moment comes, it is great and wonderful, and we know that it is grace at work and not our own doing.

The Grail Castle is the image of the self. The turrets, towers, bedrooms, kitchens, dungeons; all represent one's inner being. Perceval finds two kings within, the Grail King, and the Fisher King. The Grail King, clearly a God image, he sees only briefly but describes as "the most beautiful person he ever beheld." Perceval never sees the Grail King again, but he cannot forget what he saw. In the outer chamber of the castle is the wounded king. His name is Anfortas, from an old French word meaning Infirmity or "without strength." The two kings are the two parts of our soul, the godly part and the broken part. The godly king is the one that holds the castle together, that accepts the gospel, that always says "Yes" to God. The broken king is the part that feels obsessed, neurotic, and sick. Both parts are in us. The hero's task is not only to discover his True Self, but also to bring the two kings, the two parts, together.

"The experience of God," Richard Rohr reminds us, "is always an experience of totality. There is enough room for everything, a universal spaciousness. Nothing need be excluded. Everything is allowed space by God. That is why, in our later years, we can become holy fools. The holy fool, like the trickster, can play with the dark side of things and not be threatened. This is hard to do when one is young and building the tower and in need of clear definition."[10]

Amid the varying, speculative, and often contradictory stories associated with the quest of the Grail, none is more perplexing than the identity of the Grail itself. Pick up a book on the subject, and you may be told, with a show of erudition, that the object itself was derived from the cauldron of the Irish god Dagda, from the eye of the Egyptian god Thoth, from a symbol of

---

10. Rohr, *Quest for the Grail*, 107.

the female organ of generation, from a pearl of the Zoroastrian cult named Gohar, from a talisman of the heretical Albigensians, or from a Great Sapphire formerly preserved in the sacristy of Glastonbury Abbey.

In the Grail romance of Chrétien de Troyes, the Grail is a kind of bowl. Wolfram's Grail is a stone, either the *lapis exilis* of Alexander the Great—a stone sent to the conqueror from Paradise—or the "philosophers' stone," a legendary alchemical substance capable of turning base metals into gold or silver. On the other hand, many people are content to believe that the Grail was a holy eucharistic vessel, described as the dish from which Jesus ate the Passover lamb at the Last Supper, or as the chalice used at that event, in which later Christ's blood was caught by Joseph of Arimathea as it flowed from the wounded Savior's body.

Some accounts of the quest portray the Grail as a cornucopia, a deep dish or horn of plenty that provides guests instantly with whatever food one desired. Curiously, near the end of his account, Chrétien asserts through the mouth of a hermit that the Grail contained but a single consecrated wafer, destined for the Fisher King's father alone.[11] Other accounts portray the Grail as a talisman or magical vessel used to distinguish the chaste from the unchaste. Its custodian may be called Bron, Anfortas, Pellas, Joseph of Arimathea, or simply "the Fisher King," who may be sound of body or wounded through the thighs or in the genitals. The hero who achieves the quest may be the notoriously amorous Gawain or the chaste Galahad.

The problem of definition originates with Chrétien's use of the word "*graal*," which even the French frequently misunderstood. Note also that Chrétien calls it "*a* grail," not "*the* grail." Thus, it is not a unique object. Instead, it is one of a class, even if it is a particularly splendid example of its kind. The point is, anything can become a Grail if it open us up to the transcendent. Anything can become a symbol of ancient truth if it leads us to ask about origins, destinations, and identity.

Anfortas, the stricken king, cannot live because of his wounds, but he cannot die because of the Grail. He lives in the castle, close to the Grail, but he is still infirm and removed from it. He is caught in the middle—like many of us—unable to life fully because of a flaw in our being, yet unable to die because of our unfinished dream. The Grail says there is still something good at our core, something unfinished, and it will not let us hate ourselves or self-destruct. As long as things remain in the unconscious, we cannot

---

11. This strange reference was probably due to a mistranslation, for in the Old French, the nominative case for the words "horn" (vessel or horn of plenty) and "body" was identical, *li cors*. The First Continuation of the *Conte del Graal* illustrates the use of *cors* in both senses, as a reference to a magic horn, and to the eucharistic Corpus Christi as a sacred, miraculous food, Loomis, *Grail*, 60.

make sense of them. They need to surface, to become visible in the conscious world. We can see our soul in images; hence, we must search for the image that best reveals our soul. The Grail is that image.

In our story, a critical aspect of Perceval's experience in the Grail Castle is his failure to ask a certain expected question ("Who is served by the Grail?") that would have healed the king and broken the enchantment of his ailing kingdom. Inside the castle, there was a hushed expectancy, as everyone knew that an "innocent fool" was prophesied to ask the healing question to revive the king and the Grail. Perceval felt a great stirring within him to speak, but alas, he said nothing.

THE WASTELAND

In the morning, Perceval awakens. He is alone, bathed and naked. The castle is completely silent. His armor is beside the bed, but he has to put it on alone. He mounts his horse and crosses the drawbridge, which closes behind him. The Grail Castle vanishes and Perceval finds himself back in the world of time and space. The Grail experience is over, and he is back in the forest. What follows is a long period of wandering, the personal, existential side of what T. S. Eliot describes as "the waste land." The story contains many minor incidents and lesser characters. They are simply the symbols of what we need along the way. The underlying lesson that sustains our hero is trust. We live in a transcendent universe, and what we need will be provided.

Our hero has been touched by God in such a way that only God will do from now on. He is gripped by the truth. "He has experienced the absolute, and the relative will never again totally satisfy him. He aches for God. The aching becomes the seeking. Thus, after the Grail experience, our lives are driven in perpetual dissatisfaction. We become dissatisfied with everything: with church, with self, with America. No matter whom we elect president, we are unhappy. Ordinary life will never again be satisfactory or good enough."[12]

From now on, God is both perfectly hidden and perfectly revealed in everything. After the Grail experience, the ordinary becomes forever extraordinary. Once Parsifal has seen the Grail—even though he crosses the moat and leaves the castle—he is radically different ever after. Not that we are perfect. We sin; we betray, we act contrary to our values and beliefs; we are hypocritical, lustful, angry, and all the rest. Nevertheless, we are also gripped by the truth. As Jeremiah says, "There is something like a burning fire shut up in my bones" (Jer. 20:9). We know it is the truth, even though

---

12. Rohr, *Quest for the Grail*, 114.

we cannot live up to it. "The only sin would be to deny that it is the truth. Trying to live up to it is the rest of the Grail journey. Now the quest is real because the Grail is real."[13]

At one point Perceval meets the character called Vassal—the Dark Knight—who lives in a tomb, in a state of enchantment. A foolish maiden tries to persuade Perceval to kill the Dark Knight, which is Perceval's "shadow self."[14] Just in time, Perceval meets a wise old man, who tells him not to attack the Dark Knight or drive him back into his tomb, but instead to invite him out and make peace with him.

Insight into the shadow self is perhaps the most significant breakthrough to understanding the meaning of wholeness, mental health, and the spiritual quest. Jesus spoke of it in a number of parables, most clearly in Matthew 13, in the parable of "weeds among the wheat" (13:24–30). Someone sows good seed in his field—we are that field; we sow good seed in our fields. But by midsummer weeds appear, growing amid the wheat. Where did the weeds come from? That's the typical question we ask when we discover we are inconsistent in belief and in practice. We think of ourselves as loving and caring, yet we often lash out at others. We say we care, but we can be mean, stingy, and uncooperative. Where did these weeds come from?

The man in the parable is facing his shadow side, recognizing the weeds in the field. He asks the master, "Should I go and pull the weeds?" But Jesus replies, "No, don't pull them out. If you do, you will pull out the wheat as well. Let them grow together, and at the end they will be separated and the weeds discarded." If we do otherwise, we will mess things up. We often don't know what our gifts are, or what our sin is. The spiritual journey teaches, and it often takes the entire journey to learn, that what we think is our greatest gift when we are twenty can be our greatest sin when we are forty.

The shadow side is not our evil side. Rather, it consists of those opposing aspects of self that are difficult to acknowledge or own and that counter our conscious identity. Our shadow, then, is the unacceptable side—the side of us that, for whatever reason, whether it be family, church, or culture, we don't want to present publicly. It is not so much our opposite as our rejected twin, "to whom we are negatively bound, but bound nonetheless."[15] As a result, we are likely to project this negativity onto others rather than to face and negotiate an integration of shadow and self.

---

13. Ibid., 116.
14. The material on Vassal and the shadow self is adapted from Rohr, ibid, 125–35.
15. Rohr, ibid., 126.

Projection, however, only makes things work. What we must do is confront our shadow, befriend what we hate and fear. It is futile to say men are the problem, or women, or feminists, or patriarchy, or blacks, or whites, or gays, or strait, or Protestants, or Catholics, or atheists, or sinners. We are all saints and sinners. Growing up spiritually and emotionally means taking the lid off, entering the cave and befriending the Dark Knight within. That task will take more courage, humility, and time than any task in our lives, because it never ends. When we resist, ignore, project, bewail, confess, or sublimate our shadow, it simply goes deeper. At the end, if we are blessed, we learn to accept ourselves, "warts and all." Confrontation with the shadow teaches us to take ourselves less seriously, even to laugh at ourselves.

In the spiritual life, nothing goes away; there is no Gehenna—no heavenly garbage dump. Even forgiveness does not mean something goes away. It means we forgive it for being there. Even our demons do not go away. As Robert Bly wisely said, "You don't get rid of your demons, you just educate them." If we are wise, we start talking to our demons, particularly fear, guilt, and anger, those three great demons that dominate the lives of people who don't face their shadow.

The shadow is dangerous to the degree we are out of touch with it. The "prince of darkness" tries to persuade us to remain clueless, or to blame others for our shadow side. "Don't believe the truth about yourself," he whispers. But he is the "father of lies." However, most of the major crises in our lives are confrontations with our shadow side, something about ourselves we would rather not see. They are painful and distasteful, and we do everything we can to avoid them. In this light, church teaching about repentance, confession, and forgiveness makes sense. At some point we need to admit our darkness, for only by confronting it can we bring it into the light.

The answer, however, does not lie in repeated rituals of confession, but in letting go. In general, conservative personalities tend to repress too quickly, while liberals tend to express too quickly. Both approaches are counterproductive. What we must do is hold our shadow self in the middle—neither expressing or suppressing—but simply acknowledging. Recall Perceval lying in bed nose to nose and eye to eye with Blanche Fleur—not expressing, not repressing. That's spirituality! It is not easy; it requires wisdom, patience, and trust.

The church's primary failure might be that it does not teach us how to carry our dark side, neither our personal darkness nor the darkness of history and of institutions. Jesus was intentional. When the flattering young man came to him and said, "Good Teacher," Jesus replied, "Why do you call me good. No one is good but God alone" (Mark 10:17–18). In other words, "Stop flattering me." Flattery, a form of hypocrisy, usually involves denial of the shadow. Flatterers do not talk honestly, but we need honesty and humility more than apparent heroism, and perhaps they are heroism. This wrestling with the shadow is the game of life. It is what gives us personality. If we do not wrestle, we do not have personality; there is nothing real or authentic about us.

When we keep it real, we finally understand the first beatitude of Matthew's Sermon on the Mount: "Blessed are the poor in spirit" (Matt. 5:3). The poor in spirit are the ones who know they are no big deal, and are quite content remaining so. They are the only people who are truly free and secure. For them, the kingdom is said to be a present reality. Notice that Jesus uses the present tense: "theirs *is* the kingdom." It is theirs now because they have no boundaries of prestige, power, righteousness, greatness, moral superiority, or savedness to protect.

However, there is a right order to things. The confrontation with Vassal—with one's shadow—should be contemplated and understood only after there has been a Grail experience, only after there has been an experience of unconditional acceptance, of universal belonging. Until then, we do not have sufficient wisdom or courage to face our shadow. To put it simply, people who are not on the spiritual journey will continue, largely, to live a life of unconsciousness. We cannot face the dark until we have seen the light.

It is ironic that the people who receive the most attention, and even adulation, in our society, have so little inclination to do soul work. The politicians, actors, athletes, and captains of industry—the movers and shakers—simply do not have the time or desire to walk the interior path. These are the people we admire, who lead our world, and so few have confronted their shadow. We need a generation that will confront and befriend the Dark Knight, not ignore or try to defeat it. The only way to do so is to enter the Grail chamber, finding the image of God hidden in the depths of our unconscious. To enter the chamber, we need a mentor, a good guide to teach us how to fall, graciously, and even to trust the fall and realize it is a necessary way to learn and grow.

We in the West live in massive alienation from the center. Hence, we try to create pseudo-Grail chambers, always placing the ego at the center. When we are young, building our tower, we think we are the center. We take ourselves too seriously, thinking we are more important than we are. Then we fall, and that becomes the door or window through which the unconscious becomes conscious. We call that transformation, where the spirit erupts through our unconscious. In spiritual language, it is called conversion. There is no easy way to bring about such transformation, but pain is surely essential. Without pain and sense of loss, we surely run to that false Grail chamber, to that false security system called "ego." For some, that false chamber is a power job, a prestigious education, even a role, such as a religious vocation.

A living connection with the center needs reminders, sacraments, images, metaphors, and myths. With these symbols as vehicles, God comes to us from the center. It is all right to live at the edge, however, for as the mystics remind us, "The center is everywhere and the circumference is nowhere."

Today we find ourselves in a state of spiritual emergency. We cannot be complacent, satisfied simply with religious or denominational affiliation. We need people who, like Perceval, are prepared to go the distance. We need, in other words, a clear recognition of what the Center is, what the totality is, and how we are a part of it. Such living, serving, and knowing proceeds from the Center, and it always comes toward us before we come toward it. That's the dynamic of grace, the procession from the Grail Castle.

The classic myth of the hero involves four stages: the departure, the journey, the encounter, and finally the return. It is always full circle. We go back where we began, and, in the idiom of T. S. Eliot, know the place for the first time. Christ has died, Christ has risen—the inexorable wheel. Do not try to stop it; get on board, ride it, trust it. Trust the dying, trust the rising; live the dying, live the rising. And Christ will come, again and again. We cannot and must not get off the wheel!

PERCEVAL'S RETURN

According to myth, individuals are given two opportunities to enter the Grail Castle. The first time in their youth, a "gratuitous" opportunity to experience the potential of one's "numinous self." The second Grail Castle opportunity is not gratuitous, but coincides with a person's mid-life crisis; a time when individuals reevaluate their lives and hopefully rediscover vision and new vigor for the journey ahead.

In some of the Grail myths, after twenty or thirty years of knighthood, Perceval has earned the right to regain entry to the Grail Castle for a second time. He has untangled himself from the collective mother and patriarchal complexes and emerged as a man capable of determining his own unique destiny. When he returns, Perceval's first act in the Grail Castle is to ask the famous question, "Whom does the Grail serve?" He touches the wound of the Fisher King with the spear, and the king is healed. Immediately, the lands and people surrounding the king are healed as well. Perceval, by giving "voice" to the mystery of what is central in the kingdom, knows that the Grail is located within himself. The question "whom does it serve" means that we must give service to our virtue, honoring the noble part of ourselves.

Eventually, the Fisher King dies, and Perceval takes his place. Now he sits on the throne, and he is no longer replicating the role of the wounded Fisher King, engaging solely with the unconscious. He has walked the walk, through the fear, guilt, and anger. To use "recovery" language, he has moved beyond denial. When you become a wise warrior, magician, and lover, in submission to the king, you become a king as well. Perceval lives in the Grail Castle, marries Blanche Fleur, and lives happily ever after. He is now remembered as the greatest knight to sit at the Round Table—in the circle, that is, as one of the people.

Once we have faced our demons and won, it is the lover within that matters most. When we face the final demon, death, what matters is not what we accomplished or how much we accumulated, but rather what and whom we have loved. Love grounds the whole thing. It is the foundation of all reality. When we have loved purely, we can face death without fear. That is the heart of all religion, certainly of Christianity.

I conclude with my favorite version of the Grail myth, a version told by Robin Williams to Jeff Bridges in *The Fisher King*. In this film, Williams is Parry, a homeless history professor who lives in a fantasy world, traumatized by the murder of his wife, shot in his presence by a deranged killer. Lying naked in New York's Central Park, Williams gazes at the stars and tells Bridges a story:

> The story begins with the king as a boy, having to spend the night alone in the forest, so he can prove his courage and become a king. While he is spending the night alone, he is visited by a sacred vision. Out of the fire appears the Holy Grail, a symbol of God's divine grace. And a voice says to the boy, "You shall be keeper of the Grail, so that it may heal the hearts of men." But the boy is blinded by visions of greatness, filled with power and glory and beauty. And in this state of radical amazement, he feels for a brief moment, not like a boy but invincible, like God. So he reaches in the fire to take the Grail, and the Grail vanishes, leaving him with his hand in the fire to be terribly wounded.
>
> As this boy grows older, his wound grows deeper, until one day, life for him has lost its reason. He has no faith in others—not even in himself. He can't love, or feel loved. Sick with experience, he begins to die.
>
> One day, the boy wanders into the castle, and finds the king alone. Not being sophisticated, he doesn't recognize the king. He only sees a man alone, and in pain. And he asks the king, "What ails you, friend?" And the king replies, "I'm thirsty. I need some water to cool my throat."

So the boy takes a cup from beside the king's bed, fills it with water, and hands it to the king. As the king begins to drink, he realizes his wound is healed. He looks at his hands, and there is the Holy Grail—that which he had sought all his life.

"How could you find that which my brightest and bravest could not find?" the king asks. And the boy replies, "I don't know. I only knew that you were thirsty."

QUESTIONS FOR DISCUSSION AND REFLECTION

1. In terms of your temperament and upbringing, would you characterize yourself as a child of nature or a child of culture? Explain your answer.
2. Did your parents or guardians provide an atmosphere that was protective and secure, or one that promoted adventure, risk-taking, and ambiguity? Explain your answer.
3. In your estimation, did you complete the "tower-building phase" of your life successfully? Explain your answer.
4. Can you point to a time when the circumstances of your life (or your faith) prompted or forced you from your tower? Explain your answer.
5. Explain and assess the concept that "being cast out of the Garden teaches us to long for the Garden."
6. Did people in your life teach you the "language of departure," that is, the importance of rebelling against the status quo, or were you led by the conventional slogan: "Follow the rules"? Which of these roles did religion play during your adolescence and young adulthood?
7. Assess the merits of the statement, "When we don't have wise 'kings,' dark warriors and immature heroes dominate."
8. Was there a Red Knight encounter in your adolescent or young adulthood experience? Explain your answer.
9. Was there a Gornemant encounter in your adolescent or young adulthood experience? Explain your answer.
10. Was there a Blanche Fleur encounter in your adolescent or young adulthood experience? Explain your answer.
11. Are there two kings in the Grail Castle, or only one? Explain your answer.
12. Explain how the concept of "wasteland" applies to one's Grail quest.

13. Have you had a Dark Knight encounter? Explain your answer.
14. Must there be a "Hollywood ending" to our Grail quest? Explain you answer.
15. In your estimation, what is the primary insight gained from this chapter? Does this chapter raise any issues you might need to address in the future?

Chapter 12

The Power of Love

Today, the great quest no longer seems real or inviting. Many of us are unsure of our spiritual goals. We have difficulty reading the meaningful patterns of our existence, and many remain unconvinced or even uninterested in their divine origins. This is a major crisis of meaning that results in a loss of hope and a lack of vision.

Faith demands living with a certain degree of anxiety and holding a very real amount of tension. We have to be trained how to do this. Only two things are strong enough to accomplish this training: great love and great suffering. They are the primary spiritual teachers, more than the Bible, church, clergy, sacraments, or theology. Only love and suffering are strong enough to decentralize the ego and the superego, break down our dual thinking, and open us to Mystery. "Great suffering has the potential to open the mind space, and then the heart space. Great love has the potential to open the heart space and then the mind space."[1] Both spaces need to be opened. They are the two great doors, and we dare not leave them closed.

Authentic love is of one piece. How you love anything is how you love everything. I believe that is what Jesus meant when he said that we must love "with all our heart, all our soul, all our mind, and all our strength" (Mark 12:30), for that is the only way to love. Anything less does not appear to be love at all. That's how love works and why it leads to the giving up of control.

If we define suffering broadly, namely, as the experience of being vulnerable, powerless, or out of control, then we can see its correlation with

---

1. Rohr, *Naked Now*, 126.

love. Love is what we long for and were created for, but suffering often seems to be our opening to that need. Whenever we are inside of great love and great suffering, we have a much stronger possibility of surrendering our ego controls and opening up to the depth of life. Apart from suffering, failure, humiliation, and pain, none of us will naturally let go of our self-sufficiency. Great love makes us willing to risk everything, holding nothing back. Great suffering opens us differently, for here, things happen against our will. Ultimately, our sufficiency comes from who we are in God, who we are as part of a much larger whole, not who we are in ourselves.

Suffering, of course, can lead us in one of two directions: it can make us bitter and close us down, or it can make us better, wise, compassionate, and utterly open. It can take us to the edge of our inner resource, and often this is when we encounter grace—and with it, God! Struggling with our shadow self, facing interior conflicts and moral failures, undergoing humiliation and rejection, experiencing abuse or any form of limitation, all are gateways into deeper consciousness and the flowering of the soul. We are somehow representatives of God, and God is carrying us, not simply our good parts but also the bad parts.

If we are honest, there always will be at least one situation in our lives that we cannot fix, control, explain, change, or even understand. For Jesus and his followers, the crucifixion became the symbol of that necessary and absurd stumbling stone. Suffering is necessary not because it solves problems mechanically as much as it opens new spaces within us for learning and loving. Our False Self—our role, title, and personal image that is largely a creation of our own mind and attachments—will and must die in exact correlation to how much we want the Real. The significant question, then, is "How much False Self are we willing to shed to find our True Self?" Such necessary suffering will always feel like dying, which is what good spiritual guides must tell us. If your spiritual guides do not talk to you about dying, they are not effective.

The spiritual journey cannot be traveled alone. If there were no suffering on earth, no need, no sin or imperfection, we could each live in our isolated worlds. I would not need you or be drawn to you. I would be self-sufficient, caught up in my own perfection. This is the Gnostic temptation, condemned in some form in every century. There are two things that draw us outside of ourselves: pain in others, and the unbelievable beauty that others represent at their best; in other words, cross and resurrection.

Pain and beauty constitute the two faces of God. Unbelievable beauty, on the one hand—whether it be physical beauty or spiritual beauty—we find in human beings to which we are attracted. On the other hand, brokenness, weakness, and suffering also pull us out of ourselves. That is why St.

Francis could kiss the leper. This is why so many saints want to get near suffering, because, as they say repeatedly, they meet Christ there. Such encounter "saved" them from their smaller and untrue self.

Jesus asked his original disciples, "Are you able to drink the cup that I drink, or be baptized with the baptism that I am baptized with?" (Mark 10:38). It is not that we have a message and then suffer for it. It is much the opposite: we suffer, come through it transformed, and then we have a message. We hope to bypass suffering by being moral and ritualistic, but Christ's words remain the same today: "The cup that I drink, you will drink; and with the baptism with which I am baptized, you will be baptized" (Mark 10:39).

Enlightenment, conversion, and seeing the truth represent a journey of transformation, not a matter of membership in the right group, reciting the correct formulas, or even practicing the right morality. As Paul made so clear in his letters, legalism can give us correct information, but only God's Spirit of love can transform us. The word of God calls us to greater wisdom. God does so by making the system fall apart. It is called suffering, and that is how God shows us that life is bigger than we presently imagine.

THE FACE WE HAD BEFORE WE WERE BORN

Modern Western society presents a rosy picture: the journey ahead is upward and onward. You can be successful, and you can do it by yourself. Jesus, however, presents us with a different model, that of death and resurrection—a pattern of renewal, of daily dying to self. The True Self is who you are from the beginning, in the heart of God, the "face we had before we were born," as the Zen masters say. In this light, Carl Jung offered a momentous insight: "Life is a luminous pause between two great mysteries, which themselves are one."

Sometimes the end is the beginning, and the beginning points toward the end. Agreeing with Jung, we can affirm that the One Great Mystery is revealed at the beginning and forever beckons us toward its full realization. Many of us cannot let go of this implanted promise. Some call this homing device their soul, some call it the indwelling Holy Spirit, and others think of it as nostalgia or dreamtime. Whatever we call it, we cannot ignore it. It calls us both backward and forward, to our foundation and our future at the same time. The soul lives in such eternally deep time.

Speaking of this mystery, Richard Rohr notes that we are called forward by "a kind of deep homesickness," an inherent dissatisfaction that comes from our original and radical union with God.[2] Like loneliness, sadness, and depression, sickness, loss, and deprivation can serve as beacons to light our way home. One of the reasons the Wizard of Oz has such lasting appeal is because Dorothy is guided forward to Oz and back to Kansas by her constant love and desire for home. Restlessness and dissatisfaction in life can serve as pointers to our destiny in God. The moment that we find ourselves in the presence of God is the moment we also find ourselves inside God.

The end was planted in us at the beginning, and it gnaws at us until we get there freely and consciously. Suffering, tragedy, and all episodes of loss in our lives are potentially sacramental. As Carl Jung put it, "when you stumble and fall, there you find pure gold." God hides, and is found, precisely in the depths of everything, especially so in the deep fathoming of our pain, suffering, weakness, and failure. This "something real" is what all the world religions point to when they speak of heaven, nirvana, bliss, or enlightenment. Their only mistake is to push it off into the next world. "If heaven comes later, it is because it is first of all now."[3]

How does God operate? We really don't know. However, so many have encountered God in their weakness that we realize God's strength is God's ability to be patient, to refrain from overt use of power. From our perspective, then, we can say that God is a god of weakness, acting as much by persuasion as by direct action.

In tragedy and sickness, we are no longer in charge. That is good news, because all attempts to engineer or plan our own enlightenment are doomed to failure, since they are ego driven. The ego's job is to protect the status quo, so failure and humiliation force us to look beyond our comfort zones. Thus, we must stumble and fall. We must get out of the driver's seat for a while or we will never learn how to give up control to our soul's True Guide.

In the spiritual world, we do not really find something unless we first lose it, choose it, long for it, and personally find it again—only now on a new level. In Luke 15 we find three parables about losing something—a sheep, a coin, a son—searching for them anew, and finding them once again. This new appreciation is followed by the kind of sincere celebration that comes with any new realization.

If you desire to grow spiritually, eventually some idea, event, or relationship will enter your life that you are not equipped to handle, using your present skill set. Richard Rohr calls such a situation a "stumbling stone,"

---

2. Material in this segment is adapted from Rohr, *Falling Upward*, 65–96.
3. Rohr, *Falling Upward*, 95.

an event that causes you to leave your comfort zone in life.[4] Often such an experience involves physical or mental suffering. In this case, suffering will not solve any problem mechanically so much as it discloses the chronic problem in our lives, the refusal of our ego to let go. In such cases, suffering has a mentoring role, that of opening up new spaces within us for learning and loving. Francis of Assisi noted that when he kissed the leper, "what had been nauseating to me became sweetness and life." He marked that moment as his conversion, as the defining moment in his life, when he tasted his own insufficiency and began drawing from a different source.[5]

Catholic theologian Friedrich von Hügel, valued more highly in his day as a spiritual director than as a theologian, found practical outlets for his significant intellectual skills. At the age of eighteen, sickened with typhus fever and left practically deaf, he embarked on a theological career. While he spent most of his life as a Catholic layman dedicated to theological and philosophical writing, at the age of forty he met the Abbé Huvelin, a distinguished spiritual director serving in a Parisian parish. Through his influence, von Hügel experienced a profound spiritual transformation that led him from his intellectual pursuits into the field of spiritual counseling, and it was as a guide and counselor that he made his greatest contribution. Von Hügel's final words, written to his niece, fittingly summarize life: "Remember, no joy without suffering, no patience without trial, no humility without humiliation, no life without death."[6]

What von Hügel learned at eighteen from his own spiritual director, Father Raymond Hocking, when he decided on a career in theology, he applied as a spiritual counselor: "You want to grow in virtue, to serve God, to love Christ? Well, you will grow in and attain these things if you will make them a slow and sure, but utterly real, mountain-step plod and ascent, willing to have to camp for weeks in spiritual desolation, darkness, and emptiness at different stages in your march and growth. All demand for constant light, all attempt at eliminating or minimizing the cross and trial, is so much soft folly and puerile trifling."[7]

These words reflect what Jesus taught his followers about the cost of discipleship: "If any want to become my followers, let them deny themselves and take up their cross and follow me. For those who want to save their life will lose it, and those who lose their life for my sake and for the sake of the gospel, will save it" (Mark 8:34–35). A more realistic description of the

---

4. Ibid., 68.
5. Ibid., 69–70.
6. Steere, *Spiritual Counsel and Letters of von Hügel*, 34.
7. Ibid., 4.

Christian spiritual journey has not been recorded. However, the story does not end here, for Jesus also teaches his followers that wherever they go, he will accompany them (Matt. 28:20). Those who are yoked to Jesus experience exhilaration and joy daily, even in times of trial, for Christ's burden is light (Matt. 11:30).

THE VISION QUEST

The "vision quest," a religious ritual and a central rite of passage found in all times and across the globe, has traditionally been one of the most important ritual practices of Native American people. All important undertakings had first to be received in a vision. Any change in tribal rituals, the conduct of war, hunting practices, songs, or even the giving of names had first to be authorized in a vision. For many tribes, the vision was the source of all things sacred. Some tribes performed the vision quest as a rite of passage into adulthood.

While open to both males and females, the vision quest was expected of all males. Females quested in the community, learning their roles as life-givers and guardians of the sacred traditions. Males were expected to perform the vision quest because the quest played a central role in determining their lifestyle and lifework. It was through the vision experience, or lack of it, that each male received his relative role in the society, his place in hunting parties and war parties, his right to perform certain religious functions, and his overall status among his people.

The Sioux vision quest represents the quests performed by most Plains tribes. This important ritual began with a period of fasting, the end of the period being marked by a ritual purification to put off worldly thoughts. Following the steam bath, the young brave left camp accompanied by two assistants who prepared the hilltop on which the vision quest would take place. At the site the assistants first made a hole, into which they set a long pole. One of the helpers went about ten strides to the west, and in the same manner set up another pole. He returned to the center and picked up a third pole, and this he fixed at the north, returning to the center. In the same manner he set up poles at the east and south.

The ritual site and the manner in which it was constructed had symbolic meaning. The assistants were symbolically constructing the world. The establishment of the directions also related to the four periods of time (the day, the night, the month or moon, and the year) and the four stages of life (infancy, youth, adulthood, and old age). All of these "fours" were understood as points on a circle, and thus the vision quest site formed a circle. When the site had been prepared, the assistants returned to the tribe. The selection of the site was crucial, for where the person stood marked the symbolic center of the world.

Though the preparation was not necessarily always the same, the vision, when it came, usually included the following results: (1) a glimpse of a guardian animal (sometimes the young man would be renamed to include this animal); (2) finding a token (a feather or some item associated with the guardian animal), which became the person's most prized possession; (3) receiving a song or chant (like a mantra that he alone would sing); and (4) a promise for the tribe.

This communal element was deemed essential. A successful quest was necessary for a young person to take his or her place as a full member of the tribe. It provided direction for life, and resulted in living with a full purpose. An unsuccessful quest could limit the individual to a marginal position in the tribe or even bar one from adult roles. Vision quests, while differing in details from tribe to tribe, have been practically universal among Native Americans. They were viewed as the most sacred act that anyone could perform.

In Western religious ritual, a worship service may be viewed as a vision quest. Christian worship often ends with a benediction, and sometimes with a congregational response. In my travels as a guest preacher, I noticed that some churches end worship with the singing of the inspirational folksong, "Let There be Peace on Earth," written by Jill Jackson-Miller and Sy Miller in 1955. The prayerful lyrics state, "Let there be peace on earth, and let it begin with me. Let there be peace on earth, the peace that was meant to be. With God our Creator, family all are we. Let us walk with each other in perfect harmony." This is a good message for society. What message do you bring for our society and planet?

A HERO IS BORN

In his important book *The Myth of the Birth of the Hero*, Otto Rank declares that everyone is a hero in birth, for the newborn undergoes a tremendous psychological as well as physical transformation, from the condition of a tiny water creature living in a realm of amniotic fluid into an air-breathing mammal that will soon walk upright. That is an enormous transformation.

The mother's role is particularly heroic, for giving birth is the giving of oneself to the life of another. While the male typically has had the more conspicuous role in society, that is not the case in most primal societies. Among the Aztecs, for example, who have a number of heavens to which people's souls are assigned according to the conditions of their death, the heaven for warriors killed in battle is the same for mothers who die in childbirth.

In addition to birth, the change from infant to child, adolescent, and adult requires courage, faith, perseverance, and risk-taking. It is a heroic process, involving love, commitment, sacrifice, forgiveness, and hope on the part of the parents, whose role is also heroic.

Heroes are distinguished by two types of deeds. One is the physical deed, in which the hero performs a courageous act to save a life. The other is a spiritual deed, in which the hero experiences a series of adventures beyond the ordinary, either to recover what has been lost or to discover a hopeful message, and then returns with a hopeful message. In today's world, the spiritual hero is one who values life, while belonging to the planet.

THE ROAR OF AWAKENING

The fifth and final section of Eliot's *Waste Land*, "What the Thunder Said," is written in unpunctuated, unrhymed free verse. Readers find themselves in a dry land, among people undertaking a quest to find the Holy Grail. Much of this final section of the poem is about a desire for water. The wasteland is a land of drought where little will grow. Water is needed to restore life to the earth, to return a sterile land to fertility. It is as if the lack of water leads the speaker of this section, in his desire for water, to lapse into semi-coherent snatches of speech. The poem ends with the arrival of rain in a thunderstorm, where the sound of the thunderclap is interpreted in light of the Hindu Upanishads.

The Upanishads are Vedanta (the "end of the Vedas"). Representing the summation of the vast sacred literature of Hinduism, they also stand at the beginning of India's vast philosophical tradition, bridging religion, philosophy, and psychology—the study of the soul. The Upanishads are revolutionary "wisdom teaching" intended to transform and enlighten human consciousness. The Upanishads ask, "What is the nature of Ultimate Reality, of the soul?" The answer requires deep insight. This is not the kind of knowledge one needs to pass an exam, but rather the knowledge one needs for life.

To overcome the limitation of language and to answer the ultimate existential questions, Indian sages developed an approach we often associate with Jesus—they told parables. An old parable—"The Roar of Awakening"—helps explain self-realization and the meaning of the phrase *tat tvam asi*. Told as a fable, the story speaks of a pregnant tigress that came upon a flock of goats. With the energy she expended in pouncing upon them, she brought on the birth of her cub and her own death. The goats, meanwhile, had scattered, and they finally returned to their grazing spot, where they found the newborn tiger and its dead mother. Having strong parental instincts, they adopted the tiger cub, who grew up thinking he was a goat. Not knowing its true nature, it imitated the goats, bleating and learning to eat grass.

Eventually a large male tiger came upon the herd and, seeing the cub, grabbed it by the neck and dragged it to a still pond. Seeing its reflection in the water, the cub realized it was not a goat but . . . a tiger! At that point the tiger said, "You are like me, now *be* like me." The tiger then took the cub to a nearby cave and made him eat from a dead deer. At first the tiger cub began to choke, but then a recognition came—a tingling began from his tail to his toes—and it let out a loud roar.

The point of the story is not about the process of becoming, but about realization. The tiger is not a goat—it has always been a tiger. The function of the proper interpretation of mythological stories and symbols and meditation discipline is to awaken us to our tiger nature. When Jesus and other sages learned their tiger nature, they were often crucified. That may not happen to us externally, but it must happen internally to the False Self. What we must learn to do is change our perception, which occurs when we let go (crucify) the egocentricity that deceives us. According to Huston Smith, the dean of comparative religion, if we were to compress the Perennial Tradition into a single affirmation, it would be, "what you want you already possess."

Earlier we used the metaphor of death and resurrection to describe the transition from the first to the second half of life, from the death of the False Self to the liberation of the True Self. That's a heroic deed—the transformation from a self-serving, air-breathing, egoic existence to a wave on the water, from a somebody to a nobody, from an "I" to a "We." That is how you walk on water—by becoming the water. The amazing thing is, you are still you—a wave—and yet so much more than you—the sea itself. You no longer need to control, because something far better is present. Power cannot see that. Love can see nothing else.

QUESTIONS FOR DISCUSSION AND REFLECTION

1. Do you agree with the author's point that great love and great suffering are the two most effective spiritual teachers in our lives? Explain your answer.

2. Explain and assess the merits of the statement, "How you love anything is how you love everything."

3. How much False Self are you willing to shed to find your True Self?

4. Explain and assess the merits of the statement, "Pain and beauty constitute the two faces of God."

5. What "message" have you received from your suffering or wound?

6. Do you agree with Richard Rohr's statement that our spiritual journey (quest) is called forward by "a kind of deep homesickness"? Explain your answer.

7. Explain and assess Carl Jung's statement that "when you stumble and fall, there you find pure gold."

8. Have you experienced—or are you currently experiencing—what mystics call "the dark night of the soul"? If so, keep in mind that this is happening because you are "yoked with Christ" (see Matthew 11:30).

9. After reading "The Roar of Awakening," what did you learn about the meaning of the Sanskrit phrase, *tat tvam asi*?

10. In your estimation, what is the primary insight gained from this chapter? Does this chapter raise any issues you might need to address in the future?

11. After completing this course, what message do you bring for our society and planet?

12. After completing this course, what have you learned about "living into a new way of thinking"?

13. After completing this course, what have you learned about "walking on water"?

Appendix A

TWELVE WAYS TO PRACTICE RESURRECTION NOW

1. Choose your True Self—your radical union with God—as often as possible. Do not indulge or believe your False Self (refuse to identify with negative, blaming, antagonistic, or fearful thoughts concocted by your mind and society's expectations).
2. Emphasize inner rather than outer truth.
3. Regain a sense of wonder and gratitude.
4. Practice awareness of interdependence (non-dualistic thinking).
5. Gain greater tolerance for uncertainty; be less dogmatic and argumentative.
6. Always seek to change yourself before trying to change others.
7. Choose as much as possible to serve rather than be served.
8. Whenever possible, seek the common good over your mere private good.
9. Give preference to those in pain, excluded, or disabled in any way.
10. Seek just systems and policies over mere charity.
11. Be an agent of transformation and change.
12. Never doubt that it is all about love in the end.[1]

---

1. This list is adopted from Rohr, *Diamond*, 211–12.

Appendix B

MODERN APPROACHES TO REALITY[1]

Modern Consciousness	Postmodern Consciousness
1. Trust in human reason	1. Reason is relative and unreliable on its own
2. Belief in inevitable progress	2. Disbelief in inevitable progress
3. Individual autonomy	3. Self is understood in relation to larger natural and cultural context
4. Universal truth claims	4. Truth is relative to local community
5. Affirms metanarratives	5. Nihilistic perspective on life
6. Natural science over mystery	6. Holistic ways of knowing: affective, intuitive, and cognitive
7. Secular worldview	7. A new quest for spirituality in the marketplace

---

1. List is adapted from Grenz, *Primer on Postmodernism*, 13–15.

Bibliography

Aristotle. *The Rhetoric and Poetics of Aristotle*. New York: Modern Library, 1984.
Armstrong, Karen. *The Case for God*. New York: Anchor, 2010.
———. *A Short History of Myth*. New York: Canongate, 2005.
Barfield, Owen. *History in English Words*. London: Faber and Faber, 1962.
Borg, Marcus J. *The God We Never Knew*. New York: HarperSanFrancisco, 1998.
Bourgeault, Cynthia. *The Holy Trinity and the Law of Three*. Boston: Shambhala, 2013.
Campbell, Joseph. *The Hero's Journey: Joseph Campbell on His Life and Work*. Edited by Phil Cousineau. Novato, CA: New World Library, 2003.
———. *The Inner Reaches of Outer Space: Metaphor as Myth and as Religion*. Novato, CA: New World Library, 2002.
———. *The Power of Myth: with Bill Moyers*. New York: Doubleday, 1988.
———. *Romance of the Grail: The Magic and Mystery of Arthurian Myth*. Novato, CA: New World Library, 2015.
———. *Thou Art That: Transforming Religious Metaphor*. Novato, CA: New World Library, 2001.
Clayton, Philip, and Arthur Peacocke. *In Whom We Live and Move and Have our Being: Panentheistic Reflections on God's Presence in a Scientific World*. Grand Rapids: Eerdmans, 2004.
Clifford, Richard J. *The Wisdom Literature*. Nashville: Abingdon, 1998.
De La Torre, Miguel A. *Liberation Theology for Armchair Theologians*. Louisville: Westminster John Knox, 2013.
Edelman, Gerald M. *Second Nature: Brain Science and Human Knowledge*. New Haven: Yale University Press, 2006.
Egan, Dan. *The Death and Life of the Great Lakes*. New York: Norton, 2018.
Emerson, Ralph Waldo. "The Poet," 1–24. https://emerson.com/ebook/The%20Poet.pdf.
Geary, James. *I Is an Other: The Secret Life of Metaphor and How It Shapes the Way We See the World*. New York: HarperCollins, 2011.
Grenz, Stanley J. *A Primer on Postmodernism*. Grand Rapids: Eerdmans, 1996.
Griffin, David Ray. *Reenchantment without Supernaturalism: A Process Philosophy of Religion*. Ithaca: Cornell University Press, 2001.
Hartshorne, Charles. *Man's Vision of God*. Chicago: Willett, Clark, 1941.
———. *A Natural Theology for Our Time*. La Salle, IL: Open Court, 1967.
Haught, John F. *What is God? How to Think About the Divine*. Mahwah, NJ: Paulist, 1986.

Hughes, Richard T. *Myths America Lives By*. Urbana, IL: University of Illinois Press, 2004.
Huxley, Aldous. *The Perennial Philosophy: An Interpretation of the Great Mystics, East and West*. New York: Harper, 1945.
Johnson, Mark. *Philosophical Perspectives on Metaphor*. Minneapolis: University of Minnesota Press, 1981.
Johnson, Robert A. *He: Understanding Masculine Psychology*. Rev. ed. New York: HarperCollins, 1989.
Jones, Serene. *Call It Grace: Finding Meaning in a Fractured World*. New York: Viking, 2019.
———. *Trauma and Grace: Theology in a Ruptured World*. 3rd ed. Louisville: Westminster John Knox, 2009.
Jung, Carl G. *AION: Researches into the Phenomenology of the Self*. In *Collected Works*, 9:2. New York: Pantheon, 1953.
Keen, Sam. *Fire in the Belly: On Being a Man*. New York: Bantam, 1991.
Keen, Sam, and Anne Valley Fox. *Your Mythic Journey*. Los Angeles: Tarcher, 1989.
King, Martin Luther, Jr. *A Testament of Hope: The Essential Writings and Speeches of Martin Luther King Jr.* Edited by James Melvin Washington. San Francisco: HarperSanFrancisco, 1986.
Langer, Suzanne K. *Philosophy in a New Key*. Cambridge: Harvard University Press, 1996.
Lewis, C. S. "Bluespels and Falansferes." In *Rehabilitation and Other Essays*, 135–58. London: Oxford University Press, 1939.
Loomis, Roger Sherman. *The Grail: From Celtic Myth to Christian Symbol*. New York; Columbia University Press, 1963.
McFague, Sallie. *The Body of God: an Ecological Theology*. Minneapolis: Fortress, 1993.
McKibben, Bill. *The End of Nature*. New York: Random House, 1989.
———. *Falter: Has the Human Game Begun to Play Itself Out?* New York: Holt, 2019.
Meredith, Cara. *The Color of Life*. Grand Rapids, Zondervan, 2019.
Merton, Thomas. *New Seeds of Contemplation*. New York: New Directions, 1962.
Moltmann, Jürgen. *God in Creation: A New Theology of Creation and the Spirit of God*. Minneapolis, MN: Fortress, 1993.
Nietzsche, Friedrich. *The Complete Works of Friedrich Nietzsche*. New York: Macmillan, 1911.
Ozment, Katherine. *Grace without God: The Search for Meaning, Purpose, and Belonging in a Secular Age*. New York: Harper Wave, 2016.
Purves, Andrew. *Reconstructing Pastoral Theology: A Christological Foundation*. Louisville: Westminster John Knox, 2004.
Rohr, Richard. *Eager to Love: The Alternative Way of Francis of Assisi*. Cincinnati: Franciscan Media, 2014.
———. *Falling Upward: A Spirituality for the Two Halves of Life*. San Francisco: Jossey-Bass, 2011.
———. *Immortal Diamond: The Search for Our True Self*. San Francisco: Jossey-Bass, 2013.
———. *The Naked Now: Learning to See as the Mystics See*. New York: Crossroad, 2009.
———. *Quest for the Grail*. New York: Crossroad, 1994.
———. *The Universal Christ*. New York: Convergent, 2019.
———. *What the Mystics Know*. New York: Crossroad, 2015.

Rohr, Richard, and Joseph Martos. *The Wild Man's Journey: Reflections on Male Spirituality*. Cincinnati: St. Anthony Messenger, 1992.
Schulweis, Harold M. *For Those Who Can't Believe*. New York: Harper Perennial, 1995.
Shapiro, Rami. *Perennial Wisdom for the Spiritually Independent*. Woodstock, VT: Skylight Independent, 2013.
Smith, Huston. *Forgotten Truth: The Common Vision of the World's Religions*. New York: HarperSanFrancisco, 1976.
Spong, John Shelby. *Eternal Life: A New Vision*. New York: HarperOne, 2009.
———. *Why Christianity Must Change or Die*. New York: HarperOne, 1999.
Steere, Douglas V. *Spiritual Counsel and Letters of Baron Friedrich von Hügel*. New York: Harper & Row, 1964.
Stevens, Wallace. "Three Academic Pieces." In *The Necessary Angel: Essays on Reality and the Imagination*. New York: Vintage, 1951.
Tolle, Eckhart. *The Power of Now: A Guide to Spiritual Enlightenment*. Novato, CA: New World Library, 2004.
Vande Kappelle, Robert P. *Beyond Belief: Faith, Science, and the Value of Unknowing*. Eugene: OR: Wipf & Stock, 2012.
———. *Dark Splendor: Spiritual Fitness for the Second Half of Life*. Eugene: OR: Wipf & Stock, 2015.
Vico, Giambattista. *New Science*. London: Penguin, 2001.
Wallis, Jim. *America's Original Sin: Racism, White Privilege, and the Bridge to a New America*. Grand Rapids: Brazos, 2011.
Weston, Jessie L. *The Quest of the Holy Grail*. New York: Barnes & Noble, 1964.
Whitehead, Alfred North. *Process and Reality*. Rev. ed. New York: Free Press, 1978.
———. *Science and the Modern World*. New York: Free Press, 1967.

Index

Abelard (theologian), 129
Abraham (patriarch), 121
action, primacy of, xii, 69, 75, 112
activism, xii
Aesop's Fables, 92
afterlife, 39, 61, 62, 69, 78
Alexander the Great, 147
allegory, 93
amor, 128, 129
anima, animus, 143
Anselm (theologian), 129
anthropology, biblical, 124
Aquinas, Thomas, 38
Aristotle, ix, 34, 86
Armstrong, Karen, xvi, 120
ascension. *See* metaphor, "ascension" as
Athanasius (bishop), 4
atheist, atheism, 39, 41, 43, 67, 83, 94, 150
Atman, 73, 115
atonement, theories of, 129
attachment, 99
Augustine, 36, 53, 60, 75, 104
awareness, 13, 66–71, 72, 107
    social, 15–29

Barfield, Owen, 86
Barth, Karl, 38
belief, believe, xn2, 6, 68, 88, 102, 106, 114, 128
Blake, William, 6
Blanche Fleur, 143–44, 150, 153
Bly, Robert, 150
Bonhoeffer, Dietrich, 49
Borg, Marcus, xvi, 47–48

Bourgeault, Cynthia, 53
Brahman, 34, 73, 115
Brooks, David, 26
Buber, Martin, 37
Buddha, the, 7, 92, 99, 114, 115, 116, 118, 132
Bunyan, John, 93
butterfly, 61–62

Campbell, Joseph, xvi, 83, 91, 111n1, 117
Catherine of Siena, 79
Chautauqua Institution, xv, xvi, 19, 26, 27, 28, 35, 51, 58
Chief Seattle, 19–20
children, 6
    of God, 7
Chrétien de Troyes, 126, 127, 130, 137, 147
Clifford, Richard, 77
climate change/global warming, xvi, 16–19, 114
Coates, Ta-Nehisi, 26
compassion, compassionate, 6, 10, 22, 26, 35, 58, 68, 75, 117, 157
Constitution (U.S.), 21, 22, 24
consumerism, 79, 139
contemplation, 7, 66–67, 68, 72, 74
conversion, xii, 7, 34, 69, 151, 158
Cosmic Christ, 103, 104
Crane, Hart, 92

Dante Alighieri, 93
Dark Knight, 149–52
    See also self, shadow

death
  of False Self, 97–100, 157
  physical, xiii
  spiritual, 97, 100, 107
  See also metaphor, "death" as
detachment, 99
discipleship, 104, 160
Dostoyevsky, Fyodor, 55
dualism, dualistic thinking, 6, 35–36, 52, 53, 54, 58, 64, 66, 67, 68, 72, 73, 79, 131, 156
  See also nondualism
Dürkheim, Karlfried, 116

Easter, 97
Eberhardt, Jennifer, 23
Eckhart, Meister, xii, 59
Edelman, Gerald, 88
ego, egocentricity, xi, xii, 4, 34, 36, 58, 60, 62, 76, 96, 97, 98. 99, 100, 115, 116, 117, 124, 132, 138, 141, 151, 156, 157, 159, 160, 164
  definition of, 60
  as "Satan," 96
Einstein, Albert, 66
election, doctrine of, 115
Eliot, T. S., 11, 125, 131, 148, 152, 163
Emerson, Ralph Waldo, 87
enlightenment, 7, 100, 134, 158, 159
eternity, eternal life, 13, 69, 70
evil, 51, 149

failure, xii, 139
faith, x, xii, 36, 67, 75, 102, 107, 121, 138, 156
False Self. See self, selfhood, False
Finn MacCool, 134n11
first half of life, 10, 62, 138–39, 164
Fisher King, 130, 131, 133, 137, 145, 146, 147, 153
  wound, 131, 134–35, 147, 152, 153–54
Fourier, Jean, 90
fractals, 71
Francis of Assisi, 128, 158, 160
Freud, Sigmund, 41, 120
Frost, Robert, 90
fundamentalism, 93, 94, 115, 140

Gadamer, Hans-Georg, 42
Garden of Eden, 116
  See also metaphor, "Garden of Eden" as
Gardner, Howard, 111
Geary, James, xvi, 85, 89, 92
Giraut de Bornelh, 128
global warming. See climate change
God, xi–xii, 51, 53–54, 74, 75–76, 78, 103, 104, 148
  absence of, 47
  as aliveness, 58
  and anthropomorphic language, 90
  as Creator, 33, 36, 76, 106
  as dualist Other, 58
  experience of, 146, 157, 159
  face of, 54
  goodness of, xii
  knowing, 36–37, 38
  as love, 45, 48, 50, 53, 55
  loving. See love, for God
  masks of, xi
  as metaphor, 83–84
  metaphor for, 41–44
  as Monarch, 48, 49
  as mother, 72
  as mystery. See mystery
  and nature, 52, 72
  nearness of, 47
  as personal, 37–38, 43, 49, 55
  small, xi
  as Spirit, 48, 49, 64, 65
  as Subject, 35, 43, 57, 59, 74
  as "Totally Other," 38
  transcendence of, xi–xii, 38, 40, 51, 71
  as Trinity, 52–55, 61
  and True Self, 69
  two faces of, 157
  as Ultimate Reality, 34, 51, 58–59, 69
  views of, 37, 39
  See also panentheism
  See also theism
Goethe, Johann von, 114
Goodell, Jeff, 19
Gornemant, 142, 143
Gospels, 6, 69, 102, 142
grace, xiii, 51, 146, 152, 157

Grail, the
    enchantment theme, 132–33
    identity of, 147, 153
    quest, 123–54, 163
    romances, 117, 126–27
Grail Castle, 130, 131, 132, 133, 135, 145–48, 152
Grail King, 146, 147
Grail procession, 131, 145, 152
Griffin, David Ray, 40

Hansen, James, 19
Hartshorne, Charles, 72
Haught, John, 41, 42, 43, 44, 45
heaven, 7, 11, 39, 52, 63, 72, 78–79, 100, 105, 106, 107, 159
Heidegger, Martin, 42
hell, 11, 39, 78, 79, 100, 108
hero, 162–63
Hobbes, Thomas, 86
holons, 71
holy, holiness, 71
Holy Spirit, xii, 48, 52, 53, 65, 97, 98, 102, 103, 158
    fruit of the, 75
Hooke, Robert, 90
hope, 79, 107
Hügel, Friedrich von, 160
Hugh of St. Victor, 6
Hughes, Richard, 21, 23
Huxley, Aldous, 34

image of God, 61
incarnation, 103–4, 105, 106
    definition of, 105
    of God, 103–5
interracial marriage, 28–29
Irenaeus (bishop), 4
Irving, Debby, 23

Jacob (patriarch), 78
Jesus Christ, ix, x, 48, 50, 52, 53, 79, 98, 114, 118
    as archetypal True Self, 59, 101, 102, 104–5, 116
    as the Christ, 102, 103
    death of, 74, 139, 152
    as divine, 4, 101
    and False Self, 97
    as healer, 69
    as human, 101, 102
    mission of, 102
    as model for humanity, 4, 106
    as new Bethel, 78
    as prophet, 5
    as Savior, 102, 132
    as teacher, 5, 7, 12–13, 25, 50–51, 68, 72, 74, 92, 93, 97, 99, 149, 160
    and Ultimate Reality, 69
    walking on water ix, x
Job, book of, 76–77
John, Gospel of, ix, x, 9, 78, 97, 106–7
Johnson, Robert A., 127
Jonah, sign of, 99
Joseph of Arimathea, 127, 147
Joyce, James, 117
Julian of Norwich, 146
Jung, Carl, xvi, 102, 120, 143, 158, 159

Keene, Sam, 144
King Jr., Martin Luther, xvi, 21
kingdom of God, 7, 9, 13, 50–51, 78, 97, 105, 132, 142, 145, 151
Krishna, 36

Langer, Suzanne, 91
Lao Tzu, 35
learning
    lifelong, 8–10
Leibnitz, Gottfried, 34
Lewis, C. S., 90, 91
literalism, x, 93, 94, 106
Locke, John, 86
logos, 111, 112, 113
love, 45, 99, 100, 107, 153, 163, 164
    for God, 70, 75, 140
    great, 97, 99, 156, 157
Luke, Gospel of, 6, 50, 51, 159

Malleus Maleficarum, 143
Malory, Thomas, 127
Mark, Gospel of, x
Mary Magdalene, 99, 106–7
Maslow, Abraham, 118–19
Matthew, Gospel of, x, 149
maya, 132

McFague, Sallie, 72
McKibben, Bill, xvi, 16, 19, 20
meaning, 93, 94, 156
meditation, 67, 72, 94, 118
Meredith, Cara, 28
Meredith, James, 28
meritocracy, 21, 22, 26
Merton, Thomas, 4, 70
metaphor, 10, 53, 83–94, 114, 152
   "ascension" as, 105
   "cross" as, 99, 116, 157
   "crucifixion" as, 106, 157
   "death" as, 61, 62, 97–100, 101, 102, 103, 105, 107, 153, 157, 158, 164
   definition of, 85, 91
   "dissatisfaction" as, 148. 158–59
   "Garden of Eden" as, 116, 134, 138, 139
   "incarnation" as, 105
   "resurrection" as, 62, 85, 99, 100, 101, 102, 105–6, 107, 157, 158, 164, 167
   river-ocean, 73
   "water" as, 99, 163, 164
   wave-ocean, 73, 99, 164
   "world" as, 96
Mill, John Stuart, 38, 91
mind, 64, 65, 69, 88, 98
mindfulness, 4, 15, 68
Mirandola, Giovanni Pico della, 34
modernity, modernism, 115, 119, 120, 169
Moltmann, Jürgen, 40
Muhammad, 36, 92, 114, 118
mystery, 7, 10, 35, 41, 42, 43, 44, 47, 49, 51, 53, 67, 74, 84, 91, 102, 105, 106, 114, 115, 156, 158
mystics, mysticism, xii, 47, 49, 63, 65, 68, 78, 79, 84, 94, 152
   See also seeing mystically
myth, mythology, 10, 83–84, 93, 100, 111–21, 152
   Celtic, 125
   communal, ix
   definition of, 112
   functions of, 115
   labyrinth, 120–21
   as metaphor, 83
   tasks of, 113
mythos, 111

nature, realm of, 45, 53, 70, 84, 114, 115, 116, 130–31
   as extension of the human body, 72–73
   as God's "body," 72
Newton, John, 69
Nietzsche, Friedrich, 88, 114
nondualism, 35, 54, 72, 74, 75–76, 78, 79, 84, 86, 101–2
Novalis (poet), 116

original sin, 129
Otto, Rudolph, 42, 43, 100

panentheism, 39–45
   definition of, 40
pantheism, 39–40, 59
parable, 92–93, 149, 163
Pascal, Blaise, 146
Paul (apostle), 5, 7, 59–60, 62, 71, 74, 75, 101, 104, 124, 158
Peacocke, Arthur, 40, 45
Perceval, 131, 137–53
Perennial Philosophy/Tradition/wisdom, xii, 34, 35, 51, 52, 58, 64, 68, 69, 73, 75, 113, 164
   and Christianity, 37, 54
   definition of, 32, 34
   and False Self, 60, 62, 75
   and hope, 76–79
   and metaphor, 84
   and realm of nature, 73
   and True Self, 35, 57–79
   and Ultimate Reality, 33–55, 57, 58, 59, 60, 66, 72, 77, 78–79, 113, 163
perichoresis, 54–55, 61
person, personhood, xi, 54, 55, 61
Peter (apostle), x, 102
Picasso, Pablo, 94
Picault, Jodi, 23n7
Planck, Max, 90
Plato, 34
postmodernism, ixn1, 94, 119, 169
prayer, 72, 78
presence, 4, 49, 68–69. 70–71, 72

priming, 88
Princeton Theological Seminary, 28
process theology, 49, 72
proverb, 93
Proverbs, book of, ix
psyche, 61
Purves, Andrew, 97

quest, the, 34, 60, 117, 118, 123, 156
    for meaning, 118–19
    role of priest (pastor) in, 124
    role of prophet in, 124
    for wholeness, 119–20
    See also Grail, the, quest
    See also Vision Quest

racism, xvi. 15. 20–29
Rahner, Karl, 5, 42
Rank, Otto, 162
Red Knight, 140–41
religion, 8, 34, 50, 64, 84, 112, 113, 114
    definition of, 101
    inadequate, 7, 10, 68, 78, 79, 84, 91, 93, 98, 101, 115
    language of, 114
    mature, 66–67, 69. 97, 98
    and metaphor, 91
    and reason, 84
    and science, 9
    task of, 63, 64, 94, 103, 112
resurrection, 105, 167
    of Jesus, 74, 101
    of the Self, xiii, 101–2, 105, 106
    See also metaphor, "resurrection as"
Richard of St. Victor, 6
rites of passage, 119, 161
Robinson, Randall, 26
Rohr, Richard, xvi, 10, 35, 52, 96n1, 117, 138n1, 146, 158, 159
Russell, John, 93

sacraments, sacramental, 94, 118, 132, 152, 156, 159
salvation, 13, 68, 71, 100
Satan, 77, 96, 102, 129, 132
science, 8, 54, 83, 84, 85, 94, 106
second half of life, 10–12, 138–40, 164
seeing mystically, 5–7

self, selfhood, xi, 64–65, 106, 140
    as extension of nature, 72–73
    False, xi, 4, 60, 62, 63, 75, 96, 97, 97–100, 106, 115, 157, 158, 164
    shadow, 98, 139, 149–52, 157
        definition of, 98n4
        transformation of, 107, 164
    True, 4, 7, 57–80, 96, 97, 98, 99, 101–3, 105, 106, 107, 157, 158, 164
Sermon on the Mount, 151
Shapiro, Rami, xvi, 35, 51, 55, 57–59
Shaw, George Bernard, 84
silence, 9, 10, 68, 74, 94
sin, xiii, 76, 101, 106, 131, 140, 148, 149
Singh, Kathleen Dowling, 100
Skinner, B. G., 44
slavery
    reparations for, 26–28
Smith, Huston, xvi, 63–65, 164
soul, 4, 60, 61, 63, 64, 65, 72, 104, 115, 116, 124, 148, 158, 163
    definition of, 61
    immortality of, 61
    and the True Self, 60, 61, 62, 63
spirit (human), 59–60, 63, 64, 65, 105, 115, 118, 119, 124, 133, 151
spirituality, 8, 9, 10, 35, 64, 68, 79, 84, 98, 99, 115, 118, 130, 140, 150
Spong, Bishop John, 38–39, 50
Steuco, Agostino, 34, 58
Stevens, Wallace, 91
Stevenson, Bryan, 23–24
success, xii
suffering, 75, 77, 118, 134, 151, 159, 160
    great, 156–57, 158
Sutton, Bishop Eugene, xvi, 27–28
symbols, 94, 101
    definition of, 94

tarot playing cards, 131n9, 138n2, 145n8
temptation, 96
Tennyson, Alfred Lord, 124n3
Teresa of Ávila, 72
theism, 37, 38–39, 40, 41, 50, 83
    See also God
theology, 37, 113, 114, 156
theosis, 4–5
Thurmond, Howard, 144

Tillich, Paul, 42, 50
Tolle, Eckhart, 68
transcendence, 71, 79, 84, 106, 112, 113, 114, 115, 116, 148
  See also God, transcendence of
transformation, 7, 10, 69, 100, 118, 139, 158
  definition of, 105
  personal, 7, 13, 36, 78, 98, 100, 152, 162
  social, 13, 36, 78
  spiritual, 4, 7, 10, 13, 62, 104–5, 134, 151, 158, 160, 164
Trinity. *See* God, as Trinity
True Self. *See* self, selfhood, True
Trump, Donald, 24, 25
truth, ix, xii, 7, 60, 67, 69, 74, 84, 85, 88, 91, 93–94, 113–14, 147, 148–49, 158

ultimate (existential) questions, 33–34, 94, 123, 163
Ultimate Reality. *See* Perennial Philosophy, and Ultimate Reality
Unitarianism, 52
unknowing, 68, 74
Upanishads, 59, 163

Vassal. *See* Dark Knight
Vico, Gianbattista, 89
Vision Quest, 142, 161–62

Wagner, Richard, 124, 126
Wallis, Jim, xvi, 20, 23, 25
wasteland, 131, 133, 148–52
water. *See* metaphor, "water" as
white supremacy, 22, 23
Whitehead, Alfred North, 39, 42, 45, 49
wholeness, 71, 143, 144, 149
williams, angel Kyodo, 21, 22, 23, 26
Williams, Charles, 125
Williams, Robin, 153
wisdom, xii, 6, 67, 69, 112, 158
Wolfram von Eschenbach, 126, 127, 128, 132, 147
Wordsworth, William, 8
worship, 118, 143, 162

www.ingramcontent.com/pod-product-compliance
Lightning Source LLC
Chambersburg PA
CBHW062044220426
43662CB00010B/1638